Anatomy of the Psyche

The Mountain-Cave of the Adepts. Symbolic Résumé of the Alchemical *Opus* (Michelspacher, *Cabala*, 1654. Reprinted in Jung, *Psychology and Alchemy*).

THE REALITY OF THE PSYCHE SERIES

Anatomy of the Psyche

Alchemical Symbolism in Psychotherapy

Edward F. Edinger

OPEN COURT

LA SALLE, ILLINOIS

OPEN COURT and the above logo are registered in the U.S. Patent and Trademark Office.

Library of Congress Cataloging in Publication Data

Edinger, Edward F.
    Anatomy of the psyche.

    (The Reality of the psyche series)
    Bibliography: p.
    1. Psychoanalysis. 2. Alchemy. 3. Individuation.
I. Title. II. Series.
BF175.E297   1985   150.19'54   85-11546
ISBN: 0-8126-9009-5

THE REALITY OF THE PSYCHE SERIES

Originally published in the following issues of *Quadrant: The Journal of the C. G. Jung Foundation for Analytical Psychology*:

Chapters 1 and 2—Volume 11, Number 1 (Summer 1978)
Chapter 3—Volume 11, Number 2 (Winter 1978)
Chapter 4—Volume 12, Number 1 (Summer 1979)
Chapter 5—Volume 13, Number 1 (Spring 1980)
Chapter 6—Volume 14, Number 1 (Spring 1981)
Chapter 7—Volume 14, Number 2 (Fall 1981)
Chapter 8—Volume 15, Number 1 (Spring 1982)

Note on Abbreviations
The Collected Works of Jung are cited as *CW*.
Various versions of the Bible are abbreviated as follows:
       AV   Authorized (King James) Version
       DV   Douay Version
       RSV   Revised Standard Version
       NEB   New English Bible
       JB   Jerusalem Bible
       NAB   New American Bible

[Let us]...study that
true Bible, as we count
it, of the human body
and of the nature of man.

Andreas Vesalius

⚜ Contents ⚜

List of Illustrations/x

Preface/xix

Chapter 1/Introduction/1

Chapter 2/*Calcinatio*/17

Chapter 3/*Solutio*/47

Chapter 4/*Coagulatio*/83

Chapter 5/*Sublimatio*/117

Chapter 6/*Mortificatio*/147

Chapter 7/*Separatio*/183

Chapter 8/*Coniunctio*/211

Bibliography/233

Fire

Water

Earth.

air. ←

Death.

❧ List of Illustrations ❧

References to primary sources appear under illustration titles. For secondary sources, see captions for individual illustrations and Bibliography.

Frontispiece
The Mountain-Cave of the Adepts. Symbolic Résumé of the Alchemical *Opus*. Michelspacher, *Cabala* (1654).

1–1 (page 4)
Macrocosm and Microcosm Interconnected. Waite, A. E., trans., *The Hermetic Museum*.

1–2 (page 7)
The Alchemist Guided by God. Barchusen, *Elementa Chemiae* (1718), Paris, Bibliothèque Nationale.

1–3 (page 13)
The *Prima Materia* as Chaos. Marolles, *Tableaux du temple des muses* (1655), London, British Museum.

1–4 (page 14)
Cerberus as the Devouring and Entangling Aspect of the *Prima Materia*. (15th century), Biblioteca Apostolica Vaticana, Cod. Pal. lat. 1066, fol. 239.

2–1 (page 18)
Calcinatio of the King. The Wolf as *Prima Materia*, Devouring the Dead King. Maier, *Atalanta Fugiens* (1618).

2–2 (page 21)
Calcinatio of an Earth-Animal. MS. Sloane I. 1316 (17th century), London, British Museum.

2–3 (page 22)
Calcinatio of the Devouring Parent. *Mutus Liber* (1702).

2–4 (page 23)
The Fire of the Dragon Being Both Fanned and
Extinguished. Trismosin, *Splendor Solis* (1582).

2–5 (page 25)
The Fiery Furnace of Daniel. Bible of St. Stephen Harding
(12th Century), Dijon, Bibliothèque Municipale, MS. 14.

2–6 (page 26)
The Starry Salamander That Lives in the Fire. The Mercurial
Spirit of the *Prima Materia,* as Salamander, Frolicking in
the Fire. Maier, *Atalanta Fugiens* (1618).

2–7 (page 28)
The Violent Tortured in a Rain of Fire. Doré, *Illustrations
for Dante's Divine Comedy.*

2–8 (page 33)
Calcinatio of the Hermaphrodite. Maier, *Atalanta Fugiens*
(1618).

2–9 (page 34)
The Fire Sower. E. Jacoby.

2–10 (page 36)
Pentecost. Doré, *Bible Illustrations.*

2–11 (page 39)
Shiva Dancing in a Circle of Fire. Bronze (12th or 13th
century), Amsterdam, Museum van Aziatische Kunst.

2–12 (page 41)
St. John Boiled in Oil. Dürer, 1498.

2–13 (page 44)
Expulsion of the Demons. Engraving (17th Century).

2–14 (page 45)
The King in the Sweatbox. Maier, *Atalanta Fugiens* (1618).

3–1 (page 50)
Siegfried and the Rhine Maidens. Rackham, *Color
Illustrations for Wagner's "Ring."*

3–2 (page 51)
The King and Queen in the Bath. Mylius, *Philosophia
reformata* (1622).

3–3 (page 53
Solutio of the King. Background: Drowning King Calling
for Help. Foreground: The King Reborn. Trismosin,
Splendor Solis (1582).

3–4 (page 54)
The Birth of Aphrodite. (c. 460 B.C.), Rome, Terme Museum.

3–5 (page 55)
Hylas and the Nymphs. John William Waterhouse,
Manchester, England, City Art Gallery.

3–6 (page 56)
Bathsheba. Rembrandt, Paris, the Louvre.

3–7 (page 57)
Susanna and the Elders. Tintoretto, Vienna, Gemäldegalerie.

3–8 (page 59)
Diana and Actaeon. Titian, Edinburgh, National Gallery of
Scotland.

3–9 (page 61)
Baptism with Lunar Water While Being Bitten by Dragons.
Ashmole, ed., *Theatrum Chemicum Britannicum* (1652).

3–10 (page 62)
Bacchanal of the Andrians. Titian, Madrid, Prado.

3–11 (page 65)
Bathers. Renoir, Philadelphia, Collection of Carroll Tyson.

3–12 (page 67)
The Flood. Doré, *Bible Illustrations.*

3–13 (page 69)
"Save Me, O God; for the Waters Are Come in Unto My
Soul." Illustration for Psalm 69, *The Visconti Hours,*
Florence, National Library.

3–14 (page 73)
Pharaoh's Army Drowning in the Red Sea. *The Visconti
Hours,* Florence, National Library.

3–15 (page 74)
The Woman Washing Clothes. Maier, *Atalanta Fugiens*
(1618).

3–16 (page 76)
The Corpse of the Merged King and Queen Being Purified
and Reanimated by Heavenly Dew. *Rosarium
Philosophorum,* Frankfurt (1550).

4–1 (page 84)
Earth Nurses the *Filius Philosophorum.* Maier, *Atalanta
Fugiens* (1618).

4-2 (page 87)

Eagle Chained to a Ground Animal. Stolcius, *Viridarium Chymicum* (1624).

4-3 (page 89)

The Fall of the Rebel Angels. *Les Très Riches Heures du Duc de Berry,* Chantilly, Musée Condé.

4-4 (page 92)

The Stone of Saturn. Maier, *Atalanta Fugiens* (1618).

4-5 (page 94)

The Torture of Prometheus. Moreau.

4-6 (page 96)

Virgin and Child on Crescent Moon. Dürer.

4-7 (page 97)

Liberty Leading the People. Delacroix, Paris, the Louvre.

4-8 (page 102)

Fortune or Nemesis Carrying the Cup and Harness of Destiny. Dürer.

4-9 (page 105)

The Annunciation. Drawing by Rembrandt, Besançon, Musée Communal.

4-10 (page 106)

"Sow Your Gold in White Earth." Maier, *Atalanta Fugiens* (1618).

4-11 (page 107)

Crucifixion. Drawing from Ramsey Psalter (c. 980), London, British Museum.

4-12 (page 108)

The Mercurial Serpent Crucified. Alchimie de Flamel, MS. Français 14765, Paris, Bibliothèque Nationale.

4-13 (page 109)

Transfixion of the Mercurial Serpent and the King. "Speculum veritatis," Cod. Vaticanus Latinus 7286 (17th Century), Biblioteca Vaticana.

4-14 (page 110)

Adam and Eve. Dürer.

4-15 (page 112)

The Last Supper. Note the Tiny Black Devil Entering Judas' Mouth. *The Hours of Catherine of Cleves,* The Guennol Collection and the Pierpont Morgan Library.

5–1 (page 119)
Satellite Photograph of Cape Cod and Vicinity. *Photo Atlas of the United States.*

5–2 (page 120)
Sublimatio. Sapentia veterum philosophorum sive doctrina eorundum de summa et universali medicina (18th century), Paris, Bibliothèque de l'Arsenal, MS. 974.

5–3 (page 121)
Extraction of the White Dove. Trismosin, *Splendor Solis* (1582).

5–4 (page 122)
The Cry. Munch (1895), Oslo, National Museum.

5–5 (page 124)
Extraction of Mercurius and Coronation of the Virgin. Lower Level: Mercurius (Represented as a Monstrosity) Being Extracted from the *Prima Materia.* Upper Level: Assumption and Coronation of the Virgin, Transforming the Trinity into a Quaternity. *Speculum trinitatis* from Reusner, *Pandora* (1588).

5–6 (page 132)
Ascension of Elijah. Doré, *Bible Illustrations.*

5–7 (page 133)
Assumption of the Virgin. *The Hours of Catherine of Cleves,* The Guennol Collection and the Pierpont Morgan Library.

5–8 (page 135)
Osiris as a Ladder. From the papyrus of Ani, British Museum.

5–9 (page 138)
The Mystics' Ladder to Heaven. Icon from St. Catherine's Monastery, Mount Sinai (11th-12th century).

5–10 (page 140)
Simeon Stylites on His Column Besieged by a Serpent. Reliquary (6th century), Paris, the Louvre.

5–11 (page 141)
Dante's Ladder of Saturn. Doré, *Illustrations for Dante's Divine Comedy.*

5–12 (page 143)
The Tower of Babel. Bruegel (1563), Vienna, Kunsthistorisches Museum.

6–1 (page 148)
Skeleton as *Mortificatio* Image. Waite, A. E., trans., *The Hermetic Museum.*

6–2 (page 149)
The Triumph of Death. Fresco by Francesco Traini (c. 1350), Pisa, Camposanto.

6–3 (page 151)
Sol and Luna Kill the Dragon. Maier, *Atalanta Fugiens* (1618).

6–4 (page 152)
Death Pours a Drink for the King. Holbein, *The Dance of Death* (1538).

6–5 (page 153)
Death of the King. Stolcius, *Viridarium Chymicum* (1624).

6–6 (page 156)
Massacre of the Innocents. Alchemical drawing.

6–7 (page 157)
Death Blowing the Worm Trumpet. J. Meydenbach, *Doten Dantz* (c. 1492), Mainz.

6–8 (page 159)
Coniunctio in the Black Vas. The *Nigredo.* Paris, Bibliothèque de l'Arsenal, MS. 975, fol. 14.

6–9 (page 161)
Grain Growing from the Corpse of Osiris. From a bas-relief at Philae.

6–10 (page 162)
Grain Growing from the Grave, Symbolizing Resurrection. Waite, A. E., trans., *The Hermetic Museum.*

6–11 (page 164)
Death and the Landsknecht. Dürer.

6–12 (page 165)
The *Nigredo.* Mylius, *Philosophia reformata* (1622).

6–13 (page 166)
Salome with the Head of John the Baptist. *Les Belles Heures du Duc de Berry,* New York, The Metropolitan Museum of Art.

6–14 (page 169)
The Death Head Points to the Cosmic Sphere. Holbein, *The
Dance of Death* (1538).

6–15 (page 176)
The Scourging of Christ. Mair of Landshut (15th century),
London, British Museum.

6–16 (page 179)
Patient's Drawing.

7–1 (page 184)
God Creating the World. Manuscript illustration (13th
century), Vienna, Austrian National Library.

7–2 (page 185)
Cutting the Philosophical Egg. Maier, *Atalanta Fugiens*
(1618).

7–3 (page 186)
The Separation of Heaven and Earth: Nut Lifted Above Geb
by Shu. Drawing after an illustration in A. Jeremias, *Das
Alte Testament im Lichte des Alten Orients,* Leipzig (1904).
Turin, Egyptian Museum.

7–4 (page 190)
The Aces of the Four Tarot Suits: Swords, Staves, Coins,
and Cups. Marseilles Tarot.

7–5 (page 192)
Christ of the Apocalypse. Dürer.

7–6 (page 194)
Joust Between Sol and Luna. *Aurora Consurgens* (14th
century), Zurich, Zentralbibliothek, Cod. rhenovacensis 172,
fol. 10.

7–7 (page 195)
The Awakening of the Sleeping King as a Judgment of
Paris. Thomas Aquinas [pseud.], "De Alchemia," (16th cen-
tury), Leiden, Bibliothek der Rijksuniversiteit, Cod.
Vossianus 29, fol. 78.

7–8 (page 196)
Schismatics. Doré, *Illustrations for Dante's Divine Comedy.*

7–9 (page 198)
The Alchemist as Geometer. Maier, *Atalanta Fugiens* (1618).

7–10 (page 199)
Justice. Marseilles Tarot.

7–11 (page 201)
Moses Striking Water from the Rock. Biblia Pauperum
Bavaria (1414), Munich, Bayerische Staatsbibliothek, Clm.
8201, fol. 86v.

7–12 (page 205)
Crucifixion and Last Judgment. H. Van Eyck, New York,
The Metropolitan Museum of Art.

7–13 (page 207)
The Soul of the Deceased Is Weighed in the Balance. From
the papyrus of Ani, The British Museum.

7–14 (page 208)
The Archangel Michael Weighing Souls. Van der Weyden
(15th century), Bourgogne, Hospice de Beaume.

8–1 (page 213)
The Dragon Kills the Woman and She Kills It. Maier,
Atalanta Fugiens (1618).

8–2 (page 217)
Coniunctio in the Alchemical Vessel. (17th century), Paris,
Bibliothèque de l'Arsenal, MS. 975, fol. 13.

8–3 (page 219)
The Crucifixion as a *Coniunctio* Between Sol and Luna.
(Late 9th century), Paris, Bibliothèque Nationale, MS. lat.
257, fol. 12v.

8–4 (page 221)
The Circle of the Year as a *Coniunctio* of Sol and Luna.
Medieval Drawing, Stuttgart, Wurttembergische
Landesbibliothek, Cod. hist. fol. 415, fol. 17v.

8–5 (page 222)
The New Jerusalem as a *Coniunctio* of Sol and Luna. *The
Cloisters Apocalypse, fol. 36,* New York, the Metropolitan
Museum of Art.

8–6 (page 225)
The Heavenly Rose. Doré, *Illustrations for Dante's Divine
Comedy.*

8–7 (page 226)
Star Trails Around the Pole. Photo Yerkes Observatory.

8-8 (page 229)

Autobiography as a Mandala. Events in the Life of Opicinus de Canistris Arranged Concentrically from His Conception on March 24, 1296, to Completion of Drawing on June 3, 1336. Biblioteca Apostolica Vaticana, MS. Pal. lat. 1993, fol. 11r.

✣ Preface ✣

Jung's discovery of the reality of the psyche opens the way for a new approach to traditional material. Religious and literary scriptures, as well as the gropings of the protosciences such as alchemy, astrology, and pre-Socratic philosophy, can now be understood as the phenomenology of the objective psyche.

Continuing Jung's study of alchemy, this book attempts to bring into visibility certain experiential modes or categories of the individuation process that appear in alchemical symbolism. Although the data used for amplification derive from the most varied sources, they all serve to illustrate patterns and regularities of the objective psyche—that is, archetypal images of transformation. What I present is neither a theoretical construct nor a philosophical speculation, but rather an ordering of psychic *facts* based on the method of Jung.

These facts go to make up an *anatomy of the psyche,* which is at the same time an embryology, since we are dealing with a process of development and transformation. The great value of alchemical images is that they give us an *objective* basis from which to approach dreams and other unconscious material. With the psyche more than with any other subject it is very difficult to distinguish between objective fact and personal bias. A working knowledge of alchemical images can be very helpful in promoting this much needed objectivity. Our goal, given sufficient familiarity with archetypal symbolism and sufficient self-knowledge from personal analysis, is an anatomy of the psyche that is as objective as the anatomy of the body.

Anatomy of the Psyche

❖1 Introduction❖

THE PROCESS OF PSYCHOTHERAPY, when it goes at all deep, sets into motion profound and mysterious happenings. It is very easy for both patient and therapist to lose their way. This is why narrow and inadequate theories of the psyche are clung to so desperately—at least they provide some sense of orientation. If we are not to submit psychic phenomena to the Procrustean bed of a preconceived theory, we must seek the categories for understanding the psyche within the psyche itself. An old alchemical dictum says, "Dissolve the matter in its own water." This is what we do when we try to understand the process of psychotherapy in terms of alchemy.

As Jung has demonstrated, alchemical symbolism is largely a product of the unconscious psyche. "The real nature of matter was unknown to the alchemist; he knew it only in hints. Inasmuch as he tried to explore it he projected the unconscious into the darkness of matter in order to illuminate it.... While working on his chemical experiments the operator had certain psychic experiences which appeared to him as the particular behavior of the chemical process. Since it was a question of projection, he was naturally unconscious of the fact that the experience had nothing to do with matter itself. He experienced his projection as a property of matter; but what he was in reality experiencing was his own unconscious."[1]

As Jung studied alchemy he found that this luxuriant network of images was, indeed, the psyche's "own water" which could be used to understand the complex contents of the psyche. He wrote:

> I had very soon seen that analytical psychology coincided in a most curious way with alchemy. The experiences of the alchemists, were, in a sense, my experiences, and their world was my world. This was, of course, a momentous discovery: I had stumbled upon the historical counterpart of my psychology of the unconscious. The possibility of a comparison with alchemy, and the uninterrupted intellectual chain back to Gnosticism, gave substance

---

[1] Jung, *Psychology and Alchemy*, CW 12, pars. 345 ff.

to my psychology. When I pored over those old texts everything fell into place: the fantasy-images, the empirical material I had gathered in my practice, and the conclusions I had drawn from it. I now began to understand what these psychic contents meant when seen in historical perspective.[2]

At the end of *Mysterium Coniunctionis* he sums up the meaning of alchemy:

> ...the entire alchemical procedure...could just as well represent the individuation process of a single individual, though with the not unimportant difference that no single individual ever attains to the richness and scope of the alchemical symbolism. This has the advantage of having been built up through the centuries...It is...a difficult and thankless task to try to describe the nature of the individuation process from case material...No case in my experience is comprehensive enough to show all the aspects in such detail that it could be regarded as paradigmatic....Alchemy, therefore, has performed for me the great and invaluable service of providing material in which my experience could find sufficient room, and has thereby made it possible for me to describe the individuation process at least in its essential aspects.[3]

We can therefore say that alchemical images describe the process of depth psychotherapy which is identical with what Jung calls individuation. What I thus propose to do is to examine some of the basic images of alchemy to see how they correspond to the experiences of psychotherapy.

The term "psychotherapy" is used here in its broadest, etymological sense. The Greek word *therapeuein*, "to heal," originally meant "service to the gods." Healing thus took place at first in a sacred context. Philo tells us of a group of pre-Christian, Jewish contemplatives who called themselves *Therapeuts* "either because they profess an art of medicine more excellent than that in general use in cities (for that only heals bodies, but the other heals souls which are under the mastery of terrible and almost incurable diseases, which pleasures and appetites, fears and griefs, and covetousness, and follies, and injustice, and all the rest of the innumerable multitude of other passions and vices, have inflicted upon them), or else because they have been instructed by nature and the sacred laws to serve the living God."[4] Psychotherapy thus means, basically, service to the psyche.

What makes alchemy so valuable for psychotherapy is that its images concretize the experiences of transformation that one undergoes in psychotherapy. Taken as a whole, alchemy provides a kind of anatomy of individuation. Its images will be most meaningful, of course, to those who have had a personal experience of the unconscious.

---

[2]Jung, *Memories, Dreams, Reflections,* p. 205.

[3]*CW* 14, par. 792.

[4]Philo, "On the Contemplative Life," in *The Essential Philo,* p. 311.

THE ALCHEMICAL WORLD VIEW

For the alchemist, upper and lower and inner and outer were linked by hidden connections and identities. What happens in heaven is duplicated by what happens on earth, as indicated in this alchemical verse:

> Heaven above
> Heaven below
> Stars above
> Stars below
> All that is above
> Also is below
> Grasp this
> And rejoice.[5]

Likewise, a passage from the *Emerald Tablet* says, "What is below is like that which is above, and what is above is like that which is below, to accomplish the miracles of one thing."[6] The planets in heaven correspond to the metals in the earth: Sun = gold, Moon = silver, Mercury = quicksilver, Venus = copper, Mars = iron, Jupiter = tin, and Saturn = lead. As the planets revolve around the earth, they gradually spin their corresponding metals into the earth, which people can extract by their chemical operations (see figure 1–1).

Psychologically we can understand this image as referring to the archetypal constituents of the ego. The building blocks of the ego are divine qualities stolen from the gods or products of the dismemberment of a deity—earthly representatives of transpersonal principles. Such imagery is still alive in the modern psyche as indicated by the following dream of a middle-aged businessman and commercial artist who had no knowledge of alchemy:

> *Four metal-clad figures descend toward me from the sky. They float down over an ancient Roman wall. Each suit is made of a different metal. One is bronze, another lead, another iron, and the fourth is made of platinum. The platinum-suited figure separates himself from the others and approaches. "We are seeking metal," he says. "The metal we seek matches the material of our suits." The figures remain suspended in the air by some unique method.*

The metal-suited men correspond to the planetary deities of the alchemists. Since they have no weight, they are spirit beings and inhabitants of the sky. Thus they would represent archetypal images of the

---

[5]Cited in Jung, *The Practice of Psychotherapy*, *CW* 16, par. 384.

[6]Read, *Prelude to Chemistry: An Outline of Alchemy*, p. 54.

FIGURE 1 – 1.
Macrocosm and Microcosm Interconnected (*The Hermetic Museum,* trans. by A. E. Waite.)

objective psyche. Their descent in search of their corresponding metals indicates that each metal–spirit is seeking his own earthly embodiment. They want to be concretely actualized in the conscious experience of an individual ego. This is an archetypal dream and clearly has a collective as well as personal meaning. The gods we have lost are descending on us, demanding reconnection. Like Baucis and Philemon, modern individuals are being visited by and asked to provide hospitality for transpersonal factors with which they have lost connection. The dream is also relevant to our efforts to understand alchemy. The spirits of alchemy—the symbolic images that have come down to us—are asking for their earthly counterparts—that is, their meaningful realization in modern experience. Many gifted and devoted people offered up their whole lives to the quest for the Philosophers' Stone. By understanding the images they served we can redeem their lives from futility and recognize them to be witnesses to and carriers of the mystery of individuation.

THE OPUS

The central image of alchemy is the idea of the *opus*. The alchemist thought of himself as committed to a sacred work—a search for the supreme and ultimate value. Alchemical texts have a great deal to say about the nature of the *opus* and the attitude that should be taken towards it. Certain virtues are indispensable prerequisites. One text says, "O all ye seekers after this Art, ye can reach no useful result without a patient, laborious, and solicitous soul, persevering courage, and continuous regimen."[7] These are requirements of ego function. Patience is basic. Courage means a willingness to face anxiety. Continuous regimen means that through all shifts of mood and mental state one is willing to persevere in the effort to scrutinize and understand what is happening.

Another relevant text comes from Thomas Norton's *Ordinal of Alchemy*. For anyone who has had the experience of psychotherapy, the parallels will be immediately evident.

> Anyone who gives himself up to this search must therefore expect to meet with much vexation of spirit. He will frequently have to change his course in consequence of new discoveries which he makes....The devil will do his utmost to frustrate your search by one or the other of the three stumbling blocks, namely, haste, despair, or deception...he who is in a hurry will complete his work neither in a month, nor yet in a year; and in this Art it will always be true that the man who is in a hurry will never be without matter of complaint....If the enemy does not prevail against you by hurry, he will assault you with despondency, and will be constantly putting into your minds discouraging thoughts, how those who seek this Art are many, while they are few that find it, and how those who fail are often wiser men than yourself. He will then ask you what hope there can be of your attaining the grand arcanum; moreover, he will vex you with doubts whether your master is himself possessed of the secret which he professes to impart to you; or whether he is not concealing from you the best part of that which he knows. ...The third enemy against whom you must guard is deceit, and this is perhaps more dangerous than the other two. The servants whom you must employ to feed your furnaces are frequently most untrustworthy. Some are careless and go to sleep when they should be attending the fire; others are depraved, and do you all the harm they can; others again are either stupid or conceited and over-confident, and disobey instructions...or they are drunken, negligent, and absent-minded. Be on your guard against all these, if you wish to be spared some great loss.[8]

A prominent feature of the *opus* is that it is considered a sacred work requiring a religious attitude.

> ...this arcanum should be regarded, not only as a truly great, but as a most holy Art....Therefore, if any man desire to reach this great and unspeakable mystery, he must remember that it is obtained not only by the might of man, but by the grace of God, and that not our will or desire, but only the mercy of the Most High, can bestow it upon us. For this reason you must first of all

---

[7] Waite, trans., *Turba Philosophorum,* p. 127, dictum 39.

[8] Waite, trans., *The Hermetic Museum,* 2:22–25.

cleanse your heart, lift it to Him alone, and ask of Him this gift in true earnest, and undoubting prayer. He alone can give and bestow it.[9]

Now, the regimen is greater than is perceived by reason, except through divine inspiration.[10]

Woe unto you who fear not God, for He may deprive you of this art![11]

Our art, its theory as well as its practice, is altogether a gift of God, Who gives it when and to whom He elects: it is not of him that wills, or of him that runs, but simply through the mercy of God.[12]

Such passages as these make clear that a careful awareness of the transpersonal level of the psyche is required. This means one must be Self-oriented rather than ego-oriented. There is a paradox here—as so often in alchemy and psychotherapy. An awareness of the Self and the religious attitude that such an awareness brings are the goals of psychotherapy rather than requirements at the beginning. However, the potential at least must exist from the start. As one alchemist says, one must start with a bit of the Philosophers' Stone if one is to find it. As the process deepens, one realizes more and more that insights come by grace and that development occurs not by the will of the ego but by the urge to individuation from the Self (see figure 1–2).

Another aspect of the *opus* is that it is a highly individual work. Alchemists were decidedly solitaries. They might have had one helper but no more. This refers to the uniquely individual nature of individuation. In its deepest aspects it is experienced alone. The *opus* cannot be performed by a committee. It thus generates a certain unavoidable alienation from the world, at least for a time. "But when God grants his grace, to someone who understands (the Art). . . . this will appear incomprehensible in the eyes of the world and those who have this mystery will be scorned of men and looked down upon."[13]

This corresponds to the work of psychotherapy, which is impossible for anyone to understand from the outside. It will be scorned and ridiculed by the collective, conventional standpoint either from another person or one's own shadow. Parallel to this text are these words of Jesus: "If you belonged to the world, the world would love its own; but because you do not belong to the world, because I have chosen you out of the world, for that reason the world hates you" (John 15:19, NEB).

Another feature of the *opus* concerns its secret nature. The alche-

---

[9]Ibid., 1:127.

[10]*Turba Philosophorum*, p. 138, dictum 39.

[11]Ibid., p. 97, dictum 29.

[12]Waite, trans., *The Hermetic Museum*, 1:9.

[13]Ibid., 173.

FIGURE 1 – 2

The Alchemist Guided by God (Barchusen, *Elementa Chemiae*, 1718. Paris. Bibliothèque Nationale. Reprinted in Jung, *Psychology and Alchemy*.)

mists considered themselves to be the guardians of a mystery that was not to be divulged to the unworthy.

> Therefore you should carefully test and examine the life, character, and mental aptitude of any person who would be intitiated in this Art, and then you should bind him, by a sacred oath, not to let our Magistery be commonly or vulgarly known. Only when he begins to grow old and feeble, he may reveal it to one person, but not to more—and that one man must be virtuous, and generally approved by his fellows. For this Magistery must always remain a secret science, and the reason that compels us to be careful is obvious. If any wicked man should learn to practice this Art, the event would be fraught with great danger to Christendom. For such a man would overstep all bounds of moderation, and would remove from their hereditary thrones those legitimate princes who rule over the peoples of Christendom. And the punishment of this wickedness would fall upon him who had instructed that unworthy person in our Art. In order, then, to avoid such an outbreak of overweening pride, he who possesses the knowledge of this Art, should be scrupulously careful how he delivers it to another, and should regard it as the peculiar privilege of those who excel in virtue.[14]

Like the Eleusinian Mysteries, the alchemical secret was forbidden to be published. Understood psychologically, the matter is more subtle. A

---

[14]Ibid., 2:12.

secret that can be told is no secret. In a sense, the secret of the psyche is safe because it is not communicable to those who have not yet experienced it for themselves. The misuse of the secret referred to in the text suggests an inflation following the ego's identification with an archetypal image. If the transpersonal energies are not perceived as secret and sacred they will be channeled into personal ends and have destructive effects. Misuse of the alchemical mystery corresponds to the misuse of the Eucharistic mystery concerning which the Apostle Paul says, "Anyone who eats the bread or drinks the cup of the Lord unworthily will be guilty of desecrating the body and the blood of the Lord. A man must test (*dokimazo*—"to prove, to assay metals") himself before eating his share of the bread and drinking from the cup. For he who eats and drinks eats and drinks judgement on himself if he does not discern the Body" (1 Cor. 11:27-29, NEB).

The alchemical *opus* was considered a process begun by nature but requiring the conscious art and effort of a human being to complete.

> This state cannot be perfected by the mere progress of nature; for gold has no propensity to move itself so far; but rather chooses to remain in its constantly abiding body.[15]

> Nature serves Art with matter, and Art serves nature with suitable Instruments and method convenient for nature to produce such new forms; and although the before-mentioned Stone can only be brought to its proper form by Art, yet the form is from nature.[16]

This is a profound idea. In one sense the *opus* is against Nature, but in another sense the alchemist is helping her to do what she cannot do for herself. This surely refers to the evolution of consciousness. Although the urge to consciousness exists with nature—within the unconscious psyche—an ego is needed to realize fully that natural urge. It is required that the individual cooperate deliberately in the task of creating consciousness.

The ultimate statements about the alchemical *opus* occur in certain texts that equate it with the creation of the world. Zosimos says, "The symbol of chemistry is founded on the creation of the world."[17] The *Emerald Tablet* says at the conclusion of its alchemical recipe, "Thus the world has been created." Another text, after describing the preparation of a special water, continues as follows:

> When this has been done, take a drop of the consecrated red wine and let it fall into the water, and you will instantly perceive a fog and thick darkness on top of the water, such as also was at the first creation. Then put in two drops,

---

[15] *The Lives of the Alchemystical Philosophers*, p. 175.

[16] Trismosin, *Splendor Solis: Alchemical Treatises of Solomon Trismosin*, p. 18.

[17] Cited by Jung, *E.T.H. Seminars: Alchemy*. p. 146.

and you will see the light coming forth from the darkness; whereupon little by little put in every half of each quarter hour first three, then four, then five, then six drops, and then no more, and you will see with your own eyes one thing after another appearing by and by on top of the water, how God created all things in six days, and how it all came to pass, and such secrets as are not to be spoken aloud and I also have not power to reveal. Fall on your knees before you undertake this operation. Let your eyes judge of it: for thus was the world created.[18]

Understood psychologically, these texts are equating the individual with the world; that is, they state that individuation is a world–creating process. Schopenhauer begins his great work, *The World as Will and Idea,* with the outrageous statement, "The world is my idea." Likewise, Jung speaks of the "world–creating quality" of consciousness.[19] Such an idea is dangerously close to solipsistic inflation, and, indeed, it is a common content of psychosis—the idea that one is the whole world or the center of the universe. Nevertheless, it is an archetypal idea that the individual needs in order not to be swallowed up by collective, statistical standards. Collective thinking is revealed by preoccupation with whether or not one is normal. To the extent that one is a separate, unique world of being there can be no norms, since a norm is an average of many. The individual psyche is and must be a whole world within itself in order to stand over and against the outer world and fulfill its task of being a carrier of consciousness. For the scales to be balanced, the individual must be of equal weight to the world.

one is the center of world

This realization of the individual as a whole world often comes over me with considerable force as I am working with patients. It is a valuable counterbalance to doubts about the significance of one's efforts with only a handful of individuals as compared to the world population of several billion.

Although alchemical writings are complex, confused, and even chaotic, the basic scheme of the *opus* is quite simple. It is as follows: The purpose is to create a transcendent, miraculous substance, which is variously symbolized as the Philosophers' Stone, The Elixir of Life, or the universal medicine. The procedure is, first, to find the suitable material, the so–called *prima materia,* and then to subject it to a series of operations that will turn it into the Philosophers' Stone.

THE *PRIMA MATERIA*

The term *"prima materia"* has a long history that goes back to the pre–Socratic philosophers. These early thinkers were gripped by an a

---

[18]*Cited by Jung, Psychology and Alchemy, CW* 12, par. 347.

[19]*Mysterium Coniunctionis, CW* 14, par. 132.

priori idea—that is, an archetypal image that told them that the world derives from a single, original stuff, the so-called first matter. They differed as to the identification of this prime matter, but they agreed on its existence. Thales called the prime matter "water," Anaximander called it "the boundless" *(apeiron),* Anaximenes called it "air," and Heraclitus called it "fire."

This idea of a single, original substance has no empirical source in the outer world. Externally the world is obviously a multiplicity. Thus, the idea must be a projection of a psychic fact. According to philosophical fantasy it was then imagined that the prime matter underwent a process of differentiation whereby it was separated into the four elements, earth, air, fire, and water. It was thought that these four elements then combined in various proportions to form all the physical objects of the world. Upon the *prima materia* was imposed, as it were, a fourfold structure, a cross, representing the four elements—two sets of contraries, earth and air, fire and water. Psychologically, this image corresponds to the creation of the ego out of the undifferentiated unconscious by the process of discriminating the four functions: thinking, feeling, sensation, and intuition.

Aristotle elaborated the idea of the *prima materia* in connection with his distinction between matter and form. According to Aristotle, primary matter before it has been wedded to form or had form imposed upon it is pure potentiality—not yet actualized because the actual does not exist until it has taken on a particular form. As one commentator of Aristotle puts it, *"First matter* is the name of that entirely indeterminate power of change."[20]

The alchemists inherited the idea of the *prima materia* from ancient philosophy and applied it to their attempts at the transformation of matter. They thought that in order for a given substance to be transformed, it must first be reduced or returned to its original, undifferentiated state. "Bodies cannot be changed except by reduction into their first matter."[21] Again, "the species or forms of metals cannot be changed into gold and silver before being first reduced to their primary matter."[22]

This procedure corresponds closely to what takes place in psychotherapy. The fixed, settled aspects of the personality that are rigid and static are reduced or led back to their original, undifferentiated condition as part of the process of psychic transformation. Return to the *prima materia* is illustrated by the following dream:

---

[20]Brehier, *The History of Philosophy: The Hellenic Age,* p. 208.

[21]Kelly, *The Alchemical Writings of Edward Kelly,* p. 34.

[22]Figulus, *A Golden and Blessed Casket of Nature's Marvels,* p. 298.

*I am back in a hospital ward. I have become a child again and I
am in the ward to start my life from the beginning.*

The dreamer had recently made a suicide attempt, and this dream
indicates the symbolic meaning of that act. The child is the *prima
materia* of the adult. This patient's urge for transformation is causing
his return to the original condition. In Aristotle's terms, the form that
actualizes the present personality is being dissolved and returned to the
first matter, the formless state of pure potentiality, in order for a new
form or actuality to emerge. This idea is represented by the following
dream:

*I am having to deal with an infant. Whenever there is something
one can't understand—is blocked to—one must approach this
infant. At the moment of lack of understanding, the infant glows
a faint crimson. This faint crimson glow conveys innocence—which
is the material of the infant—and this innocence frees one to
approach the problem in terms of one's individual reality.*

Innocence corresponds to the undifferentiated state of the *prima
materia*. The dream reminds one of the saying of Jesus, "Truly, I say
unto you, unless you turn and become like children you will never enter
the kingdom of heaven" (Matt. 18:3 RSV). To become like children is to
revert to the innocent, undifferentiated state of the *prima materia*,
which is a prerequisite of transformation.

Fixed, developed aspects of the personality allow no change. They
are solid, established, and sure of their rightness. Only the indefinite,
fresh, and vital, but vulnerable and insecure, original condition symbolized by the child is open to development and hence is alive. We consider
the image of a child in dreams as one of the symbols of the Self, but it
also can symbolize the *prima materia*.

Often the texts speak of *finding* the *prima materia* rather than
making it. Its descriptions are innumerable. Here are a few typical
examples:

This Matter lies before the eyes of all; everybody sees it, touches it, loves it,
but knows it not. It is glorious and vile, precious and of small account, and is
found everywhere.... To be brief, our Matter has as many names as there are
things in the world; that is why the foolish know it not.[23]

As concerns the Matter, it is *one*, and contains within itself all that is needed.
...In the same way Arnold of Villa Nova writes in his "Flower of Flowers":
"Our stone is made out of one thing, and with one thing." To the same effect
he says to the King of Naples: "All that is in our stone is essential to it, nor
does it need any foreign ingredient. Its nature is one, and it is *one* thing."

---

[23]Waite, trans., *The Hermetic Museum*, 1:13.

And Rosinus says: "Know that the object of your desire is one thing, out of which all things are made."[24]

The substance that we first take in hand is mineral.... It is of great inward virtue, though it is vile to the sight. It is Saturn's child, do you need more; conceive it aright, for it is our first entrance. It is sable colored, with argent veins appearing intermixed in the body.... It is of a venomous nature.[25]

There is in our chemistry a certain noble substance over whose beginning affliction rules with vinegar, but over whose end joy rules with mirth.[26]

The problem of finding the *prima materia* corresponds to the problem of finding what to work on in psychotherapy. These texts give us some hints.

1. It is ubiquitous, to be found everywhere, before the eyes of all. This means that psychotherapeutic material likewise is everywhere, in all the ordinary, everyday occurrences of life. Moods and petty personal reactions of all kinds are suitable matter to be worked on by the therapeutic process.

2. Although of great inward value, the *prima materia* is vile in outer appearance and therefore despised, rejected, and thrown on the dung heap. The *prima materia* is treated like the suffering servant in Isaiah. Psychologically, this means that the *prima materia* is found in the shadow, that part of the personality that is considered most despicable. Those aspects of ourselves most painful and most humiliating are the very ones to be brought forward and worked on.

3. It appears as a multiplicity—"has as many names as there are things"—but at the same time is one. This feature corresponds to the fact that initially psychotherapy makes one aware of one's fragmented, disjointed condition. Very gradually these warring fragments are discovered to be differing aspects of one underlying unity. It is as though one sees the fingers of a hand touching a table at first only in two dimensions, as separate unconnected fingers. With three–dimensional vision, the fingers are seen as part of a larger unity, the hand.

4. The *prima materia* is undifferentiated, without definite boundaries, limits, or form. This corresponds to a certain experience of the unconscious that exposes the ego to the infinite, the *apeiron*. It may evoke the terror of dissolution or the awe of eternity. It provides a glimpse of the pleroma, the *increatum*, the chaos prior to the operation of the world–creating Logos. It is the fear of the boundless that often leads one to be content with the ego limits one has rather than risk falling

---

[24] Ibid., 12.

[25] *The Lives of the Alchemystical Philosophers*, p. 176.

[26] Cited in Jung, *Psychology and Alchemy, CW* 12, par. 387.

into the infinite by attempting to enlarge them (see figures 1–3 and 1–4).

FIGURE 1 – 3
The *Prima Materia* as Chaos (Marolles, *Tableaux du temple des muses,* 1655. London, British Museum. Reprinted in Jung, *Psychology and Alchemy.*)

FIGURE 1 – 4

Cerberus as the Devouring and Entangling Aspect of the *Prima Materia* (15th century. Biblioteca Apostolica Vaticana, Cod. Pal. lat. 1066, fol. 239. Reprinted in Derola, *The Secret Art of Alchemy*.)

THE OPERATIONS

It is very difficult to understand alchemy as we find it in the original writings. We encounter a wild, luxuriant, tangled mass of overlapping images that is maddening to the order–seeking conscious mind. My method of ordering the chaos of alchemy is to focus on the major alchemical operations. After the *prima materia* has been found, it has to submit to a series of chemical procedures in order to be transformed into the Philosophers' Stone. Practically all of alchemical imagery can be ordered around these operations, and not only alchemical imagery. Many images from myth, religion, and folklore also gather around these symbolic operations, since they all come from the same source—the archetypal psyche.

There is no exact number of alchemical operations, and many images overlap. For my purposes I have chosen seven operations as the major ones making up the alchemical transformation. They are *calcinatio, solutio, coagulatio, sublimatio, mortificatio, separatio, and coniunctio.* (I use the Latin terms instead of calcination, solution, and so on, in order to distinguish the psychological processes from the chemical procedures.) Each of these operations is found to be the center of an elaborate symbol system. These central symbols of transformation make up the major content of all culture-products. They provide basic categories by which to understand the life of the psyche, and they illustrate almost the full range of experiences that constitute individuation.

In subsequent chapters, I shall take up each of these operations in turn. Each will be accompanied by a chart indicating the major symbolic connections that cluster around the core image. The charts are an important part of my method because I want to emphasize the structural nature of each symbol system. Although I shall try to be clear and explicit, the nature of the subject requires that much be left on the level of image and symbol. In justification, I offer these remarks by Jung:

> We should not begrudge the alchemists their secret language: deeper insight into the problems of psychic development soon teaches us how much better it is to reserve judgement instead of prematurely announcing to all and sundry what's what. Of course we all have an understandable desire for crystal clarity, but we are apt to forget that in psychic matters we are dealing with processes of experience, that is, with transformations which should never be given hard and fast names if their living movement is not to petrify into something static. The protean mythologem and the shimmering symbol express the processes of the psyche far more trenchantly and, in the end, far more clearly than the clearest concept; for the symbol not only conveys a visualization of the process but—and this is perhaps just as important—it also brings a re-experiencing of it, of that twilight which we can learn to understand only through inoffensive empathy, but which too much clarity only dispels.[27]

---

[27]Jung, *Alchemical Studies,* *CW* 13, par. 199.

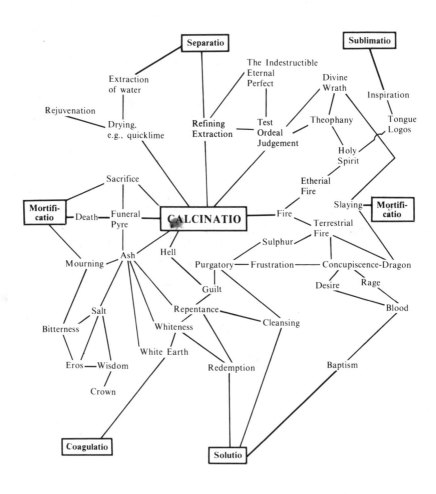

❧ 2 Calcinatio ❧

MOST LISTS OF ALCHEMICAL OPERATIONS begin with *calcinatio*. A few authors say *solutio* comes first. However, the sequence of operations (with one or two exceptions) does not seem to be psychologically significant. Any operation may be the initiating one, and the others may follow in any order.

As with most alchemical images, *calcinatio* derives in part from a chemical procedure. The chemical process of calcination entails the intense heating of a solid in order to drive off water and all other constituents that will volatilize. What remains is a fine, dry powder. The classic example of calcination, from which it derives its name (calx = lime), is the heating of limestone ($CaCO_3$) or slaked lime ($Ca(OH)_2$) to produce quicklime (CaO, *calx viva*). When water is added, quicklime has the interesting characteristic of generating heat. It was thought by the alchemists to contain fire and was sometimes equated with fire itself.[1]

The wonder of quicklime to the mind ignorant of chemistry is vividly described by Augustine:

> Let us consider the wonders of lime; for besides growing white in fire, which makes other things black, ... it has also a mysterious property of conceiving fire within it. Itself cold to the touch, it yet has a hidden store of fire, which is not at once apparent to our senses, but which experience teaches us, lies as it were slumbering within it even while unseen. And it is for this reason called "quicklime," as if the fire were the invisible soul quickening the visible substance or body. But the marvelous thing is, that this fire is kindled when it is extinguished. For to disengage the hidden fire the lime is moistened or drenched with water, and then, though it be cold before, it becomes hot by that very application which cools what is hot. As if the fire were departing from the lime and breathing its last, it no longer lies hid, but appears; and then the lime lying in the coolness of death cannot be requickened, and what we before called "quick," we now call "slaked."[2]

---

[1] *The Glory of the World* says, "Take fire, or the quicklime of the sages, which is the vital fire of all trees, and therein doth God Himself burn by divine love" (Waite, trans., *The Hermetic Museum* 1:198).

[2] Augustine, *City of God* 21:4.

Each of the four elements has its own particular operation. *Calcinatio* is the fire operation (the others: *solutio,* water; *coagulatio,* earth; *sublimatio,* air). Hence any image that contains open fire burning or affecting substances will be related to the *calcinatio.* This opens up the whole rich and complicated subject of fire symbolism. Jung has demonstrated that fire symbolizes libido.[3] This puts it very generally. In order to specify the implications of fire and its effects, we must examine the phenomenology of the image in its various ramifications.

In *The Twelve Keys* of Basil Valentine we find the following recipe for *calcinatio*: "Take a fierce gray wolf, which... is found in the valleys and mountains of the world, where he roams almost savage with hunger. Cast to him the body of the King, and when he has devoured it, burn him entirely to ashes in a great fire. By this process the King will be liberated; and when it has been performed thrice the lion has overcome the wolf, and will find nothing more to devour in him. Thus our body has been rendered fit for the first stage of our work"[4] (see figure 2-1).

FIGURE 2 – 1
Calcinatio of the King. The Wolf as *Prima Materia,* Devouring the Dead King
(From Maier, *Atalanta Fugiens,* 1618.)

---

[3]Jung, *Symbols of Transformation, CW* 5, par. 208.
[4]Waite, trans., *The Hermetic Museum* 1:325.

Read has interpreted this passage chemically. He identifies the wolf with antimony, which was called the "'wolf of metals,' because it 'devoured,' or united with, all the known metals except gold. On account of its use in purifying molten gold—the impurities being removed in the form of a scum—antimony was also called *balneum regis,* the 'bath of the King.'"[5] Thus the passage would refer to the purification of gold by melting it three times with antimony. This interpretation may be right from the strictly chemical standpoint. However, it fails to take into account the meaning of the fantasy images that are projected into the chemical process. These represent the psychic component of alchemy that is the chief interest of the psychotherapist.

The text speaks of "the body of the King." Presumably the king is already dead, having been killed in the process of *mortificatio.* The death of a king is a time of crisis and transition. Regicide is the gravest of crimes. Psychologically it would signify the death of the ruling principle of consciousness, the highest authority in the hierarchical structure of the ego. Death of the king would thus be accompanied by a regressive dissolution of the conscious personality. This course of events is indicated by the fact that the body of the king is fed to a ravening wolf; that is, the ego has been devoured by hungry desirousness. The wolf in turn is fed to the fire. But wolf = desire and desire = fire. Thus desirousness consumes itself. After a descent into hell, the ego (king) is reborn, phoenixlike, in a purified state.

As in fairy tales, the threefold repetition signifies the consummation of a temporal process.[6] The statement that "the lion has overcome the wolf" would equate the lion with the fire that consumes the wolf. The lion is the "lower sun,"[7] a theriomorphic representation of the masculine principle. There are alchemical pictures showing a lion devouring the sun. Since sun, king, and gold are equivalents, this would signify the descent of consciousness into the animal realm where it must endure the fiery energies of instinct. In chemical imagery it is the purification or refining of gold.

Our text seems to set up three levels of being. From below upward there are the level of the wolf, the level of the fire or lion, and the level of the king. If we equate the wolf with elemental desirousness, the lion with the egocentric power drive, and the king with discriminating, objective consciousness, we have a very close parallel to the stages in the transformation of instinct as formulated by Esther Harding—that is, the autos,

---

[5]Read, *Prelude to Chemistry,* p. 201.

[6]Edinger, *Ego and Archetype,* pp. 179ff.

[7]Jung, *Mysterium Coniunctionis, CW* 14, par. 21.

the ego, and the Self.[8] Although Harding uses these terms to denote successive centers of consciousness in the course of psychological development, they can also be understood as residual structural layers of the adult psyche that are subject to reactivation. The feeding of the king to the wolf, the consuming of the wolf by fire (lion), and the rebirth of the king out of the fire would then signify the regression of the ego to the original "autos" stage of autoerotic desirousness. This is followed by the "ego" or personal power stage, and finally by the return of a refined or augmented objective consciousness.

A dream that closely parallels our text was dreamed by a man of middle age facing a challenging illness:

> The Rev. X had died (a well-known minister beloved by the patient). His body was to be cremated and there was some question as to who would get the gold that would be left over after his body was burned. I saw the liquid gold, very dark in color, held in some dark stuff, perhaps ashes that were black. . . . My first thought about the gold was negative, a feeling of repugnance, then it occurred to me that he must have been something very special, and that the gold was sort of his essence, or what he left behind of value.

This dream combines several alchemical themes: *calcinatio* as cremation; the death and blackness of *mortificatio;* extraction of essence, *separatio;* and the making of gold, the goal of the *opus.* In both the text and the dream, the dead king or father figure is the object of *calcinatio.*[9] The dream suggests that a dominant life value around which the personality has been structured is undergoing reevaluation.

The calcining fire may derive from sexuality. For instance, a man who was dealing with compulsive sexuality had this dream:

> He sees his mother in a wire basket covered with fragments of hot slate. The procedure is supposed to be therapeutic but there

---

[8]Harding writes: "In the first stage. . . the focal center, the I, is completely dominated by auto-erotic desires. I have called this center the autos. In the second stage the ego becomes the center of consciousness, and the instinctive drives are modified through their relation to the new-found ego consciousness, which in turn says "I." In the third stage the ego is displaced from its central position, becoming relative in importance to the new center of consciousness, the Self, whose categorical imperative takes over ultimate control" (*Psychic Energy, Its Source and Goal,* pp. 23–24).

[9]Frances Wickes has reported a dream on the same theme, dreamed by a man with a mother problem. *The old King, whose cruelty is completely irrational, must be killed with his own sword, a bent and rusty blade. When this is done, a flame springs up from the lifeless body. As the old King is consumed to ashes, a gleaming sword appears in the center of the flame* (*The Inner World of Choice,* p. 114).

*is some question that it may become diabolical if the slate
fragments are heated so hot as to make it torture.*

The dreamer was reminded of having seen rats escaping from a basket
of burning trash. In this dream the mother represents the *prima materia*
that must undergo *calcinatio.* In other words it is the Eros realm of the
feminine principle that requires purification (see figures 2–2 and 2–3).

In another text the *calcinatio* is described as follows: "Then take out
all the faeces which remain in the retort, and are blackish like unto soot,
which faeces are called our Dragon, of which faeces calcine...in a
fervent hot fire...until it becomes a white calx, as white as snow"[10] (see
figure 2–4). Here the matter to be calcined is called dragon or "black
faeces"—that is, shadow stuff. In another text it is called the Ethiopian:
"Then will appear in the bottom of the vessel the mighty Ethiopian,
burned, calcined, bleached, altogether dead and lifeless. He asks to be
buried, to be sprinkled with his own moisture and slowly calcined till he
shall arise in glowing form from the fierce fire. ...Behold a wondrous
restoration or renewal of the Ethiopian!"[11]

The three texts quoted will suffice to demonstrate the nature of the
substance to be calcined. It is called variously a "ravening wolf," "black
faeces," a "dragon," and a "mighty Ethiopian." These terms tell us that
the *calcinatio* is performed on the primitive shadow side, which harbors

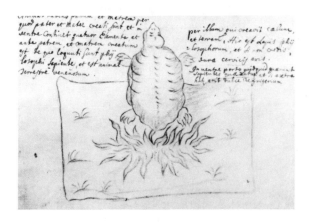

FIGURE 2 – 2
Calcinatio of an Earth–Animal (MS. Sloane I. 1316, 17th century. London,
British Museum. Reprinted in Burland, *The Arts of the Alchemists.*)

---

[10]"The Bosom Book of Sir George Ripley," in *Collectanea Chemica,* p. 126.

[11]Melchior, cited by Jung in *Psychology and Alchemy, CW* 12, pars. 484–85.

Jane Selfridge
dream - Two children
coming out of the
flames are in
embrace —

FIGURE 2 - 3
Calcinatio of the Devouring Parent (*Mutus Liber,* 1702. Reprinted in Jung,
Psychology and Alchemy.)

hungry, instinctual desirousness and is contaminated with the unconscious. The fire for the process comes from the frustration of these
instinctual desires themselves. Such an ordeal of frustrated desire is a
characteristic feature of the developmental process.

A man who endured a prolonged frustration had this dream:

> *The dreamer found himself in a cavernous place, perhaps under-
> ground. Through a door come huge, white–hot masses of lime-
> stone that slide or roll past him. Smoke and fire are all about. He*

FIGURE 2 – 4
The Fire of the Dragon Being Both Fanned and Extinguished (Trismosin, *Splendor Solis,* 1582.)

seeks for a way out but whenever he opens a door he is met by billowing smoke which drives him back.

On awakening his first associations were that this must be hell or the fiery furnace of Nebuchadnezzar. In this dream the inert limestone is in the process of being transformed into living quicklime by the *calcinatio.* The associations bring up a biblical image of the *calcinatio,* Nebuchadnezzar's fiery furnace, which makes an interesting psychological point. Nebuchadnezzar commanded everyone to fall down and worship his golden image. Shadrach, Meshach, and Abednego refused. Nebuchadnezzar in furious rage had them thrown into the fiery furnace. But they were unharmed, and in the midst of the fire four men were seen; the appearance of the fourth was "like a son of the gods" (Daniel 3:25 JB).

The account emphasizes Nebuchadnezzar's furious rage. His rage can be equated with the fiery furnace. He personifies the power motive, the arbitrary authority of the inflated ego that undergoes *calcinatio* when its overwhelming pretensions are frustrated by the presence of the trans-personal authority (the God of Shadrach, Meshach, and Abednego). Nebuchadnezzar corresponds to the king in our alchemical quotation who is fed to the wolf and then calcined. Another interesting feature is that in the furnace the three men become four. This is a clear allusion to the totality of the Self that emerges in the midst of the frustration of the ego power demands. Nebuchadnezzar's fiery furnace expresses an arche-typal situation. It is what one encounters whenever one challenges an arbitrary authority, either internal or external. Whether one gets through such a *calcinatio* depends on whether one is acting on ego motives or Self motives (see figure 2–5).

Shadrach, Meshach, and Abednego were immune to fire. This brings up a typical motif. Eliade has discussed the "mastery of fire" as a feature of shamanism and the mythology of early metallurgy.[12] The shamans were supposed to be immune to fire. They could swallow it or pick up burning coals with impunity. In this connection a woman had an interesting dream:

> The dreamer saw a woman bending over a cauldron–like vat holding a ball of fire in her hands. With complete nonchalance and no evidence of pain or harm she held, shaped, and squeezed the ball of fire as though it were a piece of laundry being washed. The dreamer watched with amazement.

The dream associated to an ancient Navajo Indian woman that the dreamer once saw making bread on a heated stone with her bare hands. The dream came at a time when the patient was starting to embark on a major creative project and indicates that the creative energies of the Self were activated[13] (see figure 2–6).

The image of invulnerability to fire indicates an immunity to identifi-cation with affect. Experience of the archetypal psyche has this effect to the extent that it enlarges and deepens ego consciousness. There is then less likelihood of identification with the emotional reactions of oneself

---

[12]Eliade, *The Forge and the Crucible,* pp. 79ff; also *Shamanism.*

[13]The interpretation of the fire–kneading woman as the Self is supported by the following amplification. "In Ephreum, the Syrian writer of hymns, John the Baptist says to Christ: 'A spark of fire in the air waits for thee over the Jordan. If thou followest it and willst be baptised, then take possession of thyself, wash thyself, for who has the power to take hold of burning fire with his hands? Thou who are wholly fire, have mercy on me' " (cited in Jung, *Psychology of the Unconscious,* p. 547 n. 61).

FIGURE 2 – 5

The Fiery Furnace of Daniel (Bible of St. Stephen Harding, 12th century. Dijon, Bibliothèque Municipale, MS. 14. Reprinted in *Medieval Manuscript Painting.)*

or others. By contrast a weak ego is very vulnerable to being consumed by encounter with intense affect. This phenomenon is described in a poem by Dorsha Hayes:

> Filled with a clutter of unsorted stuff
> a spark can set a man ablaze. What's there
> heaped high among stored rubbish at a puff
> will burst in flame. No man can be aware
> of how inflammable he is, how prone

FIGURE 2 - 6
The Starry Salamander That Lives in the Fire. The Mercurial Spirit of the
Prima Materia, as Salamander, Frolicking in the Fire (Maier, *Atalanta Fugiens,*
1618.)

to what can rage beyond control, unless
the piled up litter of his life is known
to him, and he is able to assess
what hazard he is in, what could ignite.
A man, disordered and undisciplined,
lives in the peril of a panic flight
before the onrush of a flaming wind.
    Does it now seem I seek to be profound?
    I stand on smoking ash and blackened ground![14]

The fire of the *calcinatio* is a purging, whitening fire. It acts on the black
stuff, the *nigredo,* and turns it white. Basil Valentine says, "Know that
this (*calcinatio*) is the only right and legitimate way of purifying our
substance."[15] This connects it with the symbolism of purgatory. The
doctrine of purgatory is the theological verson of *calcinatio* projected

---

[14]Hayes, "Fire Hazard," in *The Bell Branch Rings,* p. 26.

[15]Waite, trans., *The Hermetic Museum* 1:325.

onto the afterlife. The chief scriptural source for the doctrine is Paul's statement in 1 Corinthians 3:11–15 (RSV):

> For no other foundation can anyone lay than that which is laid, which is Jesus Christ. Now if anyone builds on the foundation with gold, silver, precious stones, wood, hay, stubble—each man's work will become manifest; for the Day will disclose it, because it will be revealed with fire, and the fire will test what sort of work each has done. If the work which any man has built on the foundation survives, he will receive a reward. If any man's work is burned up, he will suffer loss, though he himself will be saved, but only as through fire.

Augustine comments on this passage: The man who builds with wood, hay, and stubble is the man involved in lust and carnal desire, but "For so long as he does not prefer such affection or pleasure to Christ, Christ is his foundation, though on it he builds wood, hay, stubble; and therefore he shall be saved as by fire. For the fire of affliction shall burn such luxurious pleasures and earthly loves... and of this fire the fuel is bereavement, and all those calamities which consume these joys."[16] Again, "things are not lost without anguish when they have been loved with a possessive love. But because... he prefers to suffer the loss of these things rather than losing Christ, and does not desert Christ from fear of losing such things—even though he may grieve over his loss—'he is saved' indeed, 'yet so as by fire.' He 'burns' with grief, for the things he has loved and lost, but this does not subvert or consume him, secured as he is by the stability and the indestructability of his foundation."[17]

The doctrine of purgatory had not yet become established at the time Augustine wrote. However these remarks were later applied to purgatorial fire. Augustine makes two important psychological points. First, the fire of purgatory is caused by the frustrations of lust, desire, possessive love—in a word, concupiscence. Secondly, one can survive this fire, indeed be saved by it, if one has a solid foundation in Christ. Psychologically this would mean that psychological development will be promoted by the frustration of pleasure and power desires providing one has a basically viable relation to the Self symbolized by Christ.

Next to the doctrine of purgatory with its purging but redeeming fire is an image of perpetual *calcinatio*, the idea of eternal punitive fire. Ixion was punished for his crime of trying to seduce Hera by being bound to a perpetual wheel of fire. The notion that the wicked were punished in the afterlife was widespread in antiquity. Cumont writes: "Among all the forms of punishment that by fire predominates. The idea that the Erinyes burnt the damned with their torches is ancient, and

---

[16]Augustine, *City of God* 21:26.

[17]Augustine, *Confessions and Enchiridion* 18:68.

the Pyriphlegethon is an igneous river surrounding Tartarus. Certain authors went beyond this. Lucian in his 'True Histories' describes the island of the impious as an immense brazier whence rise sulphurous and pitchy flames"[18] (see figure 2-7).

Similarly, in Buddhism, *Avichi*, the lowest of the eight Buddhist "hot hells," is a place of torture by fire as a punishment for sin.[19] However, this image is most fully developed in the Christian doctrine of hell. One of its sources is Matthew 25:41–43 (RSV): "When he will say to those at his left hand, 'Depart from me, you cursed, into the eternal fire prepared for the devil and his angels; for I was hungry and you gave me no food, I was thirsty and you gave me no drink, I was a stranger and you did not welcome me, naked and you did not clothe me, sick and in prison and you did not visit me.' "

As did Augustine, Origen in commentary on this passage equates fire with the passions of man. Origen comments on this passage as follows:

FIGURE 2 – 7
The Violent Tortured in a Rain of Fire (Doré, *Illustrations for Dante's Divine Comedy.*)

[18]Cumont, *Afterlife in Roman Paganism,* p. 175.

[19]Hastings, *Encyclopedia of Religion and Ethics* 11:830.

Let us now see what is the meaning of threatened "eternal fire." Now we find in the prophet Isaiah that the fire by which each man is punished is described as belonging to himself. For it says, "Walk in the light of your fire and in the flame which you have kindled for yourselves" (Isaiah 50:11). These words seem to indicate that every sinner kindles for himself the flame of his own fire, and is not plunged into a fire which has been previously kindled by someone else or which existed before him. Of this fire the food and material are our sins, which are called by the apostle Paul wood and hay and stubble... in the very essence of the soul certain torments are produced from the harmful desires themselves that lead us to sin.

Consider the effect of those faults of passion which often occur in men, as when the soul is burnt up with the flames of love, or tormented by the fires of jealousy or envy, or tossed about with furious anger, or consumed with intense sadness; remembering how some men, finding the excess of these ills too heavy to bear, have deemed it more tolerable to submit to death than endure such tortures.[20]

This is a remarkably psychological interpretation of the fire of hell to have been written in the third century. It demonstrates that for the early church fathers, psychic reality and theological reality were one. Hell fire is the punishment meted out to those who are condemned in the "Last Judgement," who are "weighed in the balance and found wanting." It is the fate of that aspect of the ego that is identified with the transpersonal energies of the psyche and uses them for personal pleasure or power. This aspect of the ego, which is identified with the Self-energy, must undergo *calcinatio*. The process will be considered "eternal" only when we are dealing with a psychic split that irrevocably divides good from evil and heaven from hell.

There are many vivid expressions of the fire of the Last Judgement. For example, in Revelation 20:13–15 (RSV) we read: "And the sea gave up the dead in it, Death and Hades gave up the dead in them, and all were judged by what they had done... and if anyone's name was not found written in the book of life, he was thrown into the lake of fire."

---

[20]Origen, *On First Principles* 2:4–5. A thousand years later Thomas à Kempis expressed it this way (*The Imitation of Christ* 1:24):

What is there that the fire of hell shall feed upon, but thy sins?

The more thou sparest thyself now and followest the flesh, the more severe hereafter shall be thy punishment, and thou storest up greater fuel for that flame.

In what things a man hath sinned, in the same shall he be the more grievously punished.

There shall the slothful be pricked forward with burning goads, and the gluttons be tormented with extreme hunger and thirst.

There shall the luxurious and lovers of pleasure be bathed in burning pitch and stinking brimstone, and the envious, like mad dogs, shall howl for very grief.

There is no sin but shall have its own proper torment.

There the proud shall be filled with all confusion; the covetous shall be pinched with miserable penury.

In another place it is put this way:

> If any man worship the beast and his image, and receive his mark in his fore-
> head, or in his hand, the same shall drink of the wine of the wrath of God,
> which is poured out without mixture into the cup of his indignation; and he
> shall be tormented [βασανισθησεται] with fire and brimstone in the presence
> of the holy angels, and in the presence of the Lamb: and the smoke of their
> torment [βασανισμου] ascendeth up for ever and ever: and they have no rest
> day nor night, who worship the beast and his image; and whosoever receiveth
> the mark of his name[21] (Rev. 14:9–11, AV).

Here the punitive fire of the Last Judgement is identified with God's
wrath. The same occurs in the Sequence hymn, *Dies Irae,* in the Burial
Mass. It presents the Last Judgement quite explicitly as a *calcinatio:*

> *Dies irae, dies illa*
> *Solvet saeclum in favilla*
> *Teste David cum Sibylla*

("Oh day of wrath, Oh that day, when the world dissolves in glowing
ashes, as witness David with the Sibyl.")

The reference to the Sibyl leads to a passage in Book II of the *Sibylline Oracles:*

> And then shall a great river of flaming fire flow from heaven and consume all
> places, the earth and the great ocean and the grey sea, lakes and rivers and
> fountains, and merciless Hades and the Pole of heaven: but the lights of
> heaven shall melt together in one and into a void (desolate) shape (?). For the
> stars shall all fall from heaven into the sea (?), and all the souls of men shall
> gnash their teeth as they burn in the river of brimstone and the rush of the
> fire in the blazing plain, and ashes shall cover all things, and then shall all the
> elements of the world be laid waste, air, earth, sea, light, poles, days and
> nights, and no more shall the multitudes of birds fly in the air nor swimming
> creatures any more swim in the sea; no ship shall sail with its cargo over the
> waves; no straight-going oxen shall plow the tilled land; there shall be no
> more sound of swift winds, but he shall fuse all things together into one, and
> purge them clean.[22]

In this passage the *calcinatio* overlaps with the image of the *coniunctio.* The four elements are being fused into a quintessential one.
Multiplicity is being melted into unity. Hence it alludes to the integration
of the personality through the process of *calcinatio.* It is an example of
the widespread notion that the world will end in fire. The Stoics had the

---

[21]The Greek word for torment is βασανιζειν or βασανιμος. Jung says about this word:
"For alchemists it had a double meaning: βασανιζειν also meant 'testing on the touchstone' (βασανος). The *lapis Lydius* (touchstone) was used as a synonym for the *lapis
philosophorum.* The genuineness or incorruptibility of the stone is proved by the torment
of fire and cannot be attained without it.. This *leitmotiv* runs all through alchemy"
(*Alchemical Studies,* par. 94).

[22]James, *The Apocryphal New Testament,* p. 522.

idea, which they claimed to derive from Heraclitus, that each cosmic cycle or *magnus annus* ends in a conflagration, an ἐκπύρωσις.[23]

According to Josephus, Adam predicted that the earth would be destroyed twice, once by water and once by fire[24]—first a *solutio* and then a *calcinatio*. The same idea is expressed in 2 Peter 3:6,7 (RSV): "The world that then existed was deluged with water and perished. But by the same word the heavens and earth that now exist have been stored up for fire, being kept until the day of judgement and destruction of ungodly men."

In a poem by Robert Frost the images of fire and ice are associated with the end of the world:

> Some say the World will end in fire,
> Some say in ice.
> From what I've tasted of desire
> I hold with those who favor fire.
> But if it had to perish twice,
> I think I know enough of hate
> To say that for destruction ice
> Is also great
> And would suffice.[25]

Another modern poet uses the same image:

Fire will surely come one day to purify the earth. Fire will surely come one day to obliterate the earth. This is the Second Coming.

The Soul is a flaming tongue that licks and struggles to set the black bull of the world on fire. One day the entire universe will become a single conflagration.

Fire is the first and final mask of my God. We dance and weep between two enormous pyres.[26]

Last judgement by fire corresponds to the ordeal by fire that tests the purity of metals and refines away all impurities. There are numerous passages in the Old Testament that make use of metallurgical metaphors to describe Yahweh's testing of his chosen people. For example, Yahweh speaks:

> I will turn my hand against you, I will smelt away your dross in the furnace, I will remove all your base metal from you. (Isa. 1:24,25, JB)

> And now I have put you in the fire like silver, I have tested you in the furnace of distress. For my sake and my sake only have I acted—is my name to be profaned? Never will I yield my glory to another. (Isa. 48:10,11, JB)

---

[23]Hastings, *Encyclopedia of Religion and Ethics* 1:198.

[24]Josephus, *Antiquities of the Jews* 1:ii, 3.

[25]Frost, "Fire and Ice," in *Complete Poems of Robert Frost,* p. 268.

[26]Kazantzakis, *The Saviors of God,* p. 128.

I will lead...[them] into the fire, and refine them as silver is refined, test them as gold is tested. They will call my name and I shall listen; and I shall say: These are my people; and each will say, "Yahweh is my God!" (Zech. 13:9, JB)

You tested us, God, you refined us like silver, you let us fall into the net, you laid heavy burdens on our backs, you let people drive over our heads; but now the ordeal by fire and water is over, and you allow us once more to draw breath. (Ps. 66:10–12, JB)

Then Yahweh speaks to the refined or redeemed ones, those who have gone through the *calcinatio:* "Do not be afraid, for I have redeemed you; I have called you by your name, you are mine. Should you pass through the sea, I will be with you; or through the rivers, they will not swallow you up. Should you walk through fire, you will not be scorched and the flames will not burn you. For I am Yahweh, your God, the Holy One of Israel, your savior" (Isa. 43:1–3, JB).

This passage is paralleled by the idea found elsewhere that at death souls pass through a river or a sea of fire. It does not harm the righteous but causes suffering or destruction to the wicked. For instance, a Parsi doctrine states that all must pass through a river of fire. To the righteous it is like warm milk, but to the wicked like molten metal.[27]

Again, in the *Sibylline Oracles* we read: "And then shall all men pass through a blazing river and unquenchable flame, and the righteous shall be saved whole, all of them, but the ungodly shall perish therein unto all ages, even as many as wrought evil aforetime."[28]

Yahweh's remarks about his use of fire can be compared with Paracelsus' statements about the alchemical effects of fire:

By the element of fire all that is unpurified is destroyed and taken away.

In the absence of all ordeal by fire, there is no proving of a substance possible.

Fire separates that which is constant or fixed from that which is fugitive or volatile.[29]

Another alchemist specifically compares the fire of the alchemical *calcinatio* with the fire of divine wrath as endured by Christ. "It is not unfitly compared with Christ when the putrefied body of the Sun lies dead, inactive, like ashes in the bottom of a phial.... So also did it happen to Christ himself, when at the Mount of Olives, and on the

---

[27]Hastings, *Encyclopedia of Religion and Ethics* 5:376.

[28]James, *Apocryphal New Testament*, p. 532.

[29]Paracelsus, *The Hermetic and Alchemical Writings of Paracelsus* 1:4.

cross, he was roasted by the fire of the divine wrath (Matt. 26,27), and complained that he was utterly deserted by his heavenly Father."[30]

As early as Homeric Greece we find the image of fire as a purifier and separator of the soul. According to Rohde the body of a dead man must be burnt before his soul is released to go to Hades. "Only through fire are the souls of the dead 'appeased' (Iliad VII, 410). So long, then, as the psyche retains any vestige of 'earthliness' it possesses some feeling still, some awareness of what is going on among the living"[31] (see figure 2-8).

Everywhere fire is associated with God and therefore represents archetypal energies that transcend the ego and are experienced as numinous. The Psalmist speaks of God as he "who maketh his angels spirits; his ministers a flaming fire" (Ps. 104:4, AV). An ancient prayer to Mithra says: "Give ear to me, hear me, Lord, who has fastened the fiery bolts of heaven with thy spirit, double-bodied, fire-ruler, creator of

FIGURE 2 – 8
Calcinatio of the Hermaphrodite (Maier, *Atalanta Fugiens,* 1618.)

---

[30]Cited by Jung, *Mysterium Coniunctionis, CW* 14, par. 485. The same passage in *The Hermetic Museum* (1:102) translated by Waite omits the crucial passage—that Christ "was roasted by the fire of divine wrath."

[31]Rohde, *Psyche* 1:18ff.

light, fire-breathing, fiery-hearted, shining spirit, rejoicing in fire, beautiful light, Lord of light, fiery-bodied, giver of light, sower of fire, confounding with fire, living light, whirling fire, mover of light, hurler of thunderbolts, glorious light, multiplier of light, holder of fiery light, conqueror of the stars, etc."[32]

In several texts Christ is associated with fire. In Luke 12:49 (RSV) Christ said, "I came to cast fire upon the earth; and would that it were already kindled." In the Gnostic *Gospel of Thomas* we read, "Jesus said: He who is near me is near the fire and he who is far from me is far from the kingdom"[33] (see figure 2-9).

Characteristically, mythical thinking distinguishes two types of fire. The Stoics spoke of a terrestrial fire and an etherial fire. The latter corresponded to Nous, the divine Logos, and is analogous to the later

FIGURE 2 – 9
The Fire Sower (E. Jacoby. Reprinted in Jung, *Civilization in Transition.*)

---

[32]Dieterich, *Eine Mithrasliturgie,* cited by Jung, *Symbols of Transformation, CW* 5, par. 135.
[33]Grant, *The Secret Sayings of Jesus,* p. 180.

Christian conception of the Holy Spirit. Bevan describes the concept of etherial fire as follows: "All round the world was an envelope of the fiery ether, pure and unmixed, but it also penetrated the whole mass, as its soul. The orderly working of nature was its operation: organic beings grew according to regular types, because the Divine Reason was in them as a *logos spermatikos,* a formula of life developing from a germ. Even upon earth some of the divine fire retained its pure essence—the reasonable souls, each one a particle of fiery ether, which dwelt in the hearts of men."[34]

In Jacob Boehme we find the image of two trees of fire—one is the fire of the Holy Ghost, the other the fire of God's wrath. "The tree of life was kindled in its own quality by the fire of the *Holy Ghost,* and its quality burnt in the fire of heavenly joyfulness, in an unsearchable light and glory.... The tree of the fierce quality, which is the other part in nature, was kindled also, and burnt in the fire of *God's Wrath* in a hellish flame; and the fierce source rose up into eternity, and the prince of darkness with his legions abode in the fierce wrathful quality, as in his own kingdom."[35]

The tree of life as a tree of fire alludes to the passage in Genesis (3:24, RSV): "He drove out the man; and at the east of the garden of Eden he placed the cherubim, and a flaming sword which turned every way, to guard the way to the tree of life." The sword belongs to the symbolism of *separatio* and *mortificatio.* In this passage there is thus an overlap of the latter images with the *calcinatio.* The *Zohar* says the flaming sword symbolizes the trials with which God overwhelms man, that he may be restored to the way of goodness.[36]

For the purged ego the divine fire is more apt to be experienced as a theophany or divine inspiration. For instance, when Yahweh descended onto Mount Sinai he turned it into a lime kiln: "And Mount Sinai was wrapped in smoke, because the Lord descended upon it in fire; and the smoke of it went up like the smoke of a kiln" (Exod. 19:18, RSV).

The word of God is described as a fire. Yahweh says: "Behold, I am making my words in your mouth a fire, and this people wood, and the fire shall devour them" (Jer. 5:14, RSV). Again, "Is not my word like fire, says the Lord, and like a hammer which breaks the rocks in pieces?" (Jer. 23:29, RSV). Elsewhere, the tongue of man is said to be set on fire by hell. "And the tongue is a fire. The tongue is an unrighteous world among our members, staining the whole body, setting on fire the cycle

[34]Bevan, *Stoics and Sceptics,* p. 43.

[35]Boehme, *Aurora,* pp. 24ff.

[36]Waite, *The Holy Kabbalah,* p. 290n.

of nature, and set on fire by hell" (James 3:6 RSV). In the *Bruce Codex,* a Coptic Gnostic papyrus in the Bodleian Library, Oxford, a ritual is described called "the Baptism by Fire." The "Virgin of Life" gives the "Water of the Baptism of Fire" and the baptized ones receive on their foreheads "the seal of the Virgin of Light."[37]

In the miracle of Pentecost, as described in Acts 2:3, the Holy Spirit comes as tongues of fire (see figure 2-10). The following case is an example of the image of fire as the Holy Spirit. A young research scientist made a brilliant formulation in a scientific paper based on an important discovery. The professor who held authority over him had belittled his conclusions without reading the paper. At this point the

FIGURE 2 – 10
Pentecost (Doré, *Bible Illustrations.*)

---

[37]Mead, *Fragments of a Faith Forgotten,* p. 526.

young scientist, who was usually very mild-mannered, replied with great intensity: "Professor——, if you are going to criticize my paper you must first read it and give it careful thought." He was alarmed by the intensity of his reaction, but after an initial flare of anger the professor acknowledged his mistake, read the paper, and recognized its value.

The night before this crucial encounter, which had important consequences for the young scientist's career, he had this dream:

I am sitting at a dinner table with guests. Suddenly something spills and catches fire. Then the whole table is covered with little flames shifting around from one side to the other. It is a beautiful sight. On awakening I think of the miracle at Pentecost.

This dream refers not only to the dreamer's fiery encounter with the professor, but, more importantly, to the creative fire of the Holy Ghost that poured itself out on him and enabled him to make his brilliant formulations. The divine fire that touches the creative artist is described in the fifty-ninth sonnet of Michelangelo:

> Only through fire can the smith pull and stretch
> Metal into the shape of his design.
> Only through fire can the artist reach
> Pure gold which only furnaces refine.

> Nor can the phoenix rare itself remake
> Unless it first be burnt. For my part, I
> Hope to ascend triumphantly on high
> Where death fulfills, where time itself must break.

> The fire of which I speak has brought salvation,
> I find in it new powers and restoration
> Although I seemed already with the dead.

> Since by fire nature reaches up to heaven
> I may, through it, be reconciled, forgiven,
> For it must surely bear me overhead.[38]

The ambiguous contrast between the fire of the Holy Spirit (or the dove of Aphrodite) and the fire of concupiscence is beautifully described by T. S. Eliot:

> The dove descending breaks the air
> With flame of incandescent terror
> Of which the tongues declare
> The one discharge from sin and error.
> The only hope, or else despair

---

[38]Michelangelo, *The Sonnets of Michelangelo,* p. 95.

> Lies in the choice of pyre or pyre—
> To be redeemed from fire by fire.
>
> Who then devised the torment? Love.
> Love is the unfamiliar name
> Behind the hands that wove
> The intolerable shirt of flame
> Which human power cannot remove.
> We only live, only suspire
> Consumed by either fire or fire.[39]

The "intolerable shirt of flame" refers to an important *calcinatio* image, the shirt of Nessus in the Heracles myth. Heracles rescued Deianeira from rape by the centaur Nessus, using an arrow tipped with the poisonous blood of the hydra. Before his death, Nessus gave Deianeira a love charm composed of his own blood tainted with hydra blood. When Heracles became interested in another woman, Deianeira soaked a shirt in this potion and gave it to Heracles. When he put it on it became a "shirt of flame" which could not be removed. Heracles escaped the torment only by voluntarily consuming himself on a funeral pyre. The same image appears when Medea sends Jason's fiancée, Glauce, a robe that bursts into flame when she puts it on.

The shirt of Nessus illustrates the fact that blood is often symbolically equated with fire. Thus baptism in blood is equivalent to baptism in fire. In the taurobolium rite of Mithraism, the initiate in a pit was soaked with the blood of a bull that was sacrificed on a latticed platform above him.[40] A somewhat more refined example of the same image is found in Revelation: "Who are these, clothed in white robes, and whence have they come? ... These are they who have come out of the great tribulation; they have washed their robes and made them white in the blood of the Lamb" (Rev. 7:13–14, RSV).

Baptism in blood, like the encounter with fire, refers psychologically to the ordeal of enduring intense affect. If the ego holds, the ordeal has a refining and consolidating effect. This will be one of the reasons for primitive initiation ordeals that often generated intense anxiety.

In early times fire was the chief method of sacrifice to the gods. Fire was thought of as a connecting link between the human and divine realms. That which was *sacrificed* by burning quite literally was "made sacred." That which is burned turns largely to smoke and ascends to the upper regions. It is transferred to the gods by a process of sublimation. This is how the Greek burnt sacrifice, the *thysia,* was conceived, and also the burnt offerings of the Jews.[41] In India, Agni is the Hindu fire

---

[39]Eliot, "Little Gidding," in *Four Quartets.*

[40]Cumont, *The Mysteries of Mithra,* p. 180.

[41]Yerkes, *Sacrifice in Greek and Roman Religion and Early Judaism,* passim.

god, the one to whom sacrifice is offered. In Hindu thought, "it is through fire that man could communicate with higher states of being, with the gods and the heavenly spheres. Through fire he could take part in the cosmic life, cooperate with the gods. He could feed them through the mouth of fire. 'Agni is the mouth of the gods; through this mouth they take their breath.'" (Kapisthala-katha Samhita 31.20 and Satapabha Brahmana 3.7.)[42] (see figure 2-11).

Speaking of the sacrificial fire of the Greek *thysia*, Iamblichus says: "thus also the fire that is with us, imitating the energy of divine fire,

FIGURE 2 – 11
Shiva Dancing in a Circle of Fire (Bronze, 12th or 13th century. Amsterdam, Museum van Aziatische Kunst. Reprinted in Zimmer, *The Art of Indian Asia.*)

[42]Danielou, *Hindu Polytheism,* p. 64.

destroys everything which is material in sacrifices, purifies the things which are offered, liberates them from the bonds of matter, and renders them, through purity of nature, adapted to the communion of the gods. It likewise liberates us, after the same manner from the bonds of generation, assimilates us to the Gods, causes us to be adapted to their friendship, and conducts our material nature to an immaterial essence."[43]

Similarly, certain myths speak of the fire-bath that conveys immortality. For example, Demeter, in her sorrowful wanderings after the abduction of Persephone, accepts the hospitality of Celeus and Metaneira, king and queen of Eleusis. In gratitude she plans to make their young son Demophoön immortal by holding him in the fire. Metaneira sees this procedure and interrupts it by her screams.[44] Immortality is a quality of the archetypes. Thus the psychological meaning of the fire-bath of immortality will be that a connection is made between the ego and the archetypal psyche, making the former aware of its transpersonal, eternal, or immortal aspect.

The end product of *calcinatio* is a white ash.[45] This corresponds to the so-called "white foliated earth" of many alchemical texts. It signifies the *albedo* or whitening phase and has paradoxical associations. On the one hand ashes signify despair, mourning, or repentance.[46] On the other hand they contain the supreme value, the goal of the work. One text says, "Despise not the ashes for they are the diadem of thy heart, and the ash of things that endure."[47] Another says, "The white foliated earth is the crown of victory which is ash extracted from ash, and their second body."[48] The ash is the incorruptible "glorified body," which has survived the purifying ordeal. It is equated with the biblical image of the crown of glory. Isaiah promises to give the mourners of Zion "a crown for ashes, the oil of joy for mourning, a garment of praise for the spirit of

---

[43]Iamblichus, *On the Mysteries of the Egyptians*, p. 247.

[44]Hesiod, "Homeric Hymns to Demeter," in *The Homeric Hymns and Homerica*, p. 307.

[45]Sometimes the result is a vitreous mass; hence there is an overlap between the symbolism of ash and glass. "In Senior the ash is synonymous with *vitrum* (glass), which, on account of its incorruptibility and transparency, seemed to resemble the glorified body" (Jung, *Mysterium Coniunctionis, CW 14, par. 391).*

[46]This is a common biblical image. The book of Job provides a good example. After "the fire of God fell from heaven" (Job 1:16), Satan "afflicted Job with loathsome sores from the soles of his feet to the crown of his head. And he took a potsherd with which to scrape himself, and sat among the ashes" (Job 2:7–8). At the end of the drama, after Job has encountered Yahweh, he says, "I had heard of thee by the hearing of the ear, but now my eye sees thee; therefore I despise myself and repent in dust and ashes" (Job 42:5). The entire book of Job can be considered a symbolic description of the *calcinatio.* See Edinger, *Ego and Archetype*, p. 76ff.

[47]Jung, *Mysterium Coniunctionis, CW* 14, par. 247.

[48]Ibid., par. 318 n. 619.

grief" (Isa. 61:3, DV). St. Paul, using the analogy of athletic games, says, "Now they do it to obtain a corruptible crown; but we an incorruptible" (1 Cor. 9:25, AV). And later: "I have fought the good fight (αγων), I have finished the race, I have kept the faith. Henceforth there is laid up for me the crown of righteousness" (2 Tim. 4:7–8, RSV). An example of *calcinatio* followed by glory is found in a legend of St. John the Evangelist (see figure 2-12):

> When, after Pentecost, the apostles separated, John the Apostle and Evangelist went to Asia, and there founded many churches. The Emperor Domitian, hearing of his fame, summoned him to Rome, and had him plunged into a cauldron of boiling oil which was set up before the gate called the Porta Latina; but the saint came forth untouched, just as he had escaped the corruption of the senses. Seeing which, the emperor exiled him to the

FIGURE 2 – 12
St. John Boiled in Oil (Dürer, 1498. Reprinted in *The Complete Woodcuts of Albrecht Dürer.*)

island of Patmos where, living alone, he wrote the Apocalypse. But the cruel emperor was slain that same year, and the Senate revoked all his decrees. Thus it came about that Saint John, who had been deported as a criminal, returned to Ephesus covered with glory: the multitude ran out to meet him, crying: "Blessed is he that cometh in the name of the Lord."[49]

What turns the ashes of failure into the crown of victory is indicated by the fact that ash is alchemically equivalent to salt. The symbolism of salt has been discussed comprehensively by Jung.[50] Basically salt symbolizes Eros and appears in one of two aspects, either as bitterness or as wisdom. Jung writes: "Tears, sorrow, and disappointment are bitter, but wisdom is the comforter in all psychic suffering. Indeed, bitterness and wisdom form a pair of alternatives: where there is bitterness wisdom is lacking, and where wisdom is there can be no bitterness. Salt, as the carrier of this fateful alternative, is coordinated with the nature of woman."[51] This piece of modern wisdom has an ancient parallel in Aeschylus:

> In visions of the night, like dropping rain,
> Descend the many memories of pain
> Before the spirit's sight; through tears and dole
> Comes wisdom o'er the unwilling soul.[52]

From the simplest standpoint, *calcinatio* is a drying-out process. An important part of psychotherapy involves the drying out of water-logged unconscious complexes.[53] The fire or emotional intensity necessary for this operation seems to reside in the complex itself and becomes operative as soon as the patient attempts to make the complex conscious by sharing it with another person. All thoughts, deeds, and memories that carry shame, guilt, or anxiety need to be given full expression. The affect liberated becomes the fire that can dry out the complex and purify it of its unconscious contamination.

The necessary frustration of desirousness or concupiscence is the chief feature of the *calcinatio* stage. First the substance must be located; that is, the unconscious, unacknowledged desire, demand, expectation must be recognized and affirmed. The instinctual urge that says "I want" and "I am entitled to this" must be fully accepted by the ego. There can be no proper *calcinatio*, as distinguished from masochistic self-flagella-

---

[49]Voragine, *The Golden Legend,* p. 58.

[50]Jung, *Mysterium Coniunctionis, CW* 14, pars. 234–348.

[51]Ibid., par. 330.

[52]*Agamemnon,* in *The Complete Greek Drama,* ed. Oates and O'Neill 1:173.

[53]Heraclitus says, "A dry soul is the wisest and best" (Freeman, *Ancilla to the Pre-Socratic Philosophers,* p. 32).

tion, until the proper material is at hand. I think this fact is what under-lies the following warning of an alchemist: "A great many students make a mistake at the very outset, by performing this *calcinatio* on a wrong substance;... or they choose a false method, and corrode instead of calcining the metallic bodies on which they operate. Calcination can take place only by the means of the inward heat of the body, assisted by friendly outward warmth; but calcination by means of a heterogeneous agent can only destroy the metallic nature, in so far as it has any effect at all."[54]

The fire of the *calcinatio,* to the extent that it can be brought about by the psychotherapist, is achieved largely by expressing attitudes and reactions that frustrate the patient. This is a dangerous procedure and must be used with great care. As the text warns, the *calcinatio* may be performed on the wrong substance or by a false method, which corrodes instead of calcining. A sufficiently solid psychic foundation must be present to endure the *calcinatio,* and also an adequate rapport between the patient and therapist must exist to be able to carry frustration without generating destructive negativity. The text says, *"calcinatio* can take place only by means of the inward heat of the body"—in other words, by its own heat, by its own tendency to self-*calcinatio.* This means that the therapist must take his lead from the patient's material itself and promote frustration of a given desire only to the extent that the inner developmental tendency also contains the denial of the desire. The therapist can assist "by friendly outward warmth." But "calcination by means of a heterogeneous agent can only destroy the metallic nature." A heterogeneous agent would refer to an arbitrary attitude that is not guided by the patient's own material and condition and hence is alien and damaging to his essential nature.

As a rule, life reality, if faced, provides plenty of occasions for the *calcinatio* of frustrated desirousness. The primitive, undifferentiated desire that says "I want" operates on the implicit assumption that it is entitled to have what it wants. When denied, it becomes enraged. This is the psychological homologue of the "Divine Wrath" that roasted Christ. Reality often generates fire by challenging or denying the demanding expectations of such desires. Denied justification, the frustrated desire becomes the fire of *calcinatio.* Ripley says:

> Calcination is the purgation of our stone,
> Restoring also of his natural heat;
> Of radical moisture it leaveth none.[55]

---

[54]Waite, trans., *The Hermetic Museum* 2:256.

[55]*The Lives of the Alchemystical Philosophers,* p. 218.

Calcinatio has a purging or purifying effect. The substance is purged of radical moisture. This would correspond to the drippings of unconsciousness that accompany emerging energies. Or, in other words, the energies of the archetypal psyche first appear in identification with the ego and express themselves as desires for ego-pleasure and ego-power. The fire of *calcinatio* purges these identifications and drives off the root, or primordial moisture, leaving the content in its eternal or transpersonal state, restored of its natural heat—that is, of its own proper energy and functioning (see figures 2-13 and 2-14).

Finally, the *calcinatio* brings about a certain immunity to affect and an ability to see the archetypal aspect of existence. To the extent that one is related to the transpersonal center of one's being, affect is experienced as etherial fire (Holy Spirit) rather than terrestrial fire—the pain of frustrated desirousness. Jung describes the transformation of desirousness this way:

> In this transformation it is essential to take objects away from those animus or anima devils. They only become concerned with objects when you allow yourself to be self-indulgent. *Concupiscentia* is the term for that in the church....On this subject the great religions come together. The fire of desirousness is the element that must be fought against in Brahmanism, in Buddhism, in Tantrism, in Manicheanism, in Christianity. It is also important in psychology. When you indulge in desirousness, whether your desire

FIGURE 2 – 13
Expulsion of the demons (Engraving, 17th century. Reprinted in Jung, *Symbols of Transformation.*)

FIGURE 2 - 14
The King in the Sweatbox (Maier, *Atalanta Fugiens,* 1618.)

turns toward heaven or hell, you give the animus or anima an object; then it
comes out into the world instead of staying inside in its place.... But if you
can say: Yes, I desire it and I shall try to get it but I do not have to have it, if I
decide to renounce, I can renounce it; then there is no chance for the animus
or anima. Otherwise you are governed by your desires, you are possessed....
But if you have put your animus or anima into a bottle you are free of
possession, even though you may be having a bad time inside, because when
your devil has a bad time you have a bad time.... Of course he will rumble
around in your entrails. But after a while you will see that it was right (to
bottle him up). You will slowly become quiet and change. Then you will
discern that there is a stone growing in the bottle...insofar as self-control, or
non-indulgence, has become a habit, it is a stone...when that attitude
becomes a *fait accompli,* the stone will be a diamond.[56]

---

[56]Jung, *The Visions Seminars* 1:239.

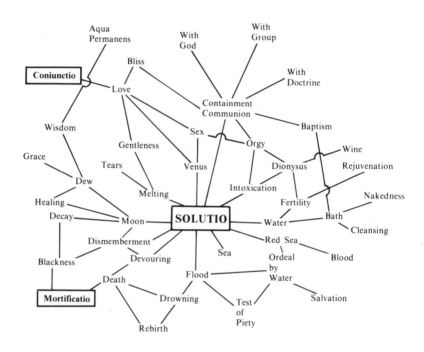

❧ **3** *Solutio* ❧

T HE OPERATION OF *SOLUTIO* is one of the major procedures in alchemy.
One text says, *"Solutio* is the root of alchemy."[1] Another says,
"Until all be made water, perform no operation."[2] In many places the
whole *opus* is summarized by the phrase "Dissolve and coagulate." Just
as *calcinatio* pertains to the element fire, *coagulatio* to the element
earth, and *sublimatio* to the element air, so *solutio* pertains to water.
Basically, *solutio* turns a solid into a liquid. The solid seems to disappear
into the solvent as if it had been swallowed up. For the alchemist,
solutio often meant the return of differentiated matter to its original
undifferentiated state—that is, to *prima materia*. Water was thought of
as the womb and *solutio* as a return to the womb for rebirth. In one text
the old king submits to the *solutio* of drowning, saying,

> Else I God's Kingdom cannot enter in:
> And therefore, that I may be Borne agen,
> I'll Humblèd be into my Mother's Breast,
> Dissolve to my First Matter, and there rest.[3]

First matter, or *prima materia,* is an idea that the alchemists inherited
from the pre-Socratic philosophers. In Thales, and also in many creation
myths, water is the original material out of which the world is created.
The alchemists thought that a substance could not be transformed
unless it were first reduced to *prima materia*. One text says, "Bodies
cannot be changed except by reduction into their first matter."[4] This
procedure corresponds to what takes place in psychotherapy. The fixed,
static aspects of the personality allow for no change. They are established
and sure of their rightness. For transformation to proceed, these fixed

---

[1]Bonus of Ferrara, *The New Pearl of Great Price,* p. 365.

[2]Read, *Prelude to Chemistry,* p. 262.

[3]Jung, *Mysterium Coniunctionis, CW* 14, par. 380.

[4]Kelly, *The Alchemical Writings of Edward Kelly,* p. 34.

aspects must first be dissolved or reduced to *prima materia*. This is done by the analytic process, which examines the products of the unconscious and puts the established ego attitudes into question.

One alchemical recipe for *solutio* is the following:

> Dissolve then sol and luna in our dissolving water, which is familiar and friendly, and the next in nature unto them, and as it were a womb, a mother, an original, the beginning and the end of their life. And that is the very reason why they are meliorated or amended in this water, because like nature rejoiceth in like nature.... Thus it behooves you to join consanguinity, or sameness of kind.... And because sol and luna have their origin from this water their mother; it is necessary therefore that they enter into it again, to wit, into their mother's womb, that they may be regenerate or born again, and made more healthy, more noble, and more strong.[5]

The chemical fact that lies behind this text is the capacity of mercury to dissolve or amalgamate with gold and silver, here referred to as Sol and Luna. In fact, this process is the basis of a very old method for extracting gold from crude ore. The ore is pulverized and treated with mercury, which dissolves the gold. The mercury is then separated from the gold by distilling with heat. However, our text has turned this chemical process into a symbolic image by superimposing a projected psychological process onto the chemical one. Sol and Luna will stand for the masculine and the feminine principles as they concretely manifest themselves in the personality at the beginning of the process. In other words the dominant conscious attitude of the ego is represented by Sol and the anima at its current state of development by Luna.[6] These two are dissolved in "friendly water"—that is, mercury—which is equated with the maternal womb and corresponds to the *prima materia*. Incest symbolism is emphasized in the phrase, "it behooves you to join consanguinity, or sameness of kind."

We have here a picture of a descent into the unconscious, which is the maternal womb from which the ego is born. It is the *prima materia* prior to the differentiation of the elements by consciousness. This text describes the procedure as a very pleasant process. There are others which express it much more negatively. For instance, consider this *solutio*-dismemberment recipe: "The body of that woman [who slays her husbands] is full of weapons and poison. Let a grave be dug for that dragon, and let that woman be buried with him, he being chained fast to that woman; and the more he winds and coils himself around her, the more will he be cut to pieces by the female weapons which are fashioned

---

[5]"Secret Book of Artephius," in *The Lives of the Alchemystical Philosophers,* pp. 145–46.

[6]This applies to a man's psychology. For a woman, Luna would represent the ego attitude and Sol the animus.

in the body of the woman. And when he sees that he is mingled with the limbs of the woman, he will be certain of death, and will be changed wholly into blood."[7]

This grisly image expresses how a fairly well-developed ego might experience *solutio*. An immature ego may find it pleasant to surrender to containment in a blissful regression; however, at a later stage of development the prospect of *solutio* will generate great anxiety because the hard-won state of ego autonomy is being threatened with dissolution. A blissful *solutio* is the most dangerous one. It corresponds to Neumann's concept of uroboric incest:

> Uroboric incest is a form of entry into the mother, of union with her, and it stands in sharp contrast to other and later forms of incest. In uroboric incest, the emphasis upon pleasure and love is in no sense active, it is more a desire to be dissolved and absorbed; passively one lets oneself be taken, sinks into the pleroma, melts away in the ocean of pleasure—a *Liebestod*. The Great Mother takes the little child back into herself, and always over uroboric incest there stand the insignia of death, signifying final dissolution in union with the Mother....
>
> Many forms of nostalgia and longing signify no more than a return to uroboric incest and self-dissolution, from the *unio mystica* of the saint to the drunkard's craving for unconsciousness, and the death-romanticism of the Germanic races. The incest we term "uroboric" is self-surrender and regression. It is the form of incest taken by the infantile ego, which is still close to the mother and has not yet come to itself; but the sick ego of the neurotic can also take this form and so can a later, exhausted ego that creeps back to the mother after having found fulfillment.[8]

An example of the longing for blissful *solutio* is Siegfried's yearning for union with Brunnhilde in Wagner's *The Ring of the Nibelung* (cf. figure 3-1):

> Before me
> a wondrous river flows
> with all my senses
> I only see
> its joyous, billowing waters...
> still would I plunge
> in the cooling water,
> myself, as I am,
> ending my pains:
> O that its billows
> Might drown me in bliss
> and quench my fire with its waves![9]

---

[7]Jung, *Mysterium Coniunctionis, CW* 14, par. 15.

[8]Neumann, *The Origins and History of Consciousness,* p. 17.

[9]Wagner, *The Ring of the Nibelung,* p. 254.

FIGURE 3 – 1
Siegfried and the Rhine Maidens (Rackham, *Color Illustrations for Wagner's "Ring."*)

Another example is the final death-song of Isolde in act 3, scene 4 of Wagner's great *solutio* drama, *Tristan and Isolde*:

> Resounding yet more clearly, wafting about me,
> are they waves of refreshing breezes?
> Are they clouds of heavenly fragrance?
> As they swell and roar around me,
> shall I breathe them, shall I listen to them?
> Shall I sip them, plunge beneath them,
> to expire in sweet perfume?
> In the surging swell, in the ringing sound,

in the vast wave of the world's breath—
to drown, to sink
unconscious—supreme bliss!

Our alchemical text is a mixture of images, as often happens in alchemy. It is a combination of *solutio* and *coniunctio*. Sol and Luna are being dissolved and united at the same time. This corresponds to a common type of alchemical picture in which the king and queen are bathing together in the mercurial fountain. An outstanding sequence of pictures of this type is found in the *Rosarium Philosophorum*[10] (cf. figure 3-2).

As our text indicates, the *solutio* has a twofold effect: it causes one form to disappear and a new regenerated form to emerge. The dissolution of the old one is often described in negative imagery and is associated with the *nigredo*. For instance, Philalethes says: "The blackness becomes more pronounced day by day until the substance assumes

FIGURE 3 – 2
The King and Queen in the Bath (Mylius, *Philosophia reformata*, 1622. Reprinted in Jung, *Psychology and Alchemy*.)

---

[10]Reproduced in Jung, "The Psychology of the Transference," in *The Practice of Psychotherapy* CW 16.

a brilliant black color. This black is a sign that the dissolution is accomplished."[11]

Solutio thus may become a *mortificatio.* This is understandable because that which is being dissolved will experience the *solutio* as an annihilation of itself. It is here that the saying of Heraclitus applies: "To souls it is death to become water."[12] However, *solutio* leads on to the emergence of a rejuvenated new form, and when this aspect is emphasized the tone is positive. For instance, *The Golden Treatise of Hermes* says: "O, blessed watery pontic form, that dissolvest the elements!... For when, by the power of the water, the composition is dissolved, it is the day of the restoration; then darkness and Death fly away from them, and Wisdom proceeds."[13]

Often *solutio* is performed on the king. There is, for instance, the image of the drowning king, since "drowning" is a synonym for *solutio* (see figure 3-3). One text has the drowning king (or king's son) say, "Whosoever will free me from the waters and lead me to dry land, him will I prosper with everlasting riches."[14] Psychologically, the meaning is that the old ruling principle, which has undergone *solutio,* is calling out to be coagulated again in a new, regenerated form, saying that it has quantities of libido (riches) at its disposal.

Another text speaks of a dropsy, an inner drowning. The king asked for a drink of water saying: "'I demand the water which is closest to my heart, and which likes me above all things.' When the servant brought it, the king drank so much that 'all his limbs were filled and all his veins inflated, and he himself became discoloured'...'I am heavy and my head hurts me, and it seems to me as though all my limbs were falling apart.' He demanded to be placed in a heated chamber where he could sweat the water out. But when, after a while, they opened the chamber he lay there as if dead."[15]

Jung comments on this text: "The king personifies a hypertrophy of the ego which calls for compensation....His thirst is due to his boundless concupiscence and egotism. But when he drinks he is overwhelmed by the water—that is, by the unconscious."[16]

---

[11]Waite, trans., *The Hermetic Museum,* 2:258.

[12]Freeman, *Ancilla to the Pre-Socratic Philosophers,* p. 27.

[13]Atwood, *Hermetic Philosophy and Alchemy,* p. 122.

[14]Jung, *Psychology and Alchemy, CW* 12, par. 434.

[15]Jung, *Mysterium Coniunctionis, CW* 14, par. 357.

[16]Ibid., par. 365.

FIGURE 3 – 3

Solutio of the King. Background: Drowning King Calling for Help. Foreground: The King Reborn. (Trismosin, *Splendor Solis,* 1582.)

As Jung suggests, the king refers to the ego—at least the dominant or ruling principle according to which the ego is structured. The king is dissolving in his own surfeit; that is, inflation is the cause and agent of *solutio*. A swollen ego is dissolved by its own excess. Its dissolution leads the way to a possible rejuvenation on a sounder basis.

In another text the king is described as drowning in the fountains of Venus. In this poem Venus is identified with the fountain, the mother and bride of the king, in which her "fixed" father is drowned:

> A stone there is, and yet no stone,
> In it doth nature work alone.

> From it there welleth forth a fount [Venus]
> In which her Sire, the Fixed, is drown'd:
> His body and life absorbed therein
> Until the soul's restored agen.[17]

In this case the agent of dissolution is the Eros principle, Venus or Aphrodite. Her mythology has important relations to water by virtue of the fact that she was born out of the sea (see figure 3-4). Her dangerous powers of *solutio* are represented by seductive mermaids or water nymphs who lure men to death by drowning. An impressive example of this theme occurred in the dream of a young man who was thinking of leaving his wife and young children to marry a seductive woman. He dreamed:

> *I am in an underpass where people pass to and fro from the beach. Here are sold the usual recreation goodies: enormous lollypops, popcorn, pretzels a foot or more in length, and crackerjacks. Two of my children are with me (the two youngest). A beautiful woman beckons me to the sea and I leave the children in*

FIGURE 3 – 4
The Birth of Aphrodite (c. 460 B.C. Rome, Terme Museum. Reprinted in Richter, *A Handbook of Greek Art*.)

---

[17]Ibid., par. 415.

a hawker's stand munching pretzels. The dream ends as I stand
midway between the sea and the stand.

A classical example of a fatal *solutio* occurs in the story of Hylas.
During the expedition of the Argonauts, Hylas, the beautiful favorite of
Heracles, was sent to fetch water. He was pulled into a pool by water
nymphs and was never seen again. Here the *solutio* image accompanies
a homoerotic entanglement, the attachment between Heracles and Hylas
(see figure 3-5).

The Old Testament provides examples of the erotic *solutio* that
combine the themes of woman, bath, and the dissolution of the masculine. David spied Bathsheba bathing (2 Sam. 11:2), and thus began the
dissolution of that man of integrity (see figure 3-6). In the apocryphal
text of Daniel and Susanna, the two elders lustfully approach Susanna
in her bath and meet their downfall after giving perjured testimony (see
figure 3-7).

These images tell us that love and/or lust are agents of *solutio*. This
corresponds to the fact that a particular psychic problem or stage of
development often remains arrested or stuck until the patient falls in
love. Then abruptly the problem is dissolved. Although new complica-
tions appear, life has begun to flow again. It has been liquified.

One alchemist defined *solutio* this way: "Solution is the action of any

FIGURE 3 – 5
Hylas and the Nymphs (John William Waterhouse. Manchester, England, City
Art Gallery. Reprinted in Grant and Hazel, *Gods and Mortals in Classical
Mythology*.)

FIGURE 3 – 6

Bathsheba (Rembrandt. Paris, the Louvre. Reprinted in *Rembrandt,* text by
Ludwig Munz.)

body, which, by certain laws of innate sympathy, assimilates anything
of a lower class to its own essence."[18] Understood psychologically, this
definition states that the dissolving agent will be a superior, more
comprehensive viewpoint—one that can act as a containing vessel for
the smaller thing. Jung's concept of "the contained and the container"
applies here. In relating to a more complex personality, he says: "the
simpler personality is surrounded, if not actually swamped, by it; he is
swallowed up in his more complex partner and cannot see his way out.
It is an almost regular occurrence for a woman to be wholly contained,
spiritually, in her husband, and for a husband to be wholly contained,
emotionally, in his wife. One could describe this as the problem of the
'contained' and the 'container.' "[19]

Whatever is larger and more comprehensive than the ego threatens to
dissolve it. Internally, the unconscious as the latent Self or totality of
the psyche can dissolve the ego. Externally, an individual with a larger

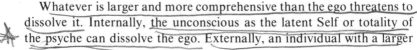

_____

[18]Kelly, *The Alchemical Writings,* p. 87.

[19]Jung, *The Development of Personality, CW* 17, par. 331.

FIGURE 3 - 7
Susanna and the Elders (Tintoretto. Vienna, Gemäldegalerie. Reprinted in
Italian Painting: The Renaissance.)

consciousness than one's own can bring about *solutio.* For instance, a
man who had recently come in contact with Jung's ideas and had fallen
under their sway had this dream: *He dreamed that he fell into the Lake
of Zurich.* A group, a school, or a party may also be the dissolving
agent. A group collective can easily attract the projection of the Self and
swallow up the individual who succumbs to it. Identification with
political parties or religious creeds would be examples of *solutio* within
a group.

In the process of psychotherapy it usually happens that the ego of the
patient encounters in the therapist a more comprehensive standpoint,
which has a dissolving effect. This happening often leads to a partial
state of containment of the patient by the therapist and is a common
cause of the transference. Whenever a one-sided attitude encounters a
larger attitude that includes the opposites, the former, if it is open to
influence, is dissolved by the latter and goes into a state of *solutio*. This
explains why a more comprehensive standpoint is often experienced as
a threat. It feels as though one were drowning, and hence it will be
resisted. Such resistance is valid and necessary and should be respected.
The psychotherapist must always be aware of the possibility that the

patient may need to be shielded from the former's more comprehensive attitude.[20] Basically it is the Self, either experienced from within or as a projection on an individual or a group from without, that is the agency of *solutio*. As Jung says: "The ego is contained in the self as it is contained in the universe of which we know only the tiniest section. [A person can serve that same containing function because] a man of greater insight and intelligence than mine can know myself, but I could not know him as long as my consciousness is inferior to his."[21]

Bath, shower, sprinkling, swimming, immersion in water, and so forth, are all symbolic equivalents for *solutio* that appear commonly in dreams. All of these images relate to the symbolism of baptism, which signifies a cleansing, rejuvenating immersion in an energy and viewpoint transcending the ego, a veritable death and rebirth. Baptism was once done by total immersion and was meant to signify drowning—an echo of the ancient primitive procedure of ordeal by water. It signified a total conversion, the death of the old life and rebirth of a new person into the community of religious believers. The ritual was considered quite literally to bring about the creation of a new personality. Eliade describes the symbolism of baptism in these words: "Immersion in water symbolizes a return to the preformal, a total regeneration, a new birth, for immersion means a dissolution of forms, a reintegration into the formlessness of pre-existence; and emerging from the water is a repetition of the act of creation in which form was first expressed."[22]

In Christian baptism the individual is united with Christ; that is, the ego is linked to the Self. The Apostle Paul says: "Do you not know that all of us who have been baptized into Christ Jesus were baptized into his death? We were buried therefore with him by baptism into death, so that as Christ was raised from the dead by the glory of the Father, we too might walk in newness of life" (Rom. 6:3-4, RSV).

Another feature of baptism is that it dissolves all separateness and individual distinctions. According to Paul: "For as many of you as were baptized into Christ have put on Christ. There is neither Jew nor Greek, there is neither slave nor free, there is neither male or female; for you are all one in Christ Jesus" (Gal. 3:27-28, RSV).

From the inner standpoint this amounts to an integration or unification of separated fragments. However, from the external standpoint—as with an outer religious ritual—it represents the collectivization of the

---

[20]An example of the effects of encountering a larger personality is found in the Moslem legend of Moses and Khidr. See Jung, *The Archetypes and the Collective Unconscious, CW* 91, pars. 244ff.

[21]Jung, *Letters* 2:194.

[22]Eliade, *Patterns in Comparative Religion,* p. 88.

individual who has his unique features dissolved by an identification
with the new viewpoint. It is also an example of a lesser standpoint
being dissolved by the greater, more comprehensive standpoint—indicated by the phrase "*in* Christ Jesus." To be "in" anything, such as in
love, or in pain, means one is surrounded, contained, and dissolved by
the containing matrix. Thus the religious faithful were described as fish
swimming in the pond containing the water of doctrine.

The ambiguous interplay of the opposites is revealed by the fact that
often *solutio* is experienced not as containment, but rather as fragmentation and dismemberment. A classic example is the myth of Actaeon
(see figure 3-8). The young hunter Actaeon unexpectedly came upon
Artemis naked in her bath. In retaliation, Artemis turned Actaeon into
a stag, and he was then dismembered by his own hounds. The dog is a
theriomorphic aspect of Artemis, therefore Artemis herself can be considered as the dismembering agency. This myth depicts the dangerous
aspect of encounter with the archetypal feminine by an immature ego. It
is thrown into a regressive *solutio* by the activation of instinctual factors
(the hounds). One way of putting it would be that Actaeon is dissolved

FIGURE 3 – 8
Diana and Actaeon (Titian. Edinburgh, National Gallery of Scotland. Reprinted
in *Titian: The Colour Library of Art.*)

by his lust. He is bitten and consumed by his animal nature. A similar idea is expressed in Plutarch's account of Isis and Osiris. According to this story, the child Maneros witnessed Isis' terrible love and grief upon seeing the dead Osiris. This awesome sight was so intolerable to Maneros that he fell out of the boat and drowned.[23] Most men, if they are honest, will acknowledge having had the experience of Maneros when confronted with a woman's intense grief, desire, or anger.

Artemis is the moon. Her dismemberment of Actaeon thus corresponds to the alchemical statement that "the *solutio* takes place in the moon"[24] (see figure 3-9). A young man who had gone as far in analysis as he was ready to once dreamed the simple statement, *Psychoanalysis is of the moon*. He awoke from this dream in panic and discontinued analysis not long thereafter. Analysis can indeed be a dissolving immersion into the dark, irrational lunar side, and the dreamer's anxiety is quite understandable.

The theme of dismemberment leads directly into the myth of Dionysus. As an infant, Dionysus was dismembered by the Titans. Also, the Maenads who worshipped him were dismemberers who tore apart whatever crossed their frenzied path. Such was the fate of Pentheus in *The Bacchae* of Euripides. Many aspects of the Dionysian principle belong to *solutio* symbolism. Walter Otto tells us: "Water is...the element in which Dionysus is at home.... The cults and myths are as explicit as they can be about the fact that Dionysus comes out of the water and returns to it, and that he has his place of refuge and home in the watery depths."[25]

 Dionysus is even described as the moisture principle itself and therefore the source of all fertility. Psychologically he is the principle of life, spontaneity, and energy as contrasted with form, measure, and restraint.

One aspect of the Dionysian *solutio* is the orgiastic instinct bath. Sometimes the yearning of the lonely, alienated ego for containment in a larger whole expresses itself as lust for orgiastic, collective sexuality (see figure 3-10). If acted out concretely, such experiences aggravate the state of psychic fragmentation. Symbolically, however, the image of a collective orgy suggests the possibility of reestablishing one's lost connection with common humanity. Group experiences of collective identification may activate this image of an orgy. For instance, a group process that I had an opportunity to observe generated in some participants definite *solutio* dreams. A beginner in the group had this dream

---

[23]Plutarch, *Moralia,* vol. 5.

[24]Bonus of Ferrara, *The New Pearl of Great Price,* p. 426.

[25]Otto, *Dionysus Myth and Cult,* p. 162.

FIGURE 3 - 9
Baptism with Lunar Water While Being Bitten by Dragons (Ashmole, ed.,
Theatrum Chemicum Britannicum, 1652.)

after being shocked by the psychological intimacies shared by group
members.

*I am looking for the group. I open a door to the room and on the
floor I see all the group members making love with each other.
One couple falls out of the door in front of me.*

Another group member had this dream:

*I am in a classroom like a chemistry classroom. With seats in
high tiers leading down to a stage-like platform. It is our group,*

FIGURE 3 – 10
Bacchanal of the Andrians (Titian. Madrid, Prado. Reprinted in *Titian:*
The Colour Library of Art.)

and the exhibit is of a beach with enormous, crashing waves,
which become abruptly real. I can see that under the waves,
along the sand, there is a strong sturdy fishing net which has
been firmly anchored into the sand in several places, obviously
to catch and hold a good haul in even rough weather, but the
waves become so real and turbulent that they splash out of the
exhibit stage and onto the audience. Several of us scramble
down from the seats to avoid getting wet. I notice that I have left
my purse behind in my hurry, and I think I will have to go back
and get it.

Water as the Dionysian fertility principle is described beautifully in
Goethe's hymn to water:

> Hail anew! Spring's burgeoning
> Leaps up within my heart, a spring
> With truth and beauty permeated—
> From the wave was all created.
> Water will all life sustain:
> Ocean, grant your endless reign!

But for clouds of your rich lending,
And the brooklets of your sending,
Rivers' courses wide extending,
Streams that reach majestic ending,
What were our world, our mountains, and our plains?
Your power the freshness of our life maintains.
'Tis you from whom the life flows in our veins.[26]

Fertility and creativity were emphasized in the phallic aspects of Dionysian rituals. Otto writes:

Inherent in the Dionysiac element of moisture is not only the power which maintains life but also the power which creates it. Thus it flows through the entire human and animal world as a fertilizing, generative substance. The learned Varro was very well informed when he declared that the sovereignty of Dionysus was not only to be recognized in the juice of fruits whose crowning glory was wine but also in the sperms of living creatures. From this sphere of the god's activity he traced the origin of the custom in which a phallus was crowned with wreaths and carried around in the god's cult. We certainly know how great a role this symbol of procreative power played in his festivals. "A wine jar, a vine, a goat, a basket of figs, and then the phallus"—this is the description Plutarch gives us of the original simplicity of the Dionysiac celebration. A song was sung to the phallus. We have inscriptional evidence for the use of a large wooden phallus in the processions of the Dionysia in Delos. Each colony sent a phallus regularly to the Athenian Dionysia.[27]

An example of Dionysian phallic symbolism linked with baptismal imagery is provided by the following dream. The dreamer was a middle-aged woman with emerging creative powers as a poet and a scholar. She dreamed:

There is a party at my mother's apartment. A strange and disturbing man, Mr. X, a poet, is the guest of honor. (After several episodes the mother leaves the party.) When she does, there's a kind of universal, spontaneous rejoicing which I also feel, though I don't know what's up. I find out soon enough, though. For almost at once X gathers all the women around him in a semi-circle, whereupon he undresses and ejaculates a huge stream of sperm which falls like a fountain on each of us. I'd thought the idea was for us to serve him in this way, but as it turns out that's only part of it. Because as the sperm shower hits us severally, we each experience our own separate and individual orgasms.

---

[26]Goethe, *Faust*, pt. 2, lines 8432–44.

[27]Otto, *Dionysus Myth and Cult*, p. 164.

This dream foreshadowed an emerging positive realization of the dreamer's creative capacities. However, sometimes one's relation to the creative power is dangerous. Nietzsche, the great exponent of the Dionysian principle, is an awesome example of the dangers of a destructive *solutio* brought about by a personal identification with Dionysian creativity. In his psychosis, Nietzsche called himself "Dionysus" and signed his letters, "Zagreus"—that is, "the dismembered one." Jung has some profound observations to make on the danger of dissolution in identification with creative powers. He says:

> [The creative forces] have you on the string and you dance to their whistling, to their melody. But in as much as you say these creative forces are in Nietzsche or in me or anywhere else, you cause an inflation, because man does not possess creative powers, he is possessed by them. That is the truth. If he allows himself to be thoroughly possessed by them without questioning, without looking at them, there is no inflation, but the moment he splits off, when he thinks, I am the fellow, an inflation follows. . . .
>
> It happens automatically that you become conscious of yourself and then you are gone, it is as if you had touched a high tension wire. Nietzsche, of course, could not help looking at the thing and then he was overwhelmed with resentments, because the creative powers steal your time, sap your strength, and what is the result? A book perhaps. But where is your personal life? All gone. Therefore, such people feel so terribly cheated, they mind it, and everybody ought to kneel down before them in order to make up for that which has been stolen by God. The creative forces have taken it out of them, and therefore they would like to personify them, imagine that they are Shiva, in order to have the delight of being creative. But if you know you are creative and enjoy being creative, you will be crucified afterwards because anybody identified with God will be dismembered. An old father of the church, the Bishop Synesius, said that the *spiritus phantasticus*, our creative spirit, can penetrate the depths or the heights of the universe like God, or like a great demon, but on account of that he will also have to undergo the divine punishment, and that would be the dismemberment of Dionysus or the crucifixion of Christ.[28]

In general, the Dionysian is daimonic and ecstatic, promoting intensity of experience rather than clear, structured meaning. It is a dissolver of limits and boundaries, bringing life without measure. In its extreme form it is wild, irrational, mad, ecstatic, boundless. It is the enemy of all conventional laws, rules, and established forms. It is in the service, not of safety, but of life and rejuvenation. The weak and immature may be destroyed by its onslaughts; the healthy will be fertilized and enlivened like the land by the flooding of the Nile (see figure 3-11).

Many clinical syndromes are due to a concretistic identification with the Dionysian principle. Alcoholism and drug addiction are obvious. Don Juanism can also be considered an identification with Dionysus, in

---

[28]Jung, *Zarathustra Seminar* 1:67.

FIGURE 3 - 11
Bathers (Renoir. Philadelphia, Collection of Carroll Tyson. Reprinted in
Craven, *A Treasury of Art Masterpieces.)*

which the individual surrounds himself with an entourage of women in
various stages of love or frenzy (Maenads). This situation threatens to
bring about his own psychological dismemberment by conflicts, obliga-
tions, and entanglements. The Dionysian takes on a compulsive quality
when it exists in a dissociated personality. Put another way, the
Dionysian destroys the Pentheus-like ego that is not related to wholeness. In favorable circumstances it promotes harmony and dissolves
differences. For instance, consider this paean to the Dionysian by
Nietzsche:

Under the charm of the Dionysian not only is the union between man and
man reaffirmed, but nature which has become alienated, hostile, or subju-
gated, celebrates once more her reconciliation with her lost son, man. Freely,
earth proffers her gifts, and peacefully the beasts of prey of the rocks and
desert approach. The chariot of Dionysus is covered with flowers and
garlands; panthers and tigers walk under its yoke. Transform Beethoven's
"Hymn to Joy" into a painting; let your imagination conceive the multitudes
bowing to the dust, awestruck—then you will approach the Dionysian. Now
the slave is a free man; now all the rigid, hostile barriers that necessity,
caprice, or "impudent convention" have fixed between man and man are
broken. Now, with the gospel of universal harmony, each one feels himself
not only united, reconciled, and fused with his neighbor, but as one with

him, as if the veil of máyá had been torn aside, and were now merely fluttering in tatters before the mysterious primordial unity.[29]

The Apostle Paul expresses approximately the same idea concerning the efficacy of the blood of Christ. In Ephesians, we read: "But now in Christ Jesus you who once were far off have been brought near in the blood of Christ. For he is our peace, who has made us both one, and has broken down the dividing wall of hostility, by abolishing in his flesh the law of commandments and ordinances, that he might create in himself one new man in place of the two, so making peace, and might reconcile us both to God in one body through the cross, thereby bringing the hostility to an end" (Eph. 2:13-16, RSV).

The wine of Dionysus and the blood of Christ are symbolically equivalent. This fact is illustrated in the dream of a young clergyman, which I have previously published in *Ego and Archetype*.[30] It is as follows:

Dream (abbreviated):

I am to celebrate communion. In the sacristy, which looks like a kitchen, the communion wine is to be prepared by mixing two separate wines–a blue wine and a red wine. The latter is in a bottle with a yellow label that looks like a Scotch label and is marked "Paul." At a round table, two men are sitting. One is a political leftist, the other a rightist. Up to now they have maintained a facade of social amenity but now they are becoming hostile to one another. I suggest that they ventilate at the gut level and resolve their feeling relationship. At this point the scene darkens as in a theatre play and a red-yellow spotlight focuses on a small table between and behind the two men. On the table is a bottle of the warm red wine with the Scotch label clearly marked "Paul." Then there is total darkness and the tinkle of glasses, sounding as though they've been clinked and perhaps broken. The sense is obvious in the dream. I think: they've drunk the red wine in their discussion, attained comradeship, become drunk in the process, fallen asleep, and dropped their glasses. My response is delight in the aesthetic way this has been portrayed and anxiety about the fact that the service needs to begin and we do not now have the ingredients for the communion wine mixture.

The dreamer's psychology is not known to me in depth; however, it is evident that Dionysian and Christian symbolism are here combined.

---

[29]Nietzsche, "The Birth of Tragedy," in *Basic Writings of Nietzsche,* p. 37.

[30]Edinger, *Ego and Archetype,* pp. 248ff.

Although the union of the two wines—perhaps Logos and Eros—remains to be achieved, a *solutio* has occurred that dissoves the opposition between leftist and rightist, although at the price of consciousness since they fall asleep. In this case, as is often true, there is a confusion between authentic reconciliation of opposites through greater consciousness and a regressive dissolution which blurs awareness of the opposites.

A cosmological version of *solutio* is the widespread myth of a cosmic catastrophe by flood (see figure 3-12). In Hebrew myth it is Noah's flood; in Greek myth, the story of Deucalion and Pyrrha. According to an ancient idea each of the four elements in turn was to be an agent of world destruction. As reported by Dio Chrysostom, the story is as follows: "The Lord of the world rides in a chariot drawn by four horses which are sacred to Zeus, Hera, Poseidon, and Hestia respectively. In other words, the four horses are the four elements, fire, air, water, and

FIGURE 3 – 12
The Flood (Doré, *Bible Illustrations.*)

earth. As a rule they are tractable, now and then, however, the first steed becomes restive and sets fire to the other three. This is the origin of the story of Phaethon told by the Greeks. Again it is the steed of Poseidon that becomes restive, and the drops of his sweat are sprinkled upon the other three. This, again, is the source from which the Greeks derived their story of Deucalion's flood," and likewise with the other two horses.[31]

This idea corresponds to the alchemical *circulatio* in which the material is to be repeatedly sublimated and coagulated, circling again and again through all the states of being until the Philosophers' Stone is created. The whole history of the world is thus seen as a vast alchemical process.

The flood myths are quite instructive psychologically. God sends a destructive flood when the world has become wicked and degenerate. It is as though humanity must be reduced through *solutio* to its *prima materia* in order for it to be transformed to something better. Another aspect of *solutio* is also demonstrated by the flood stories, namely, the theme of ordeal by water. Through this ordeal the godly men, those with authentic existence, remain intact while the wicked or inauthentic are dissolved. Psychologically this would mean that those aspects of the ego consciously related to the Self withstand *solutio*.

In the myths, the threat of a world flood was used to encourage an awareness of God. Similarly, a threat of flooding from the unconscious may have a salutary effect on a presumptuous ego and bring about an awareness of a need for a relation to the transpersonal. This state of mind is expressed in the Sixty-ninth Psalm (see figure 3-13):

> Save me, O God; for the waters are come in unto my soul. I sink in deep mire, where there is no standing: I am come into deep waters, where the floods overflow me. (1, 2, AV)

> Deliver me out of the mire, and let me not sink: let me be delivered from them that hate me, and out of the deep waters. Let not the water flood overflow me, neither let the deep swallow me up, and let not the pit shut her mouth upon me. (14, 15, AV)

Flood dreams refer to *solutio*. They represent an activation of the unconscious that threatens to dissolve the established ego structure and reduce it to *prima materia*. Major life transitions are commonly *solutio* experiences. For instance, a woman with three children who was going through a second divorce had several flood dreams, one of which was reported by Rivkah Kluger:

---

[31]Hastings, *Encyclopedia of Religion and Ethics,* 1:199–200.

FIGURE 3 – 13

"Save Me, O God; For the Waters Are Come in unto My Soul" (Illustration for Psalm 69, *The Visconti Hours.* Florence, National Library.)

From a beach house I look out and see a great wave. I call the girls in. Mary is slow but does come in time and I shut the doors. Then the wave is on us. It comes through every crack and is all around us. I am frightened about Bob, my son, who is on the beach and wonder if he has been able to escape. I know that all the swimmers will have died. There is no escape and I say to myself: "So this is how it is." I feel no real panic. Since escape is impossible, it is simply the way it is. But then the water subsides.

We run about trying to close up cracks. There is a hole in the floor, besides many cracks in the walls.... Another wave comes. It crashes over and around us but this time the room is not flooded and the cabin does not lift and roll about. We begin to run before the next one comes. I open the back door and there stands an old friend whom I have not seen in years. I hug him in joy and relief.... The country is bleak and mud is washed high up in the land. I see how lucky we have been and am so glad for the man who came to take us away.[32]

Another example is the following dream. The dreamer was a mature, middle-aged man who was going through a major life reorientation and facing a serious operation. He also later was divorced. He dreamed:

World life is seen as in a great bowl. Then there is a huge flood, something like a dam lets loose and everything is overwhelmed. It is cataclysmic, a catastrophe of huge proportions and all is washed away in the rising waters.... We flee before the deluge and some of us escape.

Then it seems as if we are in a new era. This is world life seen inside a great sphere. There are many levels connected by staircases, ramps, etc., all around an open center. Apartments and living spaces are part of the outer wall.... Before it was night, now it is day. In the middle all is earth. It is a thick layer covering over the water.

Dreams of a great flood sometimes include the experience of being rescued by a divine or transpersonal agency. In the following dream it is evident that a fatal *solutio* was avoided by the discovery of Jungian psychology:

[The dreamer] was caught in a monstrous sea. Though she was a strong and practiced swimmer, her strength was nearly exhausted, and she knew she could not hold out much longer. Just then she saw ahead a square houseboat resembling the Noah's arks of her childhood. With a tremendous last effort she made for it, and just in time she reached its side, to be hauled up half fainting by none other than Dr. Jung, whom she had never even seen at the time.[33]

A middle-aged man going through the dissolution of a dependent relationship had this dream:

I am at the center of a great city watching a vast stream of humanity pass by—individuals of every type and description. It's like the flow of a great river. I am fascinated.

---

[32]Kluger, "Flood Dreams," in *The Reality of the Psyche,* p. 51.

[33]Bertine, "The Great Flood," in *Jung's Contribution to Our Time,* p. 204.

On awakening the dreamer thought of the doctrine of Heraclitus that "all things are in flux" (*panta rhei*). The dream is thus picturing the *solutio* aspect of existence—life as perpetual change and becoming. A painful personal experience is cast in an archetypal or general context and thereby made meaningful and even fascinating.

The connection of *solutio* with salvation is indicated by the Apostle Peter's relation of Noah's flood to baptism. "Now it was long ago, when Noah was still building that ark which saved only a small group of eight people 'by water'.... That water is a type of the baptism which saves you now" (1 Pet. 3:20, 21, JB).

Because eight people were saved in the flood, the number eight became associated with baptism, the ritual repetition of the original flood. The Christians of antiquity and the Middle Ages nearly always built their baptistries in octagonal form. An inscription composed by St. Ambrose for the baptistry of the church of St. Thecla in Milan reads as follows:

> Eight are the temple's walls—O number worthy of holy
>   Actions performed at the spot; eight are the walls of the font.
> Mystical shape of the house that covers the rites of the water
>   —Rites for the saving of man—mystical number of eight,
> Rites that derive their pow'r from the light of Christ resurrected
>   Christ who set all men free, breaking the shackles of Hell,
> Who from the blemish of sin releaseth him that repenteth,
>   In the crystalline spring cleansing the bather from guilt.
> What greater proof can ye ask of the power of God who
> Acting at one small point loosens the guilt of the world?[34]

We now know that the number eight is an individuation number, an expression of wholeness. The flood and baptism symbolism is therefore telling us that by passing through the water of *solutio* we become whole—that is, related to the Self.

The exodus and passage through the Red Sea was also connected with baptism by Paul: "I want you to know, brethren, that our fathers were all under the cloud, and all passed through the sea, and all were baptized into Moses in the cloud and in the sea" (1 Cor. 10:1-2 RSV).

Jung mentions the Peratics' (a Gnostic sect's) interpretation of the Red Sea: "The Red Sea drowned the Egyptians, but the Egyptians were all 'non-knowers.'... The Red Sea is a water of death for those that are 'unconscious,' but for those that are 'conscious' it is a baptismal water of rebirth and transcendence."[35] Augustine says, "The Red Sea signifies

---

[34]Rahner, *Greek Myths and Christian Mystery*, p. 78.

[35]Jung, *Mysterium Coniunctionis*, CW 14, par. 257.

baptism," and according to Honorius of Autun, "the Red Sea is the baptism reddened by the blood of Christ, in which our enemies, namely our sins, are drowned."[36]

The alchemists used the image of the Red Sea. The tincture is said to be extracted from the Red Sea. One text speaks of the "Tyrean dye, which is extracted from our most pure Red Sea."[37] Another says, "And know that our Red Sea is more tincturing than all seas, and that [it]... penetrates all bodies."[38] The term "our Red Sea" refers to the *aqua permanens*, the universal solvent—that is, the liquid form of the Philosophers' Stone. Thus, that which has passed through the *solutio* of the Red Sea is the goal of the *opus*, the Self. Or, put another way, the Red Sea is the totality of the psyche, the agency of *solutio* that the ego must encounter and pass through on the way to individuation (see figure 3-14).

The Red Sea had several overlapping meanings to the alchemists. (1) It was the crucial transition of the exodus. The Israelites' escape from slavery was equated with the redemption of the lost value hidden in the darkness of matter and indeed with the whole alchemical process of transformation. (2) It had the general meaning of the sea—the original chaos, the creative source of all that comes to be, in psychological terms, the unconscious. (3) Its redness associated it with the color of the Philosophers' Stone and the transforming tincture. Thus the Red Sea was not only the *prima materia*, but also the goal of the *opus*. It was also connected with the redeeming blood of Christ and the "blood of the lamb" as described in Revelation. "What are these which are arrayed in white robes?... These are they which came out of great tribulation, and have washed their robes, and made then white in the blood of the Lamb. Therefore are they before the throne of God, and serve him day and night in his temple" (Rev. 7:14, 15, AV).

Literal blood baptism was practiced in the taurobolium of Mithraism. Blood is associated with the element fire; hence, blood symbolism combines fire and water—that is, both *calcinatio* and *solutio* imagery.

Baptism is basically a purification ritual that washes one clean of dirt, both literal and spiritual. Washings were frequent preliminary procedures in religious ceremonies, in the Eleusinian Mysteries for instance. Psychologically, the dirt or sin that is washed away by baptism can be understood as unconsciousness, shadow qualities of which one is unaware. Psychological cleanliness means not literal purity, but aware-

---

[36]Ibid., par. 256.

[37]Ibid., par. 259.

FIGURE 3 –14

Pharaoh's Army Drowning in the Red Sea (*The Visconti Hours,* Florence, National Library.)

ness of one's own dirt. If one is psychologically clean, one will not contaminate one's environment with shadow projections (see figure 3-15).

I cannot conclude this section on baptism symbolism without citing a beautiful quotation that equates Christ and the sun as partners in baptism. This from Melito of Sardis, a second-century theologian:

> When drawn by his fiery steeds the sun has completed his daily course, then by reason of his whirling passage he takes on the color of fire and becomes as a burning torch.... Then, almost lost from view, he descends into the ocean. ...Bathing himself in the mysterious depths he shouts mightily for joy, for water is his nourishment. He remains one and the same, yet he comes forth

FIGURE 3 - 15
The Woman Washing Clothes (Maier, *Atalanta Fugiens,* 1618.)

strengthened out of the depths, a new sun, and shines his light upon men, having been cleansed in the water....

There follow him in due course the dancing ranks of the stars and by reason of him the moon puts forth her power. They bathe in the baptistry of the sun like those who are obedient under instruction and it is only because moon and stars follow the course of the sun that they shine with a truly pure light. If then the sun and the stars and the moon all bathe together in the ocean, why should not Christ have been baptized in the River Jordan? King of Heaven, prince of creation, sun of the eastern sky who appeared both to the dead in Hades and to mortals upon earth, he, the only true Helios, arose for us out of the highest summits of Heaven.[39]

Earlier, the moon was mentioned as an agent of negative or dangerous *solutio*. It also has important connections with highly positive imagery. The moon was considered to be the source of dew—an agent of healing grace and identical with the *aqua permanens*. Isis was called "dew," and it was the dew of her tears that brought together the dismembered fragments of Osiris.[40] Jung describes moon and dew symbolism in these words:

---

[39]Rahner, *Greek Myths and Christian Mystery,* p. 115.

[40]Jung, *Mysterium Coniunctionis, CW* 14, par. 14.

Luna secretes the dew or sap of life. [According to an alchemical text,] "This Luna is the sap of the water of life, which is hidden in Mercurius!" Even the Greek alchemists supposed there was a principle in the moon which Christianos calls the "ichor of the philosopher." The relation of the moon to the soul, much stressed in antiquity, also occurs in alchemy though with a different nuance. Usually it is said that from the moon comes the dew, but the moon is also the *aqua mirifica* that extracts the souls from the bodies or gives the bodies life and soul. Together with Mercurius, Luna sprinkles the dismembered dragon with her moisture and brings him to life again, "makes him live, walk, and run about, and change his color to the nature of blood." As the water of ablution, the dew falls from heaven, purifies the body, and makes it ready to receive the soul; in other words, it brings about the *albedo*, the white state of innocence, which like the moon and a bride awaits the bridegroom.[41]

In ecclesiastical symbolism dew represents grace, and in alchemy it is the *aqua sapentiae*. An excellent example is seen in one of the *Rosarium* pictures reproduced in *The Psychology of the Transference*[42] (see figure 3-16). This picture shows the king and queen following coitus merged and dead lying on a slab. Drops of moisture are falling on them from a cloud above. Jung interprets the descending dew as the water of divine Wisdom or "Gideon's dew," a synonym for the *aqua permanens*. It "is a sign of divine intervention, it is the moisture that heralds the return of the soul."[43] This corresponds to the recovery of feeling after succumbing to the deadly, barren state of intellectual abstraction like Faust's before his encounter with Mephistopheles. As Jung tells us, "The alchemists thought that the *opus* demanded not only laboratory work, the reading of books, meditation, and patience, but also love."[44]

The dew of divine Wisdom emphasizes another aspect of *solutio*, namely, its power to answer questions or provide a *solution* to problems. Gerhard Dorn says: "The chemical putrefaction is compared to the study of the philosophers, because as the philosophers are disposed to knowledge by study, so natural things are disposed by putrefaction to solution. To this is compared philosophical knowledge, for as by solution bodies are dissolved, so by knowledge are the doubts of the philosophers resolved."[45]

The *Rubaiyat of Omar Khayyam* expresses the same idea in a style more appropriate to *solutio*.

> The Grape that can with Logic absolute
> The Two-and-Seventy jarring Sects confute:

---

[41]Ibid., par. 155.

[42]Printed in Jung, *The Practice of Psychotherapy* CW 16.

[43]Ibid., par. 487.

[44]Ibid., par. 490.

[45]Jung, *Mysterium Coniunctionis, CW* 14, par. 363.

FIGURE 3 – 16

The Corpse of the Merged King and Queen Being Purified and Reanimated by
Heavenly Dew (*Rosarium Philosophorum*, Frankfurt, 1550. Reprinted in Jung,
The Practice of Psychotherapy.)

> The sovereign alchemist that in a trice
> Life's leaden metal into Gold transmute.[46]

The *solutio* experience "solves" psychological problems by transferring
the issue to the realm of feeling. In other words, it answers "unanswer-
able" questions by dissolving the libido obstruction of which the question was a symptom.

A variant of *solutio* is *liquefactio*, the process of melting. Sometimes
it is called "ceration." About this procedure Ruland says, "Ceration is
performed upon a body which is hard and of dry humour by continual

---

[46]Fitzgerald, trans., *The Rubaiyat of Omar Khayyam,* st. 42.

inhibition until melting takes place....the sign of perfect ceration is when the medicine, being most swiftly projected upon a burning plate, resolves itself, without smoke, into the consistency of molten wax."[47]

The ability to melt upon heating, a feature of most metals, was considered to be an indicator of quality or nobility. Thus, regarding a nonfusible metal, an alchemist exclaims in disgust, "Bismuth...is not even fusible by fire—such is its earthly grossness and impurity."[48] This is an interesting psychological point. It tells us that psychic quality is indicated by its ability to soften, to melt into a liquid flowing state. Perhaps this is the root image of the idea of a *gentle*man. Lao Tse describes it beautifully:

> The best of men is like water;
> Water benefits all things
> And does not compete with them.
> It dwells in (the lowly) places that all disdain,—
> Wherein it comes near to the Tao.
>
> In his dwelling, (the Sage) loves the (lowly) earth;
> In his heart, he loves what is profound;
> In his relations with others, he loves kindness;
> In his words, he loves sincerity;
> In government, he loves peace;
> In business affairs, he loves ability;
> In his actions, he loves choosing the right time.
> It is because he does not contend
> That he is without reproach.[49]

The *I Ching* has a hexagram, number 59, which might have been named "*solutio*." Wilhelm calls it "Dispersion or Dissolution." Part of the commentary reads as follows:

Religious forces are needed to overcome the egotism that divides men. The common celebration of the great sacrificial feasts and sacred rites...was the means employed by the great rulers to unite men. The sacred music and the splendor of the ceremonies aroused a strong tide of emotion that was shared by all hearts in unison, and that awakened a consciousness of the common origin of all creatures. In this way disunity was overcome and rigidity dissolved....Egotism and cupidity isolate men. Therefore the hearts of men must be seized by a devout emotion. They must be shaken by a religious awe in face of eternity.[50]

---

[47]Ruland, *A Lexicon of Alchemy,* p. 95.

[48]Waite, trans., *The Hermetic Museum* 1:24.

[49]*Tao Teh Ching* or *The Book of Tao,* Chapter 8, Tr. Lin Yutang.

[50]Wilhelm, trans., *The I Ching or Book of Changes,* pp. 227ff.

To summarize, I have spoken of seven major aspects of *solutio* symbolism: (1) return to the womb or primal state; (2) dissolution, dispersal, dismemberment; (3) containment of a lesser thing by a greater; (4) rebirth, rejuvenation, immersion in the creative energy flow; (5) purification ordeal; (6) solution of problems; and (7) melting or softening process. These different aspects overlap. Several or all of them may make up different facets of a single experience. Basically it is the ego's confrontation with the unconscious that brings about *solutio*. Jung says:

> The analysis and interpretation of dreams confront the conscious standpoint with the statements of the unconscious, thus widening its narrow horizon. This loosening up of cramped and rigid attitudes corresponds to the solution and separation of the elements by the *aqua permanens*, which was already present in the "body" and is lured out by the art. The water is a soul or spirit, that is, a psychic "substance," which now in its turn is applied to the initial material. This corresponds to using the dream's meaning to clarify existing problems. "*Solutio*" is defined in this sense by Dorn. "As bodies are dissolved by solution, so the doubts of the philosophers are resolved by knowledge."[51]

This quotation describes the analytic process as chiefly a *solutio* for the patient. However, the therapist must also submit to *solutio*. Certain texts state this explicitly: "It is necessary therefore to convert the bodies of metals into a fluid substance; for...every tincture will tinge a thousand times more in a soft and liquid substance, than when it is in a dry one....Therefore the transmutation of imperfect metals is impossible to be done by perfect bodies while they are dry and hard: for which cause sake, they must be brought back into their first matter, which is soft and fluid."[52] Again, "that which is dry does not enter into, nor tinge anything besides itself...nor can it tinge except it be tinged."[53]

Thus, both patient and agent must be soft and fluid. This corresponds to what Jung tells us about the nature of psychotherapy:

> The relation between doctor and patient remains a personal one within the impersonal framework of professional treatment. By no device can the treatment be anything but the product of mutual influence, in which the whole being of the doctor as well as that of his patient plays its part.... Hence the personalities of doctor and patient are often infinitely more important for the outcome of the treatment than what the doctor says and thinks....For two personalities to meet is like mixing two different chemical substances: if there is any combination at all, both are transformed. In any effective psychological treatment the doctor is bound to influence the patient; but this influence can only take place if the patient has a reciprocal

---

[51]Jung, *Mysterium Coniunctionis, CW* 14, par. 306 and n. 587.

[52]*The Lives of the Alchemystical Philosophers*, p. 135.

[53]Ibid.

influence on the doctor. You can exert no influence if you are not susceptible to influence.[54]

Between doctor and patient, therefore, there are imponderable factors which bring about a mutual transformation. In the process, the stronger and more stable personality will decide the final issue. I have seen many cases where the patient assimilated the doctor in defiance of all theory and of the latter's professional intentions—generally, though not always, to the disadvantage of the doctor.[55]

Each of the alchemical operations has a lesser and a greater aspect, just as it has both a negative and a positive side. The fire of *calcinatio* can be experienced as hell fire or the inspiration of the Holy Ghost. The same applies to *solutio*. One text says: "You are to know that, although the solution is one, yet in it there may be distinguished a first, and a second.... The *first* solution is...the reduction of it to its First Matter; the *second* is that perfect solution of body and spirit at the same time, in which the solvent and the thing solved always abide together, and with this solution of the body there takes place simultaneously a consolidation of the spirit."[56]

The greater *solutio* thus involves a transposition of the opposites; the solution of the body brings about a consolidation of the spirit. Many other texts say the same thing. Kelly quotes Avicenna: "The true principle of our work is the dissolution of the Stone, because solved bodies have assumed the nature of spirits, i.e., because their quality is drier. For the solution of the body is attended with the coagulation of the spirit."[57] Another text says, "Our solucyon ys cause of our coagulacyon; For the dissolucyon on the one syde corporall causyth congelacyon on the other syde spyrytuall."[58]

This is profound and paradoxical symbolism. The most obvious meaning is that a release from concrete particulars promotes a realization of universals. However, the paradoxical play of opposites means ultimately that the procedure leads to the Self—the transpersonal center of the psyche that unites and reconciles the opposites. We are thus brought, finally, to the ultimate in *solutio* symbolism, the idea of the water that is the goal of the process. Several terms are used for this liquid version of the Philosophers' Stone: *"aqua permanens," "elixer vitae,"* "tincture," "philosophical water," "universal solvent," "divine

---

[54] *The Practice of Psychotherapy, CW* 16, par. 163.

[55] Ibid., par. 164.

[56] Waite, trans., *The Hermetic Museum* 1:40.

[57] Kelly, *The Alchemical Writings of Edward Kelly,* p. 49.

[58] *The Lives of the Alchemystical Philosophers,* p. 219.

water," and so forth. Water as the goal of the *opus* is described in this text:

> [The philosophers] say that the whole work and the substance of the whole work are nothing but the water; and that the treatment of the same also takes place in nothing but the water.... And by whatever names the philosophers have called their stone they always mean and refer to this one substance, i.e., to the water from which everything [originates] and in which everything [is contained], which rules everything, in which errors are made and in which the error is itself corrected. I call it "philosophical" water, not ordinary water but *aqua mercurialis.*[59]

Here the philosophical water in which everything takes place is both the beginning and the end of the *opus*, the *prima materia*, and the Philosophers' Stone. It is a liquid symbol of the Self containing the opposites and turning each one-sided thing into its contrary. Thus it is said, "This (divine) water makes the dead living and the living dead, it lights the darkness and darkens the light."[60]

Just as the Philosophers' Stone was identified with Christ, the divine water of the alchemists was also connected with the living water that Christ equated with himself in the Gospel of John: "Whoever drinks the water that I shall give him will never suffer thirst anymore. The water that I shall give him will be an inner spring always welling up for eternal life" (John 4:14, NEB). "If anyone is thirsty let him come to me; whoever believes in me, let him drink. As Scripture says, 'Streams of living water shall flow out from within him'" (John 7:38, NEB).

An interesting dream parallel to the "stream of living water" came to my attention. During a particular session, the analyst was especially resourceful in giving a rich amplification of the patient's dream. That night the patient dreamed that *a stream of crystal clear water was flowing from the analyst's mouth.* This episode is an excellent example of Jung's statement, "The analysis and interpretation of dreams...corresponds to the solution and separation of the elements by the *aqua permanens.*[61]

The Psalmist cries out to God, "My soul thirsteth for thee in a dry and thirsty land where no water is" (Ps. 63:1, AV). Almost in answer to this cry, an alchemical recipe for *solutio* begins with these words, "If thou knowest how to moisten this dry earth with its own water, thou wilt loosen the pores of this earth." Jung offers the following interpretation:

---

[59]Jung, *Psychology and Alchemy, CW* 12, par. 336.

[60]Jung, *Mysterium Coniunctionis, CW* 14, par. 317.

[61]Ibid., par. 306.

If you will contemplate your lack of fantasy, of inspiration and inner aliveness, which you feel as sheer stagnation and a barren wilderness, and impregnate it with the interest born of alarm at your inner death, then something can take shape in you, for your inner emptiness conceals just as great a fullness if only you will allow it to penetrate into you. If you prove receptive to this "call of the wild," the longing for fulfillment will quicken the sterile wilderness of your soul as rain quickens the dry earth.[62]

The greater *solutio* is an encounter with the *Numinosum,* which both tests and establishes the ego's relation to the Self. As the flood myths tell us explicitly, the flood comes from God; that is, *solutio* comes from the Self. What is worth saving in the ego is saved. What is not worth saving is dissolved and melted down in order to be recast in new life-forms. Thus, the ongoing life process renews itself. The ego that is committed to this transpersonal process will cooperate with it and will experience its own diminishment as a prelude to the coming of the larger personality, the wholeness of the Self.

---

[62]Ibid., par. 190.

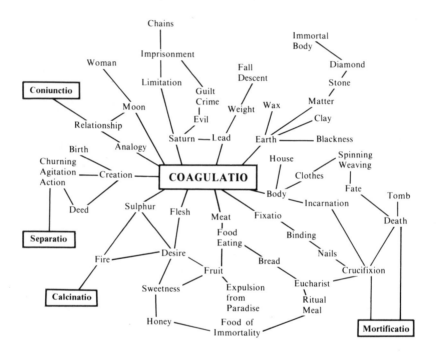

⚜ 4 Coagulatio ⚜

J UST AS *CALCINATIO* IS THE OPERATION of the element fire, *solutio* the water operation, and *sublimatio* the operation pertaining to air, so *coagulatio* belongs to the symbolism of the element earth. As with all the alchemical operations, *coagulatio* refers first of all to experience in the laboratory. Cooling can turn a liquid into a solid. A solid that has been dissolved in a solvent reappears when the solvent is evaporated.[1] Or a chemical reaction may produce a new compound that is solid—for example, the coagulation of egg white when it is heated.

In essence, *coagulatio* is the process that turns something into earth. "Earth" is thus one of the synonyms for the *coagulatio*. It is heavy and permanent, of fixed position and shape. It doesn't disappear into the air by volatilizing nor pliantly adapt itself to the shape of any container as does water. Its form and location are fixed. Thus, for a psychic content to become earth means that it has been concretized in a particular localized form; that is, *it has become attached to an ego* (see figure 4-1).

Coagulatio is often equated with creation. The *Turba Philosophorum* says, "God hath created all things by his word, having said unto them: Be, and they were made with the four other elements, earth, water, air, and fire, which He coagulated."[2] Certain creation myths use explicit images of *coagulatio*. In the cosmogony of the North American Indians, the world was often created by an "earth diver" who brought up bits of mud from the depths of the sea.[3] For example, a Cherokee myth says: "Originally the animals were crowded into the sky-world; everything was flood below. The Water-Beetle was sent on an exploration, and

---

[1]Ruland calls this "Coagulation by Segregation" and says it is "when certain portions being segregated, the rest are concreted. The operation may be termed Concretion. It is performed with heat, whereby the humour is evaporated, or exhaled, and thus the cause of fluidity is removed" (Ruland, *A Lexicon of Alchemy,* p. 107).

[2]Waite, trans., *Turba Philosophorum,* p. 25.

[3]An example is found in Eliade, *From Primitives to Zen,* p. 88.

FIGURE 4 – 1
Earth Nurses the *Filius Philosophorum* (Maier, *Atalanta Fugiens,* 1618.)

after darting about on the surface of the waters and finding no rest, it dived to the depths, whence it brought up a bit of mud, from which Earth developed by accretion. When the earth was dry...the animals came down."[4]

There is an interesting *coagulatio* image in Hindu mythology. After the flood (*solutio*) that destroyed all people except Manu, the Hindu Noah, there was need to recover valuable things lost in the deluge. "Gods and genii churned the ocean of milk, using the great serpent (Sesa-naga) as a rope and the Slow-Mountain (Mandara) as a churning rod."[5] From this churning process various objects coagulated out like butter from cream. This same image is given a psychological application in the Upanishads. "Like the butter hidden in milk, Pure Consciousness (*vijnanam:* the state of Atman as Brahman, sheer bliss) resides in every being. It is to be constantly churned, with the mind serving as the churning rod."[6] The idea that the world was coagulated into being by an

---

[4]Alexander, *The Mythology of All Races* 10:60.

[5]Danielou, *Hindu Polytheism,* p. 167.

[6]Zimmer, *Philosophies of India,* p. 369.

agitating or churning motion is also expressed by Anaximander: "There was an eternal motion, in which was brought about the origin of the worlds."[7] This "eternal motion" was thought of as a vortex taking place in the "boundless" (*apeiron*), the *prima materia,* and is very similar to the Hindu myth.

A middle-aged man who was going through a major reorientation with a "sense of the old order passing away" had this dream:

> *It is dawn, the light of the rising sun just emerging. I am up to my waist in a substance that is a mixture of black mud, slime, and shit. There is no one else around and this black expanse stretches to the horizon. It is like the beginning of the world, the first day of creation. I start to thrash my legs, to churn in the black mud with great and persistent effort. I continue doing this for hours and slowly the primeval ooze begins to harden and become firm. I notice the sun is rising into the sky and its heat is drying up the water and providing solid earth. I anticipate being able to stand on firm ground.*

These myths tell us that *coagulatio* is promoted by action (diving, churning, whirling motion). They correspond to what Faust learned from the Spirit of Mephistopheles: "In the beginning was the deed."[8] Psychologically this means that activity and psychic movement promote ego development. Exposing oneself to the storm and stress of action, the churn of reality, solidifies the personality.

The *Turba Philosophorum* gives the following alchemical recipe for *coagulatio:* "Take quicksilver, coagulate in the body of Magnesia, in Kuhul (lead), or in Sulphur which does not burn; etc." (dictum 11). This text has a recognizable chemical reference. If mercury is amalgamated with a large quantity of another metal such as lead, the amalgam solidifies. Similarly, mercury combines with sulphur to form solid mercury sulphide. However, the reference to sulphur that does not burn makes it clear that a psychic meaning has been superimposed on the chemical facts.

The substance to be coagulated is elusive quicksilver. This is the Spirit Mercurius about whom Jung has written extensively.[9] Essentially it is the autonomous spirit of the archetypal psyche, the paradoxical manifestation of the transpersonal Self. To subject the Spirit Mercurius to *coagulatio* means nothing less than the connecting of the ego with the Self, the fulfillment of individuation. Lesser aspects of the elusive

---

[7]Burnet, *Early Greek Philosophy,* p. 52.

[8]Goethe, *Faust,* pt. 1, line 1237.

[9]Jung, *Alchemical Studies, CW* 13, pars. 239ff.

Mercurius appear in the effects of all autonomous complexes. The assimilation of a complex is thus a contribution to the *coagulatio* of the Self.

The text mentions three agents of *coagulatio:* magnesia, lead, and sulphur. Magnesia had a different meaning to the alchemists than it does to us; it was a general term referring to various crude metallic ores or impure mixtures.[10] Psychologically this could refer to the union of the transpersonal spirit with ordinary human reality. Perhaps this is the meaning of Jung's remark as reported by Aniela Jaffé: "When Jung, in his eighties, was discussing at his house the process of becoming conscious with a group of young psychiatrists... he ended with the surprising words: 'And then you have to learn to become decently unconscious.'"[11]

The next agent of *coagulatio* mentioned is lead. Lead is heavy, dull, and burdensome. It is associated with the planet Saturn, which carries the qualities of depression, melancholy, and galling limitation. Thus, free, autonomous spirit must be connected with heavy reality and the limitations of personal particularity. In analytic practice this linkage with lead is often accomplished when the individual takes personal responsibility for fleeting fantasies and ideas by expressing them to the analyst or to another significant person. It is astonishing to observe the difference between an idea thought and an idea spoken. It's the difference between mercury and lead (see figure 4-2).

The third coagulating agent mentioned is sulphur. Its yellow color and inflammability associate it with the sun. On the other hand, its vapors stink and blacken most metals so that brimstone is a characteristic feature of hell. Jung summarizes his masterful discussion of the symbolism of sulphur in *Mysterium Coniunctionis* with these words:

> Sulphur represents the active substance of the sun or, in psychological language, the *motive factor in consciousness:* on the one hand the will, which can best be regarded as a dynamism subordinated to consciousness, and on the other hand compulsion, an involuntary motivation or impulse ranging from mere interest to possession proper. The unconscious dynamism would correspond to sulphur, for compulsion is the great mystery of human life. It is the thwarting of our conscious will and of our reason by an inflammable element within us, appearing now as a consuming fire and now as life-giving warmth.[12]

It is paradoxical. "As the corrupter it has affinity with the devil, while on the other hand it appears as a parallel of Christ."[13] Thus, if part of

---

[10]See Ruland, *A Lexicon of Alchemy,* "magnesia" and "marcasite."

[11]Jaffé, *The Myth of Meaning,* p. 149.

[12]Jung, *Mysterium Coniunctionis, CW* 14, par. 151.

[13]Ibid., par. 153.

FIGURE 4 - 2
Eagle Chained to a Ground Animal (Stolcius, *Viridarium Chymicum*, 1624.
Reprinted in Read, *Prelude to Chemistry*.)

the meaning of sulphur is desirousness—the striving for power and pleasure—we reach the conclusion that *desire coagulates*.

In the New Testament the flesh is explicitly equated with sinful desirousness. "For all that is in the world, the lust of the flesh and the lust of the eyes and the pride of life, is not of the Father but is of the world" (1 John 2:16, RSV). Likewise, Paul said, "Now the works of the flesh are manifest, which are these: adultery, fornication, uncleanness, lasciviousness, idolatry, witchcraft, hatred, variance, emulations, wrath, strife, seditions, heresies, envyings, murders, drunkenness, revellings, and such like" (Gal. 5:19-21, AV).

Not only is desirousness a characteristic of flesh—the coagulated aspect of the psyche—but also desire is said to initiate the incarnating process. For instance, incarnation and desire are linked in *The Tibetan Book of the Dead*. When a soul is about to be reincarnated and lodged in a womb, it has visions of mating couples and is overcome by intense desire: if a male, desire for the mother and aversion for the father, if a female, desire for the father and aversion for the mother.[14] Jacob

---

[14]Evans-Wentz, ed. *The Tibetan Book of the Dead*, pp. xlv ff.

Boehme, speaking of the manifestation of the divine nature, says: "The will by desiring contracts and becomes substantial. Thus darkness is created within the will, while without that desire there would be nothing but eternal stillness without substantiality."[15] A Neoplatonic image of the incarnation of the soul also sees it as motivated by desire. "Looking down from that highest summit and perpetual light, and having with secret desire contemplated the appetence of the body and its 'life,' so-called on earth, the soul by the very weight of this its earthly thought gradually sinks down into the nether world.... In each sphere (which it passes) it is clothed with an etherial envelopment, so that by these it is in stages reconciled to the company of this earthen garment. And thus it comes through as many deaths as it passes spheres to what here on earth is called 'life.'"[16]

In this passage the incarnating process is linked with desire, with a descent or fall from heaven, and with a putting on of clothes. The motif of the fall from heaven because of pride or passion goes back to Genesis 6:2 (AV): "The sons of God saw the daughters of men that they were fair; and they took them wives of all which they chose." Also relevant is Lucifer's rebellion and fall from heaven so beautifully described by Milton:

> He trusted to have equal'd the most High,
> If he opposed; and with ambitious aim
> Against the Throne and Monarchy of God
> Rais'd impious War in Heav'n and Battel proud
> With vain attempt. Him the almighty Power
> Hurl'd headlong flaming from th' Ethereal Skie
> With hideous ruin and combustion down
> To bottomless perdition, there to dwell
> In Adamantine chains and penal Fire,
> Who durst defie th' Omnipotent to Arms.[17]

This passage contains *calcinatio* symbolism, but its main reference is to *coagulatio*. It is a magnificent description of the initial preconscious act that lays the foundation of the ego. Angels or their equivalents still fall from heaven in modern dreams (see figure 4-3).

A young woman who had a defective ego development—a gap in awareness of her feminine identity—had this dream early in her analysis:

---

[15]Boehme, "Forty Questions," quoted in *Personal Christianity: The Doctrine of Jacob Boehme*, p. 88.

[16]Macrobius, *In Somn. Scip.*, quoted in Jonas, *The Gnostic Religion*, p. 158.

[17]Milton, "Paradise Lost," in *Milton: Complete Poetry and Selected Prose*, bk. 11, lines 40-49.

FIGURE 4–3
The Fall of the Rebel Angels (*Les Très Riches Heures du Duc de Berry*,
Chantilly, Musée Condé.)

(Abbreviated) *I was called to the window to watch a phenomenon in the sky. As I watched the moon I saw another body emerge from behind it—like a second moon. Suddenly the second body began to explode in spectacular colors that looked like an H-bomb explosion. I thought we were watching the birth of a new sun. All at once, during another explosive event, a piece of the new body was thrown into space and landed in our apartment. We ran out as fast as we could, being afraid that it might be radioactive.*

This dream encouraged me to persevere in a slow and difficult thera-peutic process. An important feature of it was the gradual development of the capacity to relate fully to a man.

Dreams of planes crashing or objects falling generally refer to *coagulatio.* For instance, a man who was in the process of developing a more authentic relation to his religion had this dream:

I am in midtown Manhattan. Tall buildings are being razed. A huge boulder from the top of one of the buildings comes crashing to the ground, almost hitting me.

The dreamer's association to the boulder was Peter, the rock upon which Christ built his church (Matt. 16:18).

Psychotherapeutic experience verifies the idea that desire promotes *coagulatio.* For those who are already driven by desirousness, *coagulatio* is not the operation needed. However, many patients have an inadequate libido investment, a weakness of desire sometimes bordering on anhe-donia. Such people don't know what they want and are afraid of their own desires. They are like unborn souls in heaven shrinking from the fall into concrete reality. These people need to cultivate their desires— seek them, nourish them, and act on them. Only thus will psychic energy be mobilized that will promote life experience and ego development. In psychotherapy, the emergence of transference desires will often indicate the beginning of a *coagulatio* process and therefore should be treated with care.

The lure of desire is the *sweetness* of fulfillment. Honey as the supreme example of sweetness is therefore an agent of *coagulatio.* Paracelsus says that "the prime matter of honey is the sweetness of the earth which resides in naturally growing things." And again, honey "is the prime materialized matter, for honey and wax are one."[18] According to the alchemist Dorn's recipe for joining the spirit (*unio mentalis*) with

---

[18]Paracelsus, *The Hermetic and Alchemical Writings of Paracelsus* 2:74.

the body, one of the required agents is honey.[19] Jung says of Dorn's use of honey:

> Thereby the mixture acquired the property not only of eliminating impurities but of changing spirit into body, and in view of the proposed conjunction of the spirit and the body this seemed a particularly promising sign. To be sure, the "sweetness of the earth" was not without its dangers, for as we have seen...the honey could change into a deadly poison. According to Paracelsus it contains "Tartarum," which as its name implies has to do with Hades. Further, Tartarum is a "calcined Saturn" and consequently had affinities with this malefic planet.[20]

Honey, because of its preservative qualities, was considered by the ancients to be a medicine of immortality and had a Eucharistic use in some early Christian communities.[21]

In modern dreams, a reference to sweets (candy, cake, cookies, and so forth) usually indicates a regressive tendency toward childish pleasure-seeking that requires reductive interpretation (*mortificatio*). Occasionally, however, it points to an authentic need for *coagulatio*. *Coagulatio* is often resisted because it is felt to be morally ambiguous and apt to lead one into pain and conflict. The classic protest is that of Hamlet: "O, that this too too solid flesh would melt,/Thaw and resolve itself into a dew" (Act 1, sc. 2, line 129). In fact, *coagulatio* is explicitly associated with evil. This is demonstrated by the alchemical connection of *coagulatio* with Saturn, the malefic principle. One text says, "the coagulation (takes place) in Saturn."[22] According to Jacob Boehme, "Saturn, that cold, sharp, austere and astringent regent, taketh its beginning and original not from the sun; for Saturn hath in its power the chamber of death, and is a drier up of all powers, from whence corporeity existeth. For as the sun is the heart of life, and an original of all spirits in the body of this world, so Saturn is a beginner of all corporeity and comprehensibility or palpability"[23] (see figure 4-4). The utterly malign nature of Saturn is expressed by Chaucer who has Saturn say:

> My course, which has so wide a way to turn,
> Has power more than any man may know.
> Mine is the drowning in the sea below;
> Mine is the dungeon underneath the moat;   /
> Mine is the hanging and strangling by the throat;

---

[19]Jung, *Mysterium Coniunctionis, CW* 14, par. 683.

[20]Ibid., par. 687.

[21]Eisler, *Orpheus the Fisher,* pp. 242ff.

[22]Bonus of Ferrara, *The New Pearl of Great Price,* p. 426.

[23]Boehme, *Aurora,* p. 687.

FIGURE 4 – 4
The Stone of Saturn (Maier, *Atalanta Fugiens,* 1618.)

> Rebellion, and the base crowd's murmuring,
> The groaning and the private poisoning,
> And vengeance and amercement—all are mine,
> While yet I dwell within the Lion's sign.
> Mine is the ruining of all high halls,
> And tumbling down of towers and of walls
> Upon the miner and the carpenter.
> I struck down Samson, that pillar shaker;
> And mine are all the maladies so cold,
> The treasons dark, the machinations old;
> My glance is father of all pestilence.[24]

Since antiquity there has been a tendency to equate matter with evil. This reached its extreme in certain Gnostic sects. The fall of the soul from its immortal state into bodily form is also often linked with a primal crime. For instance, Empedocles describes immortal spirits condemned to incarnation because of violence and perjury: "When one of the divine spirits whose portion is long life sinfully stains his own limbs with bloodshed, and following Hate has sworn a false oath—these must

---

[24]Chaucer, "The Knight's Tale," in *Canterbury Tales,* pp. 68f.

wander for thrice ten thousand seasons far from the company of the blessed, being born throughout the period into all kinds of mortal shapes, which exchange one hard way of life for another.... Of this number am I too now, a fugitive from heaven and a wanderer, because I trusted in raging Hate."[25]

According to ancient legend, behind the creation of human beings was a crime of the Titans. While playing with the infant Dionysus, they dismembered, boiled, and ate him—all except the heart, which was rescued by Zeus. In punishment, Zeus consumed the Titans by lightning and used their ashes to create the human race. Thus the "Titanic earth," containing scattered particles of the heavenly Dionysus, became the clay for human *coagulatio*—a material derived from a primal crime.

Prometheus, who taught humans how to trick the gods and take the best portion of the sacrificial animal for themselves, brought fire to people by theft and was punished by *coagulatio*—being chained to a rock (see figure 4-5). Similarly, Adam and Eve were expelled from the paradisal, pre-ego condition after the crime of eating the forbidden fruit. These examples demonstrate that ego development is associated with the experience of evil, criminality, and guilt. Thus, consciousness of one's own evil—that is, awareness of the shadow—coagulates. This can be seen as the psychological meaning of Christ's statement, "Resist not evil" (Matt. 5:39, AV). It is necessary to leave room for evil if one is to contribute to the real world. Thus Jung wrote to Richard Wilhelm: "You are *too important* to our Western world, I must keep on telling you this. You mustn't melt away or otherwise disappear, or get ill, but wicked desires should pin you to the earth so your work can go on."[26] We all know the phrase, "He was too good for this world." Saintly and spiritual people often do have a short life. In the past they often died of tuberculosis. It is dangerous to be one-sided, even one-sided in goodness.

Dreams often allude to the criminal aspect of egohood. Presuming to take on will and consciousness may be pictured as a theft. Daring to follow an inner authority may be pictured as the murder of a projected authority, perhaps a parricide. Being an ego is inextricably connected with guilt, which is punished by *coagulatio*—confinement within the limits of one's personal reality (suggested by the motif of chains and imprisonment). Although *coagulatio* is a guilt-laden process, according to one text it contains its own capacity for redemption. "Lead signifies the vexations and troubles wherewith God visits us and brings us back to repentance. For as lead burns up and removes all the imperfections of

---

[25]Empedocles, *Purifications,* fr. 115, quoted in Freeman, *Ancilla to the Pre-Socratic Philosophers,* p. 65.

[26]Jung, *Letters* 1:63.

FIGURE 4 – 5
The Torture of Prometheus (Moreau. Reprinted in *Larousse Encyclopedia of Mythology*.)

metals...so likewise tribulation in this life cleanses us from the many blemishes which we have incurred: wherefore St. Ambrose calls it the key of heaven."[27]

Coagulatio is generally followed by other processes, most often by *mortificatio* and *putrefactio*. What has become fully concretized is now subject to transformation. It has become tribulation calling out for transcendence. This is how we can understand the statements of the Apostle Paul linking body and flesh with death: "Who shall deliver me from the body of this death?" (Rom. 7:24, AV). And, "For if ye live after the flesh, ye shall die: but if ye through the Spirit do mortify the deeds of the body, ye shall live" (Rom. 8:13, AV). And again, "For those who live according to the flesh set their minds on the things of the flesh, but those who live according to the Spirit set their minds on the things of the Spirit. To set the mind on the flesh is death, but to set the mind on the Spirit is life and peace. For the mind that is set on the flesh is hostile to God; it does not submit to God's law, indeed it cannot; and those who are in the flesh cannot please God" (Rom. 8:5-8, RSV).

The body and flesh are identified with death because anything that is born into spatio-temporal existence must submit to the limitations of that existence, which include an end, death. This is the price of being real. Once a content has fully coagulated or incarnated it becomes lifeless with no further possibilities for growth. Emerson expresses this idea: "Life only avails, not the having lived. Power ceases in the instant of repose; it resides in the moment of transition from a past to a new state, in the shooting of the gulf, in the darting to an aim. This one fact the world hates; that the soul *becomes;* for that forever degrades the past, turns all riches to poverty, all reputation to shame, confounds the saint with the rogue, shoves Jesus and Judas equally aside."[28] After full *coagulatio* the *putrefactio* follows. "For he who sows to his own flesh will from the flesh reap corruption; but he who sows to the Spirit will from the Spirit reap eternal life" (Gal. 6:8, RSV). An alchemical text picks up the same theme: "The lion, the lower sun, grows corrupt through the flesh....Thus is the lion corrupted in his nature through his flesh, which follows the times of the moon, and is eclipsed. For the moon is the shadow of the sun, and with corruptible bodies she is consumed, and through her consumption is the lion eclipsed with the help of the moisture of Mercurius, yet his eclipse is changed to usefulness and to a better nature, and one more perfect than the first."[29]

The lion or lower sun is the theriomorphic aspect of masculine consciousness—the ego incarnated in pride and concupiscence. The text

---

[27]Quoted in *Mysterium Coniunctionis, CW* 14, par. 472n.

[28]Emerson, "Self Reliance," in *The Writings of Ralph Waldo Emerson,* p. 158.

[29]*Mysterium Coniunctionis, CW* 14, par. 21.

tells us that it is to be corrupted "through his flesh, which follows the times of the moon." Corruption is inherent in flesh, and both are promoted by the moon. This alludes to the fact that not only Saturn but also the moon govern *coagulatio* (see figure 4-6). According to ancient thinking the moon, as the "planet" closest to earth, was the gateway between the celestial and the earthly realms. All spiritual entities on the way to embodiment were funneled through the moon where they were materialized. Jacob Boehme says: "The seventh form is called Luna ...the property of all the six forms lies therein, and it is as a corporeal being of all the rest;...for the other forms do all cast their desire through Sol into Luna; for in Sol they are spiritual and in Luna corporeal...whatever the sun is, and makes in the spirit-life in itself, the same Luna is, and makes corporeal in itself."[30] Luna's association to *coagulatio* indicates that the latter is governed by the feminine principle. This is also indicated by the feminine nature of earth, matter (*mater*), and the fact that we can be incarnated only through a feminine womb. Any specific form, manifestation, or structure that solidifies our life energies

FIGURE 4 – 6
Virgin and Child on Crescent Moon (Dürer. Reprinted in Panofsky, *The Life and Art of Albrecht Dürer.*)

---

[30]Boehme, *The Signature of All Things,* pp. 96ff.

into particular, concrete expression is of the nature of woman. Country, church, community, institution, family, vocation, avocation, personal relationship—all enlist our commitment via the feminine principle. Even apparent abstractions such as science, wisdom, truth, beauty, liberty (see figure 4-7, *Liberty Leading the People*), and so forth, when they are served in a concrete and realistic way, are experienced as personifications of the feminine. Jung has defined the feminine principle as the principle of relatedness. Thus we can say, *relationship coagulates.* This is a very important fact for psychotherapy and warrants some discussion.

We know from clinical work the profound effect that childhood experience and personal relationships with parents have on the emerging personality of the child. We also know from such cases as the "wolf children" that if an infant lacks an environment of human relationship, no human personality develops. In such cases no ego appears. The same thing happens in those occasional cases of a child locked in a room for years and totally rejected by its parents. The child simply remains an animal. Similarly, in cases where a parent figure has been lost at an early age and not adequately replaced, a kind of hole is left in the

FIGURE 4 – 7
Liberty Leading the People (Delacroix. Paris, the Louvre. Reprinted in Craven, *A Treasury of Art Masterpieces.*)

psyche. An important archetypal image has not undergone personaliza-tion or *coagulatio* through a personal relationship and hence retains a boundless and primordial power that threatens to inundate the ego if it is approached. On the other hand there are patients who, in spite of severe deprivation at the hands of the parents, were able to find an important relationship with some marginal figure in their childhood. It may have been a maid, an aunt, a teacher, or a grandparent who was able to relate genuinely to the child and hence mediate and personalize an archetypal image. In these cases the parental inadequacies, although damaging, were not fatal to the child's development because an alternate source of human relatedness had been found. Such isolated positive relationships may have lasted only a short time, but their effects seem to be incorporated permanently into the growing personality.

Clinical experience shows that the individual realizes and relates to only those aspects of the parental archetypes that have been encountered in personal relationships. That part of the archetype that the parent's personality is able to activate, mediate, and embody will be the part that the child can incorporate most easily and build into its own personality. That part of the archetype to which the parent has no relation will be left largely unrealized in the realm of eternal forms, not yet incarnated in the child's history.

The whole early process of individual psychic development—the ego emerging from its original state of oneness with the objective psyche—can be considered a process of *coagulatio*. The experience and conscious realization of the innate archetypal images proceeds only by encounter-ing them incarnated in concrete, personal forms. Neumann alludes to this fact when he speaks of the necessary phase of secondary person-alization. Concerning this he writes:

> This principle [of secondary personalization] holds that there is a persistent tendency in man to take primary and transpersonal contents as secondary and personal, and to reduce them to personal factors. Personalization is directly connected with the growth of the ego, of consciousness and of indi-viduality...through which...the ego emerges from the torrent of transper-sonal and collective events....Secondary personalization brings a steady decrease in the effective power of the transpersonal and a steady increase in the importance of the ego and personality.[31]

This describes *coagulatio,* whereby archetypal contents fall out of heaven and are egoized.

Childhood personal relationship coagulates the archetypes but also limits and distorts them. If the particular aspects that have been coagu-lated are too one-sidely negative or otherwise inimical to growth they

---

[31]Neumann, *The Origins and History of Consciousness,* p. 336.

will have to be broken up and be recoagulated under more favorable circumstances. A woman who had such an experience had this dream:

> *She sees four square concrete slabs with circles in them. They are cracked and broken. A voice says, "These are your erroneous attitudes about femininity which are now destroyed."*

Coagulatio is promoted by an active, responsive, participating approach on the part of the psychotherapist. Certain patients require this approach and are threatened by anything that encourages *solutio*. The extreme case of failure of the archetypal images to become concretized is found in overt schizophrenia. The ego is literally inundated by boundless, primordial, archetypal images. Such an individual has had inadequate opportunity to experience the archetypes mediated and personalized through human relationships.

The vital need for the personalization of the archetype accounts for the way in which many patients cling obstinately to their original experience of the parents. If, for instance, there has been a largely negative, destructive parental experience, the patient may find it very difficult to accept and endure a positive parent experience. I have gotten the distinct impression that a person will persist in, say, a negative orientation to the father archetype simply because that is the aspect of the image which has been *coagulated* in his or her own life and therefore has an element of safety and security, even though it is negative. For such a person to encounter the positive aspect of the archetype is threatening because, since this side has never been personalized, it carries a transpersonal magnitude that threatens to dissolve the established boundaries of the ego. Emily Dickinson describes that state of affairs:

> I can wade Grief—
> Whole pools of it—
> I'm used to that—
> But the least push of Joy
> Breaks up my feet—
> And I tip-drunken—
> Let no Pebble-smile—
> 'Twas the New Liquor—
> That was all![32]

Not only does external relationship coagulate, but also inner relationship does so. An example of this is found in an alchemical text: "The igneous spirit of the natural fire is corporified in the substances which are *analogous* to it. Our stone is an astral fire, which sympathizes

---

[32]Dickinson, *The Complete Poems of Emily Dickinson,* p. 115.

with the natural fire, and which as a true salamander receives its nativity, is nourished and grows in the elementary fire, which is *geometrically proportional* to it."[33]

The text speaks of two fires, an astral fire and a natural fire; it seems to say that natural fire is proportional to astral fire and, therefore, the former corporifies or *coagulates* the latter. The term "geometrical proportion" undoubtedly refers to the passage in Plato's *Timaeus* where the creation of the *body* of the universe is described:

> Now that which comes to be must be bodily, and so visible and tangible; and nothing can be visible without fire, or tangible without something solid, and nothing is solid without earth. Hence the god, when he began to put together the body of the universe, set about making it of fire and earth. But two things alone cannot be satisfactorily united without a third; for there must be some bond between them drawing them together. And of all bonds the best is that which makes itself and the terms it connects a unity in the fullest sense; and it is of the nature of a continued geometrical proportion (*analogia*) to effect this most perfectly.[34]

In essence this passage says that the body of the universe is created (that is, coagulated) by means of proportion or analogy. Analogy is a process of relationship, a making of connections by "as if." These texts tell us that analogy corporifies or coagulates spirit. This is what makes alchemy so valuable for depth psychology. It is a treasury of analogies that corporify or embody the objective psyche and the processes it undergoes in development. The same applies to religion and mythology. The importance of analogy for realization of the psyche can hardly be overestimated. It gives form and visibility to that which was previously invisible, intangible, not yet coagulated.

Concepts and abstractions don't coagulate. They make air, not earth. They are agents of *sublimatio*. The images of dreams and active imagination do coagulate. They connect the outer world with the inner world by means of proportional or analogous images and thus coagulate soul-stuff. Moods and affects toss us about wildly until they coagulate into something visible and tangible; then we can relate to them objectively. Jung says in his memoirs: "To the extent that I managed to translate the emotions into images—that is to say, to find the images which were concealed in the emotions—I was inwardly calmed and reassured."[35]

The ancients considered human existence to be controlled by a certain inexorable factor variously called fate, destiny, lot, or portion. The image of spinning and weaving was used. The three Fates spin one's

---

[33] *The Lives of the Alchemystical Philosophers,* p. 216.

[34] Cornford, *Plato's Cosmology,* p. 43ff.

[35] Jung, *Memories, Dreams, Reflections,* p. 177.

existence into being. Clotho spins the thread, Lachesis measures it, and Atropos cuts it. One's destiny was considered a woven fabric or a garment, a rope, a chain, or a yoke that confined one mercilessly to predetermined limits.[36] Pindar invokes this *coagulatio* factor as the goddess of birth: "Goddess of birth, that art enthroned beside the brooding Destinies! Listen thou daughter of mighty Hera, thou that createst offspring. Without thine aid we see not the light, no nor the dark gloom, ere we attain unto thy sister, Hebe with glowing limbs. Yet it is not for equal aims that all of us draw our breath, for various indeed are the fates that fetter mortals in the chain of destiny."[37]

When Agamemnon decides, despite her pitiful pleas, to obey the prophecy and sacrifice his daughter Iphigenia in exchange for favorable winds to Troy, Aeschylus says, "Thus on his neck he took/Fate's hard compelling yoke." Or, by another translation, "Then he put on/The harness of necessity."[38] *Coagulatio* is experienced as a bondage because it confines individuals to their actual reality, the portion they were given by destiny. Perhaps this accounts for the phrase, "he was *bound* to do that." Language is stating that destiny is bondage (see figure 4–8).

Embodied existence is even described as a prison or tomb. Plato speaks of the soul as being "enshrined in the living tomb which we carry about, now that we are imprisoned in the body, like an oyster in his shell" (*Phaedrus,* 250). Less negatively, the body is described as the house or temple of the soul. Oliver Wendell Holmes uses this image in his poem *The Chambered Nautilus.*

> Build thee more stately mansions, O my soul,
> As the swift seasons roll!
> Leave thy low–vaulted past!
> Let each new temple, nobler than the last
> Shut thee from heaven with a dome more vast,
> Till thou at length are free,
> Leaving thine outgrown shell by life's unresting sea!

Clothes are also images of the incarnated condition. The flesh is a vesture acquired during the descent of the soul through the planetary spheres. Although Jung usually interpreted clothes in dreams as referring to the persona, they can also quite properly be understood as modes of *coagulatio.* The idea of incarnated life as a woven fabric or tapestry is found in a dream brought me by a woman who had just become pregnant for the first time. She had this dream six days after

[36]Onians, *The Origins of European Thought,* passim.

[37]*Nemean Odes* 7, 1–8, in *The Odes of Pindar,* p. 381.

[38]Oates and O'Neill, eds. "Agamemnon" in *The Complete Greek Drama,* line 318.

FIGURE 4 - 8
Fortune or Nemesis Carrying the Cup and Harness of Destiny (Dürer.
Reprinted in *The Complete Engravings, Etchings and Drypoints
of Albrecht Dürer.*)

missing her first period and three days before learning that her pregnancy test was positive.

A tapestry is being brought down from the attic. It is in two separate parts which are to be joined—the burlap backing and the threaded design. First the burlap backing is brought downstairs. Next the threaded design was to be brought down. We were supposed to study the design of the tapestry in order to understand it. This would involve the counting of the threads. The design was very rich and complex.

This dream is of considerable interest as an example of the reaction of the unconscious to the biological fact of conception. It has several similarities with the myths. First, the event is described as a fall, a descent from the attic. Secondly, there is a distinction made between the material ground (the burlap) and the image of meaning (threaded design) to be superimposed on it. This would correspond to the distinction between the soul and the flesh, which will house it, or the material, which will carry the stamp of its image. In addition, the counting of the threads would correspond to the measuring function of the second Fate, Lachesis.

Coagulatio dreams sometimes occur at the approach of death, as though to express the meaning of the incarnation now ending. An eighty-two-year-old woman had this dream a few weeks before her sudden death:

I was in the kitchen and looked into the oven. There was a beautiful roast completely cooked, perhaps a little dry. A voice said, "You left it in too long, didn't you?" I acknowledged that I had.

Another example is a woman's report of the death of her grandfather. "Before my grandfather died, he was in a nursing home for eight or ten years, so senile that he seemed to recognize no one. Everyone kept asking, "Why doesn't he die?" Everyone kept saying how much better it would have been if he could have died when his active life was over; always he had found meaning only in work and activity. The night before his death, one of his daughters (my aunt) dreamed

that she saw hanging before her a very large and very beautiful intricately and colorfully woven Oriental carpet. At the top rim she saw the final thread being woven into place. She understood that this carpet was her father's soul-work, which he had been weaving silently for the past eight or ten years, and now that it was finished, he was free to go.

The next day my grandfather died."[39]

It is particularly impressive how dreams concerning clothes come up at a time of death. For instance, a few days before her death, a woman who knew she was mortally ill dreamed *that she was going to attend a fashion show*.[40] A few days before the death of his father, a man dreamed *that he saw his father dressed very nattily in new clothes*. These dreams seem to refer to an ultimate *coagulatio*,the acquisition of an immortal body. In the *Book of Enoch* we read:

> And the righteous and elect shall have risen from the earth,
> And ceased to be of downcast countenance.
> And they shall have been clothed with garments of glory.
> And these shall be the garments of Life from the Lord of Spirits:
> And your garments shall not grow old,
> Nor your glory pass away before the Lord of Spirits. (62:15–16)[41]

Paul uses the same image. "For we know if the earthly tent we live in is destroyed, we have a building from God, a house not made with hands, eternal in the heavens. Here indeed we groan, and long to put on our heavenly dwelling, so that by putting it on we may not be found naked. For while we are still in this tent, we sigh with anxiety; not that we would be unclothed, but that we would be further clothed, so that what is mortal may be swallowed up by life" (2 Cor. 5:1-4, RSV).

The idea of an immortal body, expressing an ultimate *coagulatio* of the spirit, is a boundary image whose meaning can be only dimly sensed. It corresponds to the paradoxical symbol of the Philosophers' Stone and seems to refer to the final goal of individuation.

The grandest symbol of *coagulatio* is the Christian myth of the Incarnation of the Divine Logos. "And the Word became flesh and dwelt among us" (John 1:14, RSV)(see figure 4-9). This subject requires a separate treatment of its own. However, a few aspects of the life of Christ can be noted as particularly relevant. Christ was born of a virgin; that is, he was incarnated by means of pure earth. The Virgin Mary corresponds to the alchemical notion of the "white foliated earth." Alchemy says, "Sow your gold in white foliated earth" (see figure 4-10). White earth corresponds to the ash that has survived *calcinatio*. It is a contradiction because earth is typically black. As we have noted, the principle of materiality that promotes *coagulatio* has a bad name. This is black earth. But in the symbolism of Christianity, and more explicitly in alchemy, there arose the symbolic image of white earth, a purified materiality principle. Psychologically this means the possibility of a new

---

[39]I am indebted to Robin van Loben Sels for this report.

[40]I am indebted to Edward Whitmont for this dream.

[41]Charles, *The Apocrypha and Pseudepigrapha of the Old Testament* 2:228.

FIGURE 4 – 9
The Annunciation (Drawing by Rembrandt. Besançon, Musée Communal.
Reprinted in *Rembrandt's Life of Christ*.)

and purified attitude toward materiality. It means the discovery of the
transpersonal value of the ego. What purifies is consciousness. The
black earth of ego desirousness becomes the white foliated earth that
incarnates the Self.

The lowly circumstances of Christ's birth correspond to the ordinary
and commonplace aspects of being concretely real. The events of the
Passion also apply. Christ's condemnation and execution with criminals
present him as a willing carrier of evil. His carrying the cross represents
the realization of the burden of one's being. The outstanding image is
the crucifixion itself—being nailed to matter (see figure 4–11). In alchemical terms, the cross represents the four elements from which all
manifest being is made. *Fixatio* is one of the synonyms for *coagulatio*,
and the alchemists had pictures of the mercurial serpent fixed to the
cross or transfixed to a tree (see figures 4–12 and 4–13). The Manicheans
universalized this image to the greatest extent in their doctrine of *Jesus
patibilis,* the suffering Jesus "who 'hangs from every tree,' 'is served up
bound in every dish,' 'every day is born, suffers and dies,' and is

FIGURE 4 – 10
"Sow Your Gold in White Earth" (Maier, *Atalanta Fugiens,* 1618.)

dispersed in all creation."[42] The uncoagulated spirit is free, it can entertain any image without consequences. But to be a concretely realized ego means one is nailed to the cross of the created world.

Of particular interest concerning the Christian incarnation myth is the stated purpose of the whole drama. The purpose is redemption or rescue of the sinful human race. There is a parallel Gnostic incarnation tale that states a similar purpose. In the apocryphal *Acts of Thomas*[43] is found the so–called "Hymn of the Pearl" or "Hymn of the Soul." It describes how the royal son is required to leave the heavenly palace of his parents, take off his robe of glory, and descend to the land of Egypt in order to recover "the one pearl which lies in the middle of the sea which is encircled by the snorting serpent." After helpful reminders from heaven, the royal son accomplishes his rescue mission, returns to his heavenly home, and dons his heavenly garment. In both the Christian and Gnostic myths, incarnation or descent into flesh is for the purpose of rescue. In the one case the endangered value is humanity lost in sin; in

---

[42]Jonas, *The Gnostic Religion,* p. 229.

[43]James, *The Apocryphal New Testament,* p. 411; also in Jonas, *Gnostic Religion,* p. 113.

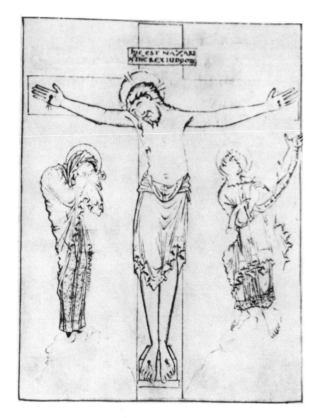

FIGURE 4 – 11
Crucifixion (Drawing from Ramsey Psalter, c. 980. London, British Museum. Reprinted in Clark, *Civilization.*)

the other case it is a pearl in the possession of a serpent. These myths hint at the idea that egohood serves a redemptive function for a lost value. In alchemy it is made more explicit that the value to be redeemed is an aspect of deity.

A curious variant of this image of the rescuing power of flesh has become part of the lore associated with the diamond. In India or Ceylon there is supposed to exist a deep valley of diamonds infested with deadly serpents. In order to acquire the diamonds, *pieces of flesh* are thrown into the valley. The diamonds adhere to the flesh, and vultures carry the flesh back to the top of the gorge where they are retrieved.[44] This legend is a quaint variation of the theme "incarnation for the purpose of

---

[44]Kunz, *The Curious Lore of Precious Stones,* p. 75.

FIGURE 4 – 12

The Mercurial Serpent Crucified (Alchimie de Flamel, MS. Français 14765. Paris, Bibliothèque Nationale. Reprinted in Jung, *Psychology and Alchemy*.)

redemption." The essential feature of the story is that diamonds adhere to flesh. We have here, I think, a tantalizing glimpse into the meaning of egohood. The diamond in its hardness is the supreme representative of the "flesh" principle in its incorruptible state and is one of the symbols of the Self. A parallel image occurred in the dream of a woman eight weeks pregnant.

> *I am on the lower level of the subway system. A young black woman hands me a diamond. I put it deep within my pocket, not wanting people to know for fear they will steal it. When I reach the upper level I feel safer.*

The association to the diamond was her pregnancy.

FIGURE 4 -13
Transfixion of the Mercurial Serpent and the King ("Speculum veritatis," Cod. Vaticanus Latinus 7286, 17th century. Biblioteca Vaticana. Reprinted in Jung, *Psychology and Alchemy*.)

Just as the terms "body" and "flesh" refer to *coagulatio*, so, that which nourishes the body—food and meal imagery—belongs to the same symbolism. Eating the forbidden fruit brought Adam and Eve into the painful world of spatio–temporal reality. The Old Testament speaks of "the bread of tears" (Ps. 80:5), "the bread of wickedness" (Prov. 4:17), "the bread of deceit" (Prov. 20:17), "the bread of idleness" (Prov. 31:2), and "the bread of adversity" (Isa. 30:20). These phrases refer to the *realization* of the conditions mentioned. They become lived experiences, not abstract ideas.

To eat something means to incorporate it—literally, to turn it into body. Hence, dreams in which the dreamer is offered something to eat indicate that an unconscious content is ready for *coagulatio*, assimilation by the ego. A woman of fragile ego had an invasion of the unconscious that required daily psychotherapy. After a month of intense encounter with the unconscious, she had this dream: (Summarized)

A woman is cooking a mysterious substance in a rectangular container. She opens it a bit and says, "It is ready." It was a

*strange material. The upper part had gelled into a green sub-
stance apparently made of fruits. Below this layer was a dark
ungelled liquid. I ate a small piece of the green stuff. It had no
taste. A man in a black suit came into the room. He went directly
to the container, filled eight jars with the gelled material and
walked out with them. He was like a strange messenger. There
was something uncanny about him.*

This dream represents a critical process of ego development. It has
similarities to the eating in the Garden of Eden, especially the reference
to the fruit and the black–suited man who associated to the Devil (see
figure 4–14). The filling of *eight* jars (double quaternity) indicates that
this is an individuation dream concerning the core and totality of the
psyche.

FIGURE 4 – 14
Adam and Eve (Dürer. Reprinted in *The Complete Woodcuts of Albrecht
Dürer.*)

A young man who had come to the end of his analysis and was in the process of taking on more substantial life responsibilities had this dream:

> I go out for dinner at a very special place. It is not really a restaurant, but the basement of a monastery. The food is served by monks. For dessert they serve "cow-dung cookies"—supposedly a delicacy like filet mignon. However they warn me to be careful, for some may not have crystallized out of their prior form. The idea of eating them causes me great distress.

Whenever food is offered one in a dream, the general rule is that it should be eaten no matter how unpleasant it seems. Sometimes, as in this dream, it will have strange or miraculous qualities, indicating that it is coming from the archetypal level of the psyche. Biblical examples are the manna from heaven sent to the Israelites in the wilderness (Exod. 16:12) and the feeding of the four thousand (Matt. 15:32). In some cases the food to be eaten clearly symbolizes the need to assimilate a relation to the Self. Isaiah speaks of the word of God as bread to be eaten. He has Yahweh say, "For as the rain and snow come down from heaven, and return not thither but water the earth, making it bring forth and sprout, giving seed to the sower and bread to the eater, so shall my word be that goes forth from my mouth (55:10–11, RSV). Christ says, "My meat is to do the will of him that sent me, and to finish his work" (John 4:34, AV).

All food dreams have at least a distant reference to Eucharistic symbolism, although at times it seems more like a black Mass (see figure 4–15). When the offered food clearly relates to the Self it becomes the *food of immortality* about which Christ speaks. "I am the bread of life. Your fathers ate the manna in the wilderness, and they died. This is the bread which comes down from heaven that a man may eat of it and not die. I am the living bread which came down from heaven; if anyone eats of this bread, he will live forever; and the bread which I shall give for the life of the world is my flesh" (John 6:48–51, RSV).

The Christian sacrament of Holy Communion is a *coagulatio* rite. It is interesting to note that several of the other sacraments are also linked with the symbolism of alchemical operations. The sacrament of baptism pertains to *solutio,* the sacrament of extreme unction to *mortificatio,* and the sacrament of matrimony to *coniunctio.* However, the Eucharist is the central ritual of Christianity and, as Jung has observed, can be considered to be the "rite of the individuation process."[45] From the standpoint of *coagulatio* symbolism, to partake of the Eucharistic meal signifies the ego's incorporation of a relation to the Self.

---

[45]Jung, *Psychology and Religion: West and East, CW* 11, par. 414.

FIGURE 4 – 15

The Last Supper. Note the Tiny Black Devil Entering Judas' Mouth (*The Hours of Catherine of Cleves*. The Guennol Collection and the Pierpont Morgan Library.)

Henry Vaughn's poem "The Incarnation and the Passion" makes use of several *coagulatio* images and again illustrates the theme of desire (love) as the motive of incarnation.

> Lord! when thou didst thy selfe undresse
> Laying by thy robes of glory,
> To make us more, thou wouldst be lesse,
> And becam'st wofull story.

> To put on Clouds instead of light,
> And cloath the morning–starre with dust,
> Was a translation of such height
> As, but in thee, was ne'r exprest;

> Brave wormes, and Earth! that thus could have
> A God Enclosed within your Cell,

Your maker pent up in a grave,
Life lockt in death, heaven in a shell;

Ah, my deare Lord! what couldst thou spye
In this impure, rebellious clay,
That made thee thus resolve to dye
For those that kill thee every day?

O what strange wonders could thee move
To slight thy precious bloud, and breath!
Sure it was *Love*, my Lord; for *Love*
Is only stronger far than death.[46]

As a final illustration of *coagulatio* symbolism, I shall present the most remarkable dream on this theme that I have yet encountered. The dreamer, a man in his early thirties, was characterized by a striking discrepancy between his high potential for psychological development and the limitations imposed by the severe psychic deprivation of his childhood environment. The result was that a sizable portion of ego development, which ordinarily occurs in childhood, was delayed and took place in adulthood during a lengthy course of psychotherapy. The following dream, which occurred after two years of about a ten–year treatment, presents the essence of that process. It can be seen as a kind of micromyth of ego development. The dream is as follows:

I am sitting before an ancient intaglio of a crucifixion. It is metal but it is partially covered with a waxlike substance which leads me to discover that there are candles above it, one on each side, and I realize I am to light these, and make the wax run down into the intaglio and that this has something to do with the ritual-like meal I am about to eat. I light the candles and the wax does run down into the empty form of the crucifixion. When it is full I take it down from the wall above me and am at my meal. I have taken the head of the image which has been formed by filling up the intaglio and am eating it. It is a substance like lead—very heavy—and I begin to wonder if I can digest it. I wonder if humans can digest lead. I realize we eat a little every day, and that we eat silver, too. I think, therefore, that it is a safe thing to have eaten, but I am wary of eating too much. The dream ends while I am at the meal.

This dream contains several *coagulatio* themes: solidification of a liquid, lead, eating, and the crucifixion. The ancient crucifixion intaglio symbolizes the innate archetype of the Self, an empty form waiting to

---

[46] *The Complete Poetry of Henry Vaughn,* p. 163.

be realized by an influx of living matter. The dream illustrates nicely Jung's statement that "archetypes are not determined as regards their content, but only as regards their form and then only to a very limited degree. A primordial image is determined as to its content only when it has become conscious and is therefore filled out with the material of conscious experience.... The archetype in itself is empty and purely formal, nothing but a *facultas praeformandi*, a possibility of representation which is given *a priori*."[47]

The two lighted candles provide the molten wax that fills the empty form. They represent the psychic life process itself. This is suggested by such phrases as "burning the candle at both ends," or "out, out brief candle."[48] The burning candle generates not only light but also molten matter, as though the living process of the psyche generates *substance—* a *coagulatio* of spirit. But why are there *two* candles? Adler reports this dream of a patient.

> I carry two lighted candles of which I blow out one and keep the other alight, saying: "This is life and death."[49]

Adler associates these two candles to the two torch bearers who flank Mithras in the conventional representations of him. One has his torch upright, the other, pointing downward. Perhaps the two candles will indicate the interplay of opposites, and the flowing of the two molten streams into one shape will signify a *coniunctio* of the opposites.

The eating of the wax figure corresponds to well-known ritual meals in which the participant eats a representation of the deity—for example, the Christian Eucharist. In the early church, wax was used as a symbol for the flesh of the *Agnus Dei*. "It was customary in Rome and in the whole Occident to make little lambs out of the consecrated wax of the Paschal candle and to keep them for the octave of Easter, when they were distributed to the communicants after the Lord's supper."[50] Amalarius of Trier gives the following explanation of this rite: "The wax symbolizes, as Gregory (the Great) says in his sermons, the humanity of the Christ; for the honeycomb consists of honey in wax; the honey in wax, however, is the divinity in the humanity. The lambs, which the Romans make (of wax), symbolize the immaculate Lamb, which was made for our benefit."[51]

---

[47]Jung, *The Archetypes and the Collective Unconscious, CW* 9i, par. 155.

[48]*Macbeth*, Act 5, sc. 5, line 23.

[49]Adler, *The Living Symbol*, p. 157.

[50]Eisler, *Orpheus the Fisher*, p. 248.

[51]Ibid.

The concern regarding the digestibility of the substance is characteristic. How much reality can the ego stand? This is an urgent question for us all. The dream seems to advise regular small doses of this bitter medicine.

In summary, this dream pictures ego development as a process in which the latent, preexistent totality, the Self, is first incarnated and then assimilated through the living efforts of the individual. It demonstrates Jung's statement that, "The self, like the unconscious, is an *a priori* existent out of which the ego evolves. It is, so to speak, an unconscious prefiguration of the ego."[52]

In conclusion, the alchemical operation of *coagulatio,* together with the imagery that clusters around this idea, constitutes an elaborate symbol system that expresses the archetypal process of ego formation. When the ego's relation to the Self is being realized—that is, when the ego is approaching the *coagulatio* of the psyche in its totality—then the symbolism of ego development becomes identical with that of individuation. Jung puts it better:

> God wants to be born in the flame of man's consciousness, leaping ever higher. And what if this has no roots in the earth? If it is not a house of stone where the fire of God can dwell, but a wretched straw hut that flares up and vanishes? Could God then be born? One must be able to suffer God. That is the supreme task for the carrier of ideas. He must be the advocate of the earth. God will take care of himself. My inner principle is: Deus *et* homo. God needs man in order to become conscious, just as he needs limitation in time and space. Let us therefore be for him limitation in time and space, an earthly tabernacle.[53]

---

[52]Jung, *Psychology and Religion: West and East. CW* 11, par. 391.

[53]Jung, *Letters* 1:65ff.

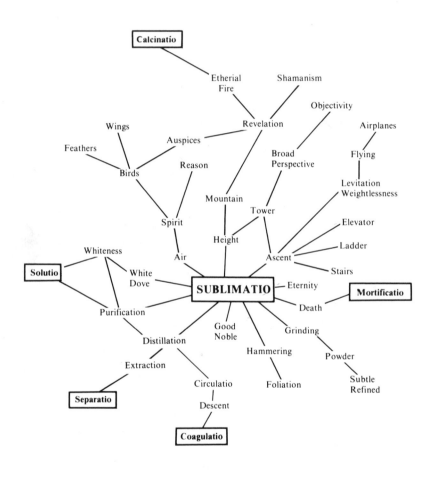

❖ **5** *Sublimatio* ❖

J UST AS *CALCINATIO* PERTAINS TO FIRE, *solutio* to water, and *coagulatio* to earth, so *sublimatio* is the operation pertaining to air. It turns the material into air by volatilizing and elevating it. The image derives from the chemical process of sublimation in which a solid, when heated, passes directly into a gaseous state and ascends to the top of the vessel, where it resolidifies on the upper, cooler region. Distillation is a similar process, in which a liquid vaporizes on heating and condenses again in a cooler area.

The term "sublimation" derives from the Latin *sublimis*, meaning "high." This indicates that the crucial feature of *sublimatio* is an elevating process whereby a low substance is translated into a higher form by an ascending movement. Earth is transformed into air; a fixed body is volatilized; that which is inferior is changed into something superior (*inferus*, below; *superus*, above). All images that refer to upward movement—ladders, stairs, elevators, climbing, mountains, flying, and so forth—belong to *sublimatio* symbolism, as do all the psychological and value connotations associated with being high rather than low. An alchemical text says, "The spirit, therefore, by the help of the water and the soul, is drawn forth from the bodies themselves, and the body thereby is made spiritual; for that at the same instant of time, the spirit, with the soul of the bodies, ascend on high to the superior part, which is the perfection of the stone, and is called sublimation."[1]

According to this text, the body is "made perfect" by spiritualizing it. Psychologically, this corresponds to a way of dealing with a concrete problem. One gets "above" it by seeing it objectively. We abstract a general meaning from it and see it as a particular example of a larger issue. Just to find suitable words or concepts for a psychic state may be sufficient for a person to get out of it enough to look down on it from

---

[1] *The Lives of the Alchemystical Philosophers,* p. 138.

above. For instance, to label a resentful mood an "anima possession" may release the grip of the mood. To identify a man's reaction to his wife as an example of his mother problem, or a reaction to his boss as part of a father complex, conceptualizes the experience and helps him to get above it. A striking example of such word power is that of a priest who had anxiety while celebrating the Eucharist. He experienced a definite alleviation of symptoms upon learning that he had a well-known condition called performance anxiety.

Sublimatio is an ascent that raises us above the confining entanglements of immediate, earthy existence and its concrete, personal particulars. The higher we go the grander and more comprehensive is our perspective, but also the more remote we become from actual life and the less able we will be to have an effect on what we perceive. We become magnificent but impotent spectators (see figure 5-1). Heaven is the abode of the eternal Platonic forms, the universals, the archetypal images. Hence, whenever a dream or life situation is interpreted from the archetypal standpoint, it is promoting *sublimatio*. The success of such interpretations may be expressed in dreams by the escape or release of caged birds or some other auspicious upward movement.

It should be stated at the outset that the symbolism of the alchemical *sublimatio* has nothing to do with Freudian theory of sublimation. According to Hinsie and Campbell's *Psychiatric Dictionary*, the term "sublimation" as used in psychoanalysis is defined as, "... the process of modifying an instinctual impulse in such a way as to conform to the demands of society. Sublimation is a substitute activity which gives some measure of gratification to the infantile impulse which has been repudiated in its original form.... Unlike the usual defenses, in sublimation the ego is not acting in opposition to the id; on the contrary, it is helping the id to gain external expression. Sublimation, in other words, does not involve repression."[2]

Jung distinguishes Freudian sublimation from the alchemical *sublimatio* in this passage from his letters: "*Sublimatio* is part of the royal art where the true gold is made. Of this Freud knows nothing, worse still, he barricades all the paths that could lead to the true *sublimatio*. This is just about the opposite of what Freud understands by sublimation. It is not a *voluntary and forcible* channeling of instinct into a spurious field of application, but an *alchymical transformation* for which *fire* and the black *prima materia* are needed. *Sublimatio* is a great mystery. Freud has appropriated this concept and usurped it for the sphere of the will and the bourgeois, rationalistic ethos."[3]

---

[2]Hinsie and Campbell, *Psychiatric Dictionary*, pp. 699f.

[3]Jung, *Letters*, 1:171.

FIGURE 5 – 1

Satellite Photograph of Cape Cod and Vicinity (*Photo Atlas of the United States.*)

For the alchemist, the process of sublimation was experienced in symbolic images. He, for example, might see a bird flying up from the matter in the lower part of the vessel to the upper regions. The alchemical vessel was equated with the macrocosm, its lower part being the earth and its upper part, heaven. The sublimate flees earth and is transported to heaven. A text says, "At the end of the sublimation there germinates through the mediation of the spirit, a shining white soul [*anima candida*] which flies up to heaven with the spirit. This is clearly and manifestly the stone"[4] (see figure 5-2).

This "white soul" is often represented by a white bird being released from the material being heated. One picture shows a man being cooked in a water bath with a white bird emerging from his head (see figure 5-

FIGURE 5 – 2

Sublimatio. (Sapentia veterum philosophorum sive doctrina eorundum de summa et universali medicina, 18th century. Paris, Bibliothèque de l'Arsenal, MS. 974. Reprinted in Derola, *The Secret Art of Alchemy.*)

---

[4]Quoted in Jung, *Psychology and Alchemy, CW* 12, par. 462.

FIGURE 5 – 3
Extraction of the White Dove (Trismosin, *Splendor Solis,* 1582.)

3). A parallel to this picture occurred in the case of a young woman who was enduring an intense and painful activation of the unconscious. She dreamed,

> *I am in a hospital, pregnant but not quite ready for birth. I go to sleep and when I wake up it is very dark. I feel something pressing on my ribs very hard and it seems as if this unseen exterior pressure is forcing me to give birth. A voice says, "How would you like to have a son?"* As I woke up the imagery *continued. I saw a girl like the one in Munch's lithograph, "The Cry." Her mouth is a circular opening. She is in a white circle surrounded by more circles of black lines. Out of her mouth comes a horde of doves or white pigeons* (see figure 5-4).

This dream informs the patient that the anxiety she is enduring is part of a larger transformation process, in which the ego is heated by

FIGURE 5 – 4

The Cry (Munch, 1895. Oslo, National Museum. Reprinted in *Graphic Works of Edvard Munch.*)

horror in order to bring forth a new birth, the "sublimate," represented by the flock of doves. Dreams of birds generally refer to *sublimatio*, and bird phobias may indicate fear of a necessary *sublimatio*. They are also often connected with a fear of death, death being the ultimate *sublimatio* whereby the soul is separated from the body.

One aspect of *sublimatio* overlaps with *separatio* symbolism—namely, its use as an extraction procedure. For instance, mercury can be extracted from certain compounds by heating. It vaporizes, sublimates, and reappears on the cooler portion of the vessel. An early text alludes to this process: "Go to the waters of the Nile and there you will find a stone that has a spirit (*pneuma*). Take this, divide it, thrust in your hand and draw out its heart: for its soul (*psyche*) is in its heart. [An interpolator adds:] There, he says you will find this stone that has a spirit, which refers to the expulsion of the quicksilver (*exhydrargyrosis*)."[5]

This "expulsion of the quicksilver" is done by *sublimatio*, which releases the spirit hidden in matter. In the largest sense, this refers psychologically to the redemption of the Self from its original unconscious state. The expulsion of the quicksilver can also be experienced in lesser ways as the extraction of *meaning* from heavy moods, from concrete events, or from the factuality of nature (see figure 5-5).

Berthelot points out that the Greek word that the Latin alchemists translated as "*sublimatio*" was *rhinisma*, which originally meant "filings." This expressed the idea of the extreme attenuation of matter. The same idea was attached later to the term "alcoolisation" which signifies reduction to the state of an impalpable powder.[6] A text says, "If you do not make the bodies subtle, so that they may be impalpable to touch, you will not gain your end. If they have not been ground, repeat your operation, and see that they are ground and subtilized."[7]

Thus, *sublimatio* can mean "grinding" or "hammering" to bring about an attenuation of the material. Very fine powder approaches a gas in its consistency. Note also that the symbolism of grinding contains the moral categories of good and bad. Powder made up of small particles is called "fine," that with large particles is "coarse." To be good is to be well pulverized. Encounter with the *numinosum* may have a pulverizing effect, as indicated by the saying, "Though the mills of God grind slowly, yet they grind exceeding small." "Foliation" has the same implication. A recipe mentioned earlier reads, "Sow your gold in white foliated earth"—that is, in sublimated earth. Foliation is done by hammering. These lines by Rilke can thus be considered as announcing an impending *sublimatio*:

> What locks itself in endurance grows rigid; sheltered
> in unassuming greyness, does it feel safe?
> Wait, from the distance hardness is menaced
>   by something still harder.
> Alas—: a remote hammer is poised to strike.[8]

In Shakespeare's *Antony and Cleopatra*, as Enobarbus commits suicide in remorse for his defection from Antony, this image of *sublimatio* by pulverization is wrung from him. He is speaking to the moon.

---

[5]Ibid., par. 405.

[6]Berthelot, *Collection des Anciens Alchemistes Grecs*, 1:210.

[7]Kelly, *The Alchemical Writings of Edward Kelly*, p. 34.

[8]Rilke, *Sonnets to Orpheus*, pt. 2, sonnet 12. (I have not been able to locate the source of this translation, but see *Sonnets to Orpheus*, trans. C. F. MacIntyre, cited in the Bibliography.)

FIGURE 5 – 5

Extraction of Mercurius and Coronation of the Virgin. Lower Level: Mercurius
(Represented as a Monstrosity) Being Extracted from the *Prima Materia*. Upper Level: Assumption and Coronation of the Virgin, Transforming the Trinity
into a Quaternity (*Speculum trinitatis* from Reusner, *Pandora,* 1588. Reprinted
in Jung, *Psychology and Alchemy.*)

O sovereign mistress of true melancholy,
The poisonous damp of night disponge upon me,
That life, a very rebel to my will,
May hang no longer on me; throw my heart
Against the flint and hardness of my fault,
Which, being dried with grief, will break to powder,
And finish all foul thoughts.

(Act 4, sc. 9, lines 12–18)

A text from Paracelsus says, "For, as from all phlegmatic and watery objects, water ascends in distillation, and is separated from its body, so, in the process of sublimation, in dry substances such as minerals, the spiritual is raised from the corporeal, subtilised, and the pure separated from the impure."[9]

Here *sublimatio* is described as a purification. When matter and spirit are intermixed in a state of unconscious contamination, they must be purified by separation. In this impure state, the spirit must first seek its own purity and will see all that pertains to flesh and matter—the concrete, the personal, the desire-laden—as the enemy to be overcome. The whole history of cultural evolution can be seen as a great *sublimatio* process in which human beings learn how to see themselves and their world objectively. Stoic philosophy was one vast effort to teach humans how to achieve the Stoic goal of *apathia* by getting above the passions that tie them to the earth. Similarly, Plato's idealism, as well as all later idealistic systems, strive to present life in terms of eternal forms and universal ideas in order to overcome the galling human bondage to the contingencies of matter. Reason, which gives people a standpoint outside their personal likes and dislikes, becomes an indispensable agent of *sublimatio* by teaching them how to be reflective spectators of themselves. Schopenhauer puts it beautifully:

[It is] indeed wonderful to see, how man, besides his life in the concrete, always lives a second life in the abstract. In the former he is abandoned to all the storms of reality and to the influence of the present; he must struggle, suffer, and die like the animal. But his life in the abstract, as it stands before his rational consciousness, is the calm reflection of his life in the concrete, and of the world in which he lives.... Here in the sphere of calm deliberation, what previously possessed him completely and moved him intensely appears to him cold, colorless, and, for the moment, foreign and strange; he is a mere spectator and observer. In respect of this withdrawal into reflection, he is like an actor who has played his part in one scene, and takes his place in the audience until he must appear again. In the audience he quietly looks on at whatever may happen, even though it be the preparation for his own death [in the play]; but then he goes on the stage, and acts and suffers as he must.[10]

---

[9]Paracelsus, *The Hermetic and Alchemical Writings of Paracelsus*, 1:152.

[10]Schopenhauer, *The World as Will and Representation*, p. 152.

The capacity to get above and see oneself objectively is the ability to dissociate. The use of this word immediately indicates the danger of *sublimatio*. Each of the alchemical operations has its own pathological symptomatology when carried to extremes, but modern individuals probably misuse *sublimatio* more than the others. The ability of the psyche to dissociate is both the source of ego consciousness and the cause of mental illness. As a single example, I recall a young man whom I saw while working at Rockland State Hospital. He was a brilliant student of mathematics. However, he had had no friends or social relations, and he did not even learn that there are anatomical differences between boys and girls until he went to college. He was unemployed and living with his mother until hospitalized following an outburst of violence at his mother for not having the television set repaired. When I asked him about his dreams, he told me the following:

> *I once dreamed that I had climbed a ladder to a high platform, and that then somebody removed the ladder so that I was left stranded on the height with no way of getting down again.*

> *Another time I was climbing a ladder miles above the earth's surface with something impelling me onward. I dared not to look down for fear of becoming dizzy and letting go of the rung.*

> *Another time I was spread-eagled on the glass floor of a wall-less elevator. There was no shaft. A hydraulic piston was pushing the floor ever upwards. I was fearfully peering over the edge of the floor, watching the earth recede in the distance.*

This young man was tragically caught in the archetypal dynamism of *sublimatio* as an autonomous process of dissociation. It impelled him further and further from personal, earthy reality until the inevitable enantiodromia sent him crashing to the ground.

A dream with similar imagery but vastly different outcome is reported by Emerson. In 1840 at the age of 37 while preparing his *Essays: First Series* for publication he dreamed:

> *I floated at will in the great Ether, and I saw this world floating also not far off, but diminished to the size of an apple. Then an angel took it in his hand and brought it to me and said "This must thou eat." And I ate the world.*[11]

A dream of floating in the "great Ether" seems symbolically appropriate for the author of Emersonian transcendentalism. This dream is grand rather than grandiose. In contrast to the previous dreams, this one

---

[11] *The Journals and Miscellaneous Notebooks of Ralph Waldo Emerson*, 7:525.

contains its own corrective factor. The extreme *sublimatio* is compensated by the *coagulatio* image of eating the apple of the world.

A beautiful poetic evocation of the *sublimatio* mood is found in these lines from Milton's *Il Penseroso*:

> Or let my lamp at midnight hour,
> Be seen in some high lonely Tower,
> Where I may oft out-watch the Bear,
> With thrice great Hermes, or unsphere
> The spirit of Plato to unfold
> What worlds, or what vast Regions hold
> Th' immortal mind that hath forsook
> Her mansion in this fleshly nook.

The image of the tower is a typical *sublimatio* symbol. Hexagram 20 of the *I Ching* entitled "Contemplation (View)" represents a tower and describes the same kind of contemplation of the archetypal realm as does Milton. The *I Ching* speaks of those who contemplate "the meaning underlying the workings of the universe" and "apprehend the mysterious and divine laws of life, and by means of profoundest inner concentration they give expression to these laws in their own persons."[12]

The tower image came up in a dream of mine after attending an impressive lecture on mythology. I dreamed:

I see a stupendously high tower. It is a broadcasting tower for a radio network. One climbs it by a ladder built on the outside. A man is there whose job it is to operate the tower. Each day he climbs to the top in the morning and descends again at night. I ask him if it isn't difficult. He says, "not at all." I realize that I would be very reluctant to climb to such a height.

The dream pictures my reaction to the lecture. I was dazzled by its brilliance and broad perspective. Ascent to a height gives one a perspective view not available from the ground. Thus in mythological and religious imagery ascension often accompanies revelation of the divine realm. God meets humanity on the mountain—for example, Moses on Sinai. The person who is vouchsafed a revelation from God is often "lifted up" and transported to heaven. For instance, a vision of Ezekiel begins, "Then I beheld, and lo, a form that had the appearance of a man; below what appeared to be his loins it was fire, and above his loins it was like the appearance of brightness, like gleaming bronze. He put forth the form of a hand, and took me by a lock of my hair; and the Spirit lifted me up between earth and heaven, and brought me in visions of God to Jerusalem" (Ezek. 8:2, 3, RSV).

---

[12]Wilhelm, trans., *I Ching or Book of Changes*, p. 33.

Enoch is another figure who receives a revelation by ascension. In the pseudepigraphal *Secrets of Enoch* he is lifted up by angels and given a guided tour through the ten heavens, and finally he sees God himself. According to popular legend, Mohammad was transported bodily through the seven heavens to the presence of God for the purposes of revelation. The symbolism of shamanism also has the motif of ascent to revelation. The shaman climbs the world pillar, or the cosmic ladder, or makes a magical flight in search of a supernatural revelation.[13]

A good example of *sublimatio* symbolism is found in an ancient Mithraic ritual of initiation. This same ritual contains the image of the sun's phallus that first led Jung to the discovery of the archetypes.[14] The ritual begins with a prayer: "O Providence, O Fortune, bestow on me Thy grace—imparting these the mysteries a Father only may hand on, and that, too, to a son alone—his immortality—[a Son] initiate, worthy of this our craft, with which Sun Mithras, the Great God, commanded me to be endowed by his archangel; so that I Eagle (as I am by my own self) alone may soar to Heaven, and contemplate all things."

After further prayers, the ritual proceeds with these instructions:

Take from the [sun-] rays breath, inhaling thrice [as deeply] as thou canst; and thou shalt see thyself being raised aloft, and soaring towards the Height, so that thou seem'st to be in midst of air. Thou shalt hear naught, nor man nor beast; nor shalt thou see aught of the sights upon the earth, in that same hour; but all things thou shalt see will be immortal. For thou shalt see, in that same day and hour, the Disposition of the Gods—the ruling Gods ascending heavenwards, the other ones descending. And through his disc— the God's, my Father's—there shall be seen the Way-of-going of the Gods accessible to sight.

This is followed by encounters with various divine figures and culminates in the apotheosis of the initiate with these words: "O Lord, being born again, I pass away in being made Great, and, having been made Great, I die. Being born from out the state of birth-and-death that giveth birth to (mortal) lives, I now, set free, pass to the state transcending birth, as Thou hast stablished it, according as Thou hast ordained and made the Mystery."[15]

This ritual was meant to bring about a revelation of the divine realm and to confer immortality on the initiate by means of an ascent to heaven. In psychological terms, it is a revelation of the archetypal psyche which releases one from a personal ego-attitude, enabling one to experience oneself as an immortal—that is, as living with archetypal

---

[13]Eliade, *Shamanism: Archaic Techniques of Ecstasy*, pp. 259ff.

[14]Jung, *The Symbolic Life, CW* 18, pars. 85ff.

[15]Dieterich, *A Mithraic Ritual.*

realities and making a contribution to the archetypal psyche. Similar experiences of revelation occur in modern dreams and visions. For example, Dr. Liliane Frey had been thinking deeply about death and her own myth concerning death as a transformation. She writes: "Death consists of the miracle of transformation into a new form of existence. Death is for me the gate to a new birth, and the breaking-through of the transcendental realm into our empirical existence. I am convinced that we experience a complete transformation of our being in the last moments of our life. Simultaneously with the death of body and ego-personality, something new gets born which is neither matter nor spirit but both together in an indeterminable way."[16] While developing these thoughts she had a very impressive dream in which

> *she was flying higher and higher in a plane especially constructed for her and she had a wonderful view of the Alps, all immersed in deep blue.*[17]

J. B. Priestley reported this very impressive *sublimatio*-revelation dream:

> *I dreamt that I was standing at the top of a very high tower, alone, looking down upon myriads of birds all flying in one direction; every kind of bird was there, all the birds in the world. It was a noble sight, this vast aerial river of birds. But now in some mysterious fashion the gear was changed, and time speeded up, so that I saw generations of birds, watched them break their shells, flutter into life, mate, weaken, falter, and die. Wings grew only to crumble; bodies were sleek and then, in a flash, bled and shrivelled; and death struck everywhere at every second. What was the use of all this blind struggle towards life, this eager trying of wings, this hurried mating, this flight and surge, all this gigantic meaningless biological effort? As I stared down, seeming to see every creature's ignoble little history almost at a glance, I felt sick at heart. It would be better if not one of them, if not one of us all, had been born, if the struggle ceased forever. I stood on my tower, still alone, desperately unhappy. But now the gear was changed again, and time went faster still, and it was rushing by at such a rate, that the birds could not show any movement, but were like an enormous plain sown with feathers. But along this plain, flickering through the bodies themselves, there now passed a sort of white flame, trembling, dancing, then hurrying on; and*

---

[16] *A Well of Living Waters*, pp. 13f.

[17] Ibid., p. 14.

*as soon as I saw it I knew that this white flame was life itself, the
very quintessence of being; and then it came to me in a rocket-
burst of ecstacy, that nothing mattered, nothing could ever
matter, because nothing else was real, but this quivering and
hurrying lambency of being. Birds, men or creatures not yet
shaped and colored, all were of no account except so far as this
flame of life travelled through them. It left nothing to mourn
over behind it; what I had thought was tragedy was mere emptiness or a shadow show; for now all real feeling was caught and
purified and danced on ecstatically with the white flame of life.*[18]

A similar vision of the process of human history as though seen from
a vast height was experienced by a woman who is a poet:

*I saw the earth covered by a single great tree whose multiple
roots fed on the inner sun of gold, the* lumen naturae. *It was a
tree whose limbs were made of light and the branches were
lovingly entangled so that it made of itself a network of beaute-
ous love. And it seemed as if it were lifting itself out of the
broken seeds of many, countless egos who had now allowed the
one Self to break forth. And when one beheld this, the sun and
the moon and the planets turned out to be something quite, quite
other than one had thought. From what I could make out, the
Lord Himself was the Alchemist and out of the collective swarm-
ing and suffering, ignorance and pollution, He was "trying" the
gold.*[19]

Another example of a *sublimation* revelation comes from the LSD
experience of a professional woman who is also the mother of three
children. She describes her experience in these words:

I knew I was on my way when a releasing and delicious sense of floating in
the atmosphere took over and engulfed my entire being. My sense of being
contained by body dissolved. I laughed with delight and said out loud, "Now
I remember what it's like to be without a body." I was in contact with some
level of being, fully conscious but without embodiment. An awareness took
form in my mind that I had resisted being born into the world in my present
incarnation. I understood why. Air is my true element, the matrix of my
being. The ecstacy of being free of body, the aging process, backaches,
headaches, creaky joints lasted an eternity. I was no longer confined by the
space-time dimensions of earth. How amazing to be "me," fully aware and
conscious, and yet without any physical vehicle.

This was followed by other experiences, including the reliving of her
own birth, and then came this final vision:

---

[18]Quoted in Adler, *Studies in Analytical Psychology*, p. 143.

[19]I am indebted to Alice Howell for permission to quote.

Then began a complex cycle of laughter and tears; the laughter usually connected with an opening of the arms and legs, the weeping with a contraction and closing of the body. I moved back in time through countless ages of mankind, experiencing in my body countless birth, death, and rebirth cycles. I found myself in different parts of the world (mainly Europe), more with simple peasants, farmers, craftsmen than kings and nobles. I was buried or buried others dear to me, having my eyelids closed and arms crossed or performing this ritual for others. The plain wooden box is lowered into the grave, the dirt is sprinkled over the box, the mourners grieve. Then I am a woman giving birth or assisting in the process. There is the cry of the newborn infant, the circular sweep of the mother's arms to gather the child to her breast. Birth cries and death rattles intermingle in a flicker of an eyelash. I realize that my own place in the rhythmic pattern of death and birth is but a moving instant—and that is more than enough. The sense of oneness with the universe, with the birth-death process experienced through my Body-Self totality overwhelms me with grace. It is as though I have been given a gift so precious I need never ask again, "What is the meaning of my life?"[20]

The remarkable similarity between this LSD vision and Priestley's dream indicates that such experiences have an objective validity; that is, they bear witness to the reality of the psyche.

Another aspect of ascent symbolism is the theme of translation to eternity. For instance, Heracles ascended to Olympus from his funeral pyre, a quite literal *sublimatio*. He disappeared from the earth and reappeared on a higher level as a result of being heated. The same thing happened to Elijah (2 Kings 2:11, RSV): "Behold, a chariot of fire and horses of fire separated the two of them [Elisha and Elijah]. And Elijah went up by a whirlwind into heaven" (see figure 5-6).

Fire also sublimates Elijah. According to 1 Maccabees 2:58, it was Elijah's fiery religious intensity that accounted for his ascension. "Elijah for his consuming fervour for the law was caught up to heaven itself" (JB). Christ ascended to heaven forty days after his resurrection (Acts 1:9). According to legend, the Virgin Mary ascended into heaven at the time of her death, and the Feast of the Assumption of the Virgin has been on the Church calendar (August 15) since the seventh century, although the assumption was not proclaimed as dogma until 1950 (see figure 5-7).

The origin of the symbolism of translation to eternity is probably Egypt. In early Egyptian religion the dead were thought to be turned into stars or companions of the sun. James Breasted writes: "In the splendor of the mighty heavens the Nile-dweller...saw the host of those who had preceded him; thither they had flown as birds, rising above all foes of the air, and received by Re as the companions of his celestial barque, they now swept across the sky as eternal stars."[21]

---

[20]I want to thank the author of this account for her generosity in sharing this important experience.

[21]Breasted, *A History of Egypt*, p. 64.

FIGURE 5 – 6
Ascension of Elijah (Doré, *Bible Illustrations.*)

A pyramid text describes the translation of the dead king to the heavenly realm in these words: "The king ascends to the sky among the gods dwelling in the sky.... He [Re] gives thee his arm on the stairway to the sky. 'He who knows his place comes,' say the gods. O Pure One, assume thy throne in the barque of Re and sail thou the sky.... Sail thou with the imperishable stars, sail thou with the Unwearied Stars."[22]

And E. A. Wallis Budge writes the following:

The primitive Egyptians believed that the floor of heaven, which also formed the sky of this world, was made of an immense plate of iron, rectangular in shape, the four corners of which rested upon four pillars which served to mark the cardinal points. On this plate of iron lived the gods and the blessed dead, and it was the aim of every good Egyptian to go there after death. At

---

[22]Breasted, *Development of Religion and Thought in Ancient Egypt*, p. 136.

FIGURE 5 – 7

Assumption of the Virgin (*The Hours of Catherine of Cleves*. The Guennol Collection and the Pierpont Morgan Library.)

certain sacred spots the edge of the plate was so near the tops of the mountains that the deceased might easily clamber on to it and so obtain admission into heaven, but at others the distance between it and the earth was so great that he needed help to reach it. There existed the belief that Osiris himself experienced some difficulty in getting up to the iron plate, and that it was only by means of the ladder which his father Ra provided that he at length ascended into heaven. On one side of the ladder stood Ra, and on the other stood Horus, the son of Isis, and each god assisted Osiris to mount it. Originally the two guardians of the ladder were Horus the Elder and Set, and there are several references in the early texts to the help which they rendered to the deceased, who was, of course, identified with the god Osiris. But, with a view either of reminding these gods of their supposed duty, or of compelling them to do it, the model of a ladder was often placed on or near the dead body in the tomb, and a special composition was prepared which had the effect of making the ladder become the means of the ascent of the deceased into heaven. Thus in the text written for Pepi the deceased is made to address the ladder in these words: "Homage to thee, O divine Ladder! Homage to thee, O Ladder of Set! Stand thou upright, O divine Ladder! Stand thou upright, O Ladder of Set! Stand thou upright, O Ladder of Horus, whereby Osiris came forth into heaven."[23]

The injunction to stand upright is reminiscent of the *Djed* or *Tet* pillar. This classic image of the resurrected Osiris looks remarkably like a ladder in some pictures (see figure 5-8). The process of translation to eternity was graphically represented in antiquity by the image of ascending the ladder of the planetary spheres. When a soul is born into an earthly body it descends from heaven through the planetary spheres and acquires the qualities pertaining to each. Macrobius writes:

> By the impulse of the first weight the soul, having started on its downward course from the intersection of the zodiac and the Milky Way to the successive spheres lying beneath, as it passes through these spheres...acquires each of the attributes which it will exercise later. In the sphere of Saturn it obtains reason and understanding, called *logistikon* and *theoretikon*; in Jupiter's sphere, the power to act, called *praktikon*; in Mars' sphere, a bold spirit or *thymikon*; in the sun's sphere, sense-perception and imagination, *aisthetikon* and *phantastikon*; in Venus' sphere, the impulse of passion, *epithymetikon*; in Mercury's sphere, the ability to speak and interpret, *hermeneutikon*; and in the lunar sphere, the function of molding and increasing bodies, *phytikon*. This last function being the farthest removed from the gods, is the first in us and all the earthly creation.[24]

When the soul has purified itself it may ascend the ladder of the planetary spheres, "for when it has rid itself completely of all taint of evil and has deserved to be sublimated, it again leaves the body and, fully recovering its former state, returns to the splendor of everlasting life."[25] The ascent of the spheres is described in a poem by Henry Vaughn:

> The power of my soul is such, I can
> Expire, and so analyse all that's man.
> First my dull clay I give unto the Earth,
> Our common Mother, which gives all their birth.
> My growing faculties I send as soon
> Whence first I took them, to the humid Moon.
> All subtilties and every cunning art
> To witty Mercury I do impart.

---

[23]Quoted in Cook, *Zeus: A Study in Ancient Religion*, 2:125f; see also Budge, *Osiris: The Egyptian Religion of the Resurrection*, 2:167.

[24]Macrobius, *Commentary on the Dream of Scipio*, pp. 136f.

[25]Ibid., p. 137.

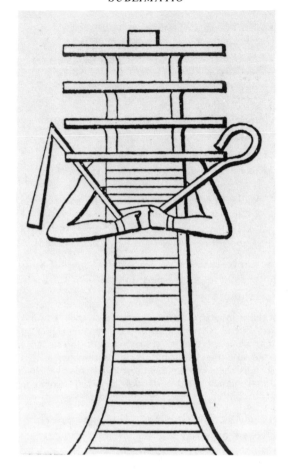

FIGURE 5 – 8

Osiris as a Ladder (From the papyrus of Ani, British Museum. Reprinted
in Budge, *Osiris: The Egyptian Religion of
Resurrection.*)

Those fond affections which made me a slave
To handsome faces, Venus thou shall have.
And saucy pride (if there was aught in me,)
Sol, I return it to thy royalty.
My daring rashness and presumptions be
To Mars himself an equal legacy.
My ill-plac'd avarice (sure 'tis but small;)
Jove, to thy flames I do bequeath it all.
And my false magic, which I did believe,
And mystic lyes to Saturn I do give.
My dark imaginations rest you there,
This is your grave and superstitious sphere.

> Get up my disintangled soul, thy fire
> Is now refined and nothing left to tire,
> Or clog thy wings. Now my auspicious flight
> Hath brought me to the Empyrean light.
> I am a sep'rate essence and can see
> The emanations of the Deity.[26]

It is also Henry Vaughn who wrote these well-known lines describing a *sublimatio* experience:

> I saw Eternity the other night
> Like a great Ring of pure and endless light,
>   All calm as it was bright,
> And round beneath it, Time in hours, days, years
>   Driv'n by the spheres
> Like a vast shadow mov'd, In which the world
>   And all her train were hurl'd.[27]

There is a kabbalistic parallel to the theme of returning to the planetary archons the qualities pertaining to each, as indicated in this passage by Gershom Scholem:

> The task of the Kabbalah is to help guide the soul back to its native home in the Godhead. For each single *Sefirah* there is a corresponding ethical attribute in human behavior, and he who achieves this on earth is integrated into the mystic life and the harmonic world of the *Sefirot*....The kabbalists unanimously agreed on the supreme rank attainable by the soul at the end of its mystical path, namely, that of *devekut*, mystical cleaving to God....(This is achieved by climbing) the ladder of *devekut*.[28]

The state of *devekut*, or cleaving to God, was thought by the kabbalists to be achieved by prayer:

> The worshipper uses the fixed words of the prayer as a banister during his meditation which he grasps on his road of ascension so that he should not be confused or distracted. Such meditation results in the joining of human thought to the divine thought or the divine will....The thought expands and ascends to its origin, so that when it reaches it, it ends and cannot ascend any further...therefore the pious men of old raised their thought to its origin while pronouncing the precepts and words of prayer. As a result of this procedure and the state of adhesion (devekut) which their thought had attained, their words became blessed, multiplied, full of (divine) influx.[29]

Certain Hasidic sayings use the image of the ladder, such as the following: "The souls descended from the realm of heaven to earth, on a

---

[26]"The Importunate Fortune," in *The Complete Poetry of Henry Vaughn*, pp. 384f.

[27]"The World," *op. cit.*, p. 231.

[28]Scholem, *Kabbalah*, pp. 174f.

[29]Ibid., p. 370.

long ladder. Then it was taken away. Now, up there, they are calling home the souls. Some do not budge from the spot, for how can one get to heaven without a ladder? Others leap and fall and leap again, and give up. But there are those who know very well that they cannot achieve it, but try and try over and over again until God catches hold of them and pulls them up."[30]

Another saying states, "Man is a ladder placed on the earth and the top of it touches heaven. And all his movements and doings and words leave traces in the upper world."[31]

The image of the spiritual ladder was used extensively by ascetic Christian mystics (see figure 5-9). It derives probably from the passage in Augustine's *Confessions* concerning the ascent of the soul to the heavenly Jerusalem. "We ascend thy ladder which is in our heart, and we sing a canticle of degrees; we glow inwardly with thy fire—with thy good fire—and we go forward because we go up to the peace of Jerusalem" (13, 9).

Several Christian martyrs are associated with the image of a ladder. Most notable is St. Perpetua, who had the following dream while in prison shortly before her martyrdom in the arena of Carthage in the year A.D. 203:

> I beheld a ladder of brass, of miraculous size, which reached up to heaven, and was so narrow that it could only be ascended singly. On either side of the ladder, all manner of iron implements were fastened–swords, lances, hooks, daggers and spears–so that anyone who was careless, or did not hold himself erect while climbing, was torn to pieces and remained hanging. Beneath the ladder lay a gigantic dragon, lying in wait for the climbers and frightening them away. Saturus, however, went up before me (just as he later chose to be put to death first, for love of us, because it was he who had taught us but afterwards was not with us when we were thrown into prison). And he reached the top of the ladder and, turning to me, spake: "Perpetua, I am holding thee, but see that the dragon does not bite thee." And I answered: "He shall not harm me, in the name of Jesus Christ." And the dragon slowly lifted his head out from under the ladder, as if in fear of me, and I trod on it, as though I were treading on the first rung of the ladder, and ascended to the top. And I beheld a vast garden and seated in the centre of it, a tall white-haired man, in shepherd's dress, who was milking sheep, and

---

[30]Buber, *Ten Rungs: Hasidic Sayings*, p. 40.
[31]Ibid.

FIGURE 5 – 9

The Mystics' Ladder to Heaven (Icon from St. Catherine's Monastery, Mount
Sinai, 11th–12th century. Reprinted in Weitzmann, *The Icon*.)

round about him many thousands of people clad in white. And he raised his head, looked at me, and spake: "It is well that thou art come, child!" And he called me to him and gave me also a morsel of the cheese which he was milking, and I received it with folded hands and ate. And all who stood around said, "Amen." And at the sound of this invocation I awoke, and was aware that I was still eating something sweet, I know not what. And I immediately reported the vision to my brother, and we understood that it meant the coming passion. And from that time we began to put no more hope in this world.[32]

This awesome dream illustrates the *Zeitgeist* of the Christian era then just beginning. The new Christian spirit was the spirit of *sublimatio* (see figure 5-10). This is illustrated in the following passage from the Syrian poet, Jacob of Batnae, who uses the idea of Jacob's ladder as a prefiguration of Christ's cross. "The cross is set up as a wonderful ladder upon which mankind is in truth led up to heaven.... Christ arose upon earth as a ladder of many steps, and raised himself on high, so that all earthly beings might be exalted through Him.... In the ladder, Jacob truly perceived the crucified one.... On the mountain, He (the Lord) made fast the mysterious cross, like a ladder, set Himself on the top of it and from thence blessed all the nations.... At that time, the cross was set up as a guiding ideal, as it were a ladder, and served all peoples as a path leading up to God."[33]

In Dante's *Paradiso* there is a beautiful example of the *sublimatio* ladder. In canto 21, accompanied by Beatrice, Dante is shown the seventh heaven of Saturn, the abode of contemplative souls (see figure 5-11).

> Within the crystal that bears round the world
> the name of its great king in that golden age
> When evil's flag had not yet been unfurled,
>
> like polished gold ablaze in full sunlight,
> I saw a ladder rise so far above me
> it soared beyond the reaches of my sight.
>
> And I saw so many splendors make their way
> down its bright rungs, I thought that every lamp
> in all of heaven was pouring forth its ray.[34]

In the foregoing I have given a number of examples of the symbolic theme of transition to eternity. Now comes the question, What does this

---

[32]Quoted in von Franz, *The Passion of Perpetua*, pp. 10f.

[33]Ibid., p. 95.

[34]Dante, *The Paradiso*, trans. John Ciardi, pp. 235ff.

FIGURE 5 – 10

Simeon Stylites on His Column Besieged by a Serpent (Reliquary, 6th century. Paris, the Louvre. Reprinted in *The Early Christian and Byzantine World.*)

mean psychologically? We are speaking here of the greater *sublimatio* as contrasted with the lesser one. The lesser *sublimatio* must always be followed by a descent, whereas the greater *sublimatio* is a culminating process, the final translation into eternity of that which has been created in time. What does it mean psychologically to translate into eternity that which has been created in time? Individual consciousness or realization of wholeness is the psychological product of the temporal process of individuation. For that to be made eternal is a mysterious idea. It seems to imply that consciousness achieved by individuals becomes a permanent addition to the archetypal psyche. There is indeed evidence for this idea.[35] For instance, Jung had *sublimatio* visions when close to

---

[35]See Edinger, *The Creation of Consciousness,* p. 23ff.

FIGURE 5 – 11
Dante's Ladder of Saturn (Doré, *Illustrations for Dante's Divine Comedy.*)

death in 1944. He found himself elevated far above the earth and stripped down to an "objective form":

> I had the feeling that everything was being sloughed away; everything I aimed at or wished for or thought, the whole phantasmagoria of earthly existence fell away or was stripped from me—an extremely painful process. Nevertheless something remained; it was as if I now carried along with me everything I had ever experienced or done, everything that had happened around me. I might also say: it was with me and I was it. I consisted of all that, so to speak. I consisted of my own history, and I felt with great certainty: this is what I am. "I am this bundle of what has been, and what has been accomplished."
>
> This experience gave me a feeling of extreme poverty, but at the same time of great fullness. There was no longer anything I wanted or desired. I existed in an objective form; I was what I had been and lived. At first the sense of annihilation predominated, of having been stripped or pillaged; but suddenly that became of no consequence. Everything seemed to be past; what remained was a *fait accompli*, without any reference back to what had

been. There was no longer any regret that something had dropped away or been taken away. On the contrary: I had everything that I was, and that was everything.[36]

I understand this passage to be a description of the greater *sublimatio* in its total and ultimate form. Partial aspects of the same process occur, I think, whenever an item in one's personal psychology is decisively objectified. It then becomes an eternal fact, untouchable by joy or grief or change.

The majority of *sublimatio* images we encounter as therapists belong to the lesser *sublimatio*. In fact, for contemporary patients, images of ascent, heights, and flying almost always indicate the need for a downgoing. Modern individuals have had entirely too much *sublimatio*, at least of the lesser kind. They need descent and *coagulatio* (see figure 5-12). The relative freedom of the sublimated state is an important achievement in psychic development, but only a part. It can be disastrous to be stuck in the sky. Ascent and descent are both needed. As an alchemical dictum says, "Sublimate the body and coagulate the spirit."

Just as ascending birds represent *sublimatio* and translation from the temporal to the eternal, so descending birds represent contents from the archetypal world that are incarnating by breaking into the personal ego realm. The dove of the Holy Spirit descended on Christ at the time of his baptism, indicating the incarnation process. An eagle descended on Tarquin Priscus on his way to Rome signifying his destined kingship. For ages birds have been considered the messengers of God. In ancient times the auspices (from *avis*, "bird" and *specio* "to look at") were taken by examining the behavior of birds. Psychotic patients have told me that they receive messages from God delivered by birds. Upward movement eternalizes; downward movement personalizes. When these two movements are combined, we get another alchemical process, namely, *circulatio*. A paragraph from the *Emerald Tablet of Hermes* refers to *circulatio:* "It ascends from the earth to the heaven, and descends again to the earth, and receives the power of the above and below. Thus you will have the glory of the whole world. Therefore all darkness will flee from you."

In astrological imagery, *circulatio* refers to the repeated ascent and descent of the planetary spheres whereby each of the archetypal principles, symbolized by the planetary archons, is encountered successively. Chemically, *circulatio* refers to the process in which a substance is heated in a reflux flask. The vapors ascend and condense; then the condensed fluid is fed back into the belly of the flask, where the cycle is

---

[36]Jung, *Memories, Dreams, Reflections*, pp. 290f.

FIGURE 5 - 12
The Tower of Babel (Bruegel, 1563. Vienna, Kunsthistorisches Museum.
Reprinted in *The World of Bruegel.*)

repeated. *Sublimatio* and *coagulatio* are thus repeated alternately, again
and again.

Psychologically, *circulatio* is the repeated circuit of all aspects of
one's being, which gradually generates awareness of a transpersonal
center uniting the conflicting factors. There is a transit through the
opposites, which are experienced alternately again and again, leading
finally to their reconciliation. Jung describes *circulatio* in these words:

> Ascent and descent, above and below, up and down, represent an emotional
> realization of opposites, and this realization gradually leads, or should lead,
> to their equilibrium. This motif occurs very frequently in dreams, in the form
> of going up- and downhill, climbing stairs, going up or down in a lift,
> balloon, aeroplane, etc. It corresponds to the struggle between the winged and
> the wingless dragon, i.e., the uroboros.... This vacillating between the oppo-
> sites and being tossed back and forth means being contained *in* the oppo-
> sites. They become a vessel in which what was previously now one thing and
> now another floats vibrating, so that the painful suspension between oppo-
> sites gradually changes into the bilateral activity of the point in the centre.[37]

---

[37]Jung, *Mysterium Coniunctionis, CW* 14, par. 296.

Circulatio is an important idea in psychotherapy. Circular motion around a center and up and down are common in dreams. One must make the circuit of one's complexes again and again in the course of their transformation. The "powers of the above and the below" are combined to the extent that the unified personality is created that connects the personal psyche (below) with the archetypal psyche (above).

The above passage from the *Emerald Tablet* gives a clear expression of the difference between the alchemical attitude and the Christian religious attitude. Jung emphasizes this point since it makes clear the nature of the psychological-empirical standpoint of which the alchemists were forerunners. He writes, "[In the *Emerald Tablet*] it is not a question of a one-way ascent to heaven, but, in contrast to the route followed by the Christian Redeemer, who comes from above to below and from there returns to the above, the *filius macrocosmi* starts from below, ascends on high, and, with the powers of Above and Below united in himself, returns to earth again. He carries out the reverse movement and thereby manifests a nature contrary to that of Christ and the Gnostic Redeemers."[38]

The difference in the images corresponds to the difference between religious faith and psychological empiricism. In another place Jung puts it this way: "[From the religious viewpoint]...man attributes to himself the need of redemption and leaves the work of redemption, the actual *athlon* or *opus,* to the autonomous divine figure;...[From the alchemical viewpoint] man takes upon himself the duty of carrying out the redeeming *opus,* and attributes the state of suffering and consequent need of redemption to the *anima mundi* imprisoned in matter."[39] And again, "[The alchemist's] attention is not directed to his own salvation through God's grace, but to the liberation of God from the darkness of matter."[40]

The alchemical *filius philosophorum* begins and ends on earth. This suggests that primary importance is given to the concrete, spatio-temporal reality of the ego. The fulfillment of the limited human condition is placed above ideal perfection. Nevertheless, this distinction must not be pushed too far. Very interestingly, our chief scriptural reference to the ascension of Christ (Acts 1:9-11) is immediately followed by a statement concerning his return to earth: "...as they were looking on, he was lifted up, and a cloud took him out of their sight. And while they were gazing into heaven as he went, behold, two men stood by them in white robes, and said, 'Men of Galilee, why do you stand looking into heaven?

---

[38]Jung, *Alchemical Studies, CW* 13, par. 280.

[39]Jung, *Psychology and Alchemy, CW* 12, par. 414.

[40]Ibid., par. 420.

This Jesus, who was taken up from you into heaven will come in the same way as you saw him go into heaven'" (RSV).

In spite of the danger of *sublimatio* for the modern mind, its symbolism remains at the core of all human effort for development. All that evokes our better, "higher" nature, indeed, all morality partakes of *sublimatio* imagery. This is well expressed by Longfellow, from whose poem "The Ladder of St. Augustine" I shall quote a few stanzas to conclude this chapter:

St. Augustine! well hast thou said,
That of our vices we can frame
A ladder, if we will but tread
Beneath our feet each deed of shame!

All common things, each day's events,
That with the hour begin and end,
Our pleasures and our discontents,
Are rounds by which we may ascend.

. . . .

The longing for ignoble things;
The strife for triumph more than truth;
The hardening of the heart that brings
Irreverence for the dreams of youth;

. . . .

All these must first be trampled down
Beneath our feet, if we would gain
In the bright fields of fair renown
The right of eminent domain.

. . . .

Standing on what too long we bore
With shoulders bent and downcast eyes,
We may discern—unseen before—
A path to higher destinies.

Nor deem the irrevocable Past,
As wholly wasted, wholly vain
If, rising on its wrecks, at last
To something nobler we attain.

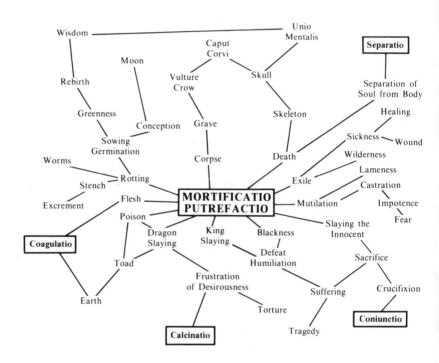

MORTIFICATIO
PUTREFACTIO

Wisdom

Unio
Mentalis

Caput
Corvi

Moon

Separatio

Vulture
Crow

Skull

Rebirth

Separation of
Soul from Body

Greenness

Skeleton

Healing

Conception

Grave

Sickness — Wound

Sowing
Germination

Wilderness

Worms

Corpse

Death

Lameness

Stench

Rotting

Exile

Castration

Excrement

Flesh

Mutilation

Impotence

Poison

Fear

Coagulatio

Blackness

Slaying the
Innocent

Dragon
Slaying

King
Slaying

Toad

Defeat
Humiliation

Sacrifice

Frustration
of Desirousness

Earth

Suffering

Crucifixion

Torture

Coniunctio

Calcinatio

Tragedy

⚜ **6** *Mortificatio* ⚜

J UNG GIVES US AN EXCELLENT RÉSUMÉ of the alchemical *opus* in a 1952 interview:

> Alchemy represents the projection of a drama both cosmic and spiritual in laboratory terms. The *opus magnum* had two aims: the rescue of the human soul and the salvation of the cosmos....This work is difficult and strewn with obstacles; the alchemical opus is dangerous. Right at the beginning you meet the "dragon," the chthonic spirit, the "devil" or, as the alchemists called it, the "blackness," the *nigredo*, and this encounter produces suffering....In the language of the alchemists, matter suffers until the *nigredo* disappears, when the "dawn" *(aurora)* will be announced by the "peacock's tail" *(cauda pavonis)* and a new day will break, the *leukosis* or *albedo*. But in this state of "whiteness" one does not *live* in the true sense of the word, it is a sort of abstract, ideal state. In order to make it come alive it must have "blood," it must have what the alchemists call the *rubedo,* the "redness" of life. Only the total experience of being can transform this ideal state of the *albedo* into a fully human mode of existence. Blood alone can reanimate a glorious state of consciousness in which the last trace of blackness is dissolved, in which the devil no longer has an autonomous existence but rejoins the profound unity of the psyche. Then the *opus magnum* is finished, the human soul is completely integrated.[1]

According to this passage the alchemical *opus* has three stages: *nigredo, albedo,* and *rubedo:* the blackening, the whitening, and the reddening. This chapter is concerned with the first of these, the *nigredo* or blackening, which belongs to the operation called *mortificatio* (see figure 6-1).

The two terms *"mortificatio"* and *"putrefactio"* are overlapping ones and refer to different aspects of the same operation. *Mortificatio* has no chemical reference at all. Literally it means "killing" and hence will refer to the experience of death. As used in religious asceticism it means "subjection of the passions and appetites by penance, abstinence, or

---

[1]Jung, *C. G. Jung Speaking,* pp. 228f.

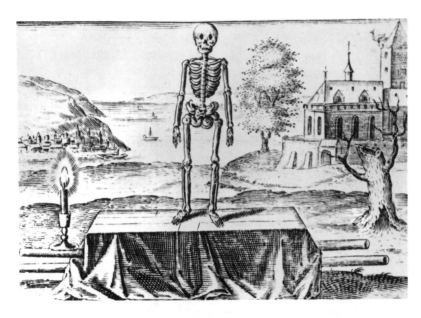

FIGURE 6 – 1
Skeleton as *Mortificatio* Image (*The Hermetic Museum,* trans. by A. E. Waite.)

painful severities inflicted on the body" (Webster). To describe a chemical process as *mortificatio* is a complete projection of a psychological image. This did in fact happen. The material in the flask was personified, and the operations performed on it were thought of as torture.

Putrefactio is "rotting," the decomposition that breaks down dead organic bodies. It, likewise, is not something that would occur in the operations of inorganic chemistry with which the alchemists were largely concerned. However, witnessing the putrefaction of a dead body, especially a human corpse, which was not an unusual experience in the Middle Ages, would have a powerful psychological impact. The effects of this experience might then be projected into the alchemical process (see figure 6-2).

Mortificatio is the most negative operation in alchemy. It has to do with darkness, defeat, torture, mutilation, death, and rotting. However, these dark images often lead over to highly positive ones—growth, resurrection, rebirth—but the hallmark of *mortificatio* is the color black. Let us begin by sampling a few texts.

> That which does not make black cannot make white, because blackness is the beginning of whiteness, and a sign of putrefaction and alteration, and that the body is now penetrated and mortified.[2]

----

[2]*The Lives of the Alchemystical Philosophers,* p. 145.

FIGURE 6 – 2
The Triumph of Death (Fresco by Francesco Traini, c. 1350. Pisa, Camposanto.
Reprinted in *The Picture History of Painting.*)

O happy gate of blackness, cries the sage, which art the passage to this so glorious change. Study, therefore, whosoever appliest thyself to this Art, only to know this secret, for to know this is to know all, but to be ignorant of this is to be ignorant of all. For putrefaction precedes the generation of every new form into existence.[3]

Putrefaction is of so great efficacy that it blots out the old nature and transmutes everything into another new nature, and bears another new fruit. All living things die in it, all dead things decay, and then all these dead things regain life. Putrefaction takes away the acridity from all corrosive spirits of salt, renders them soft and sweet.[4]

In psychological terms blackness refers to the shadow. These texts that speak positively of blackness would thus be alluding, on the personal level, to the positive consequences of being aware of one's shadow. On the archetypal level it is also desirable to be aware of evil "because blackness is the beginning of whiteness." By the law of opposites, an intense awareness of one side constellates its contrary. Out of

---

[3]Scholia to "The Golden Treatise of Hermes," quoted in Atwood, *Hermetic Philosophy and Alchemy,* pp. 126f.

[4]Paracelsus, *Hermetic and Alchemical Writings,* 1:153.

darkness is born the light. In contrast, dreams that emphasize blackness usually occur when the conscious ego is one-sidedly identified with the light. For example, a white man who was very active in the black civil rights movement had this dream:

> *I am in Hades and trying repeatedly to escape without success. There is some sort of wild sexual orgy. Everyone is covered with black tar.*

This patient had exteriorized his personal need to accept blackness by engaging in social action to force society to accept blacks. This was done very self-righteously by projecting the shadow on all who did not agree with him. Although in his conscious life he was involved in demonstrations to overcome discrimination against blacks in white restaurants, he had dreams that he was in black restaurants that discriminated against whites.

The blackness, when it is not the original condition, is brought about by the slaying of something. Most commonly it is the dragon that is to be killed (see figure 6-3). The dragon is "a personification of the instinctual psyche"[5] and is one of the synonyms for the *prima materia*. This image links the alchemical *opus* with the myth of the hero who slays the dragon. Just as the hero rescues the captive maiden from the dragon, so the alchemist redeems the *anima mundi* from her imprisonment in matter by *mortificatio* of the *prima materia*. Or, as Jung puts it, "the slaying of the dragon [is] the *mortificatio* of the first, dangerous, poisonous stage of the anima (= Mercurius), freed from her imprisonment in the *prima materia*."[6] The *mortificatio* of the first, dangerous, poisonous stage of the anima (women read "animus") is an important part of the process of psychotherapy. Outbursts of affect, resentment, pleasure, and power demands—all these must undergo *mortificatio* if the libido trapped in primitive, infantile forms is to be transformed.

Another frequent subject for *mortificatio* is the "king" (see figure 6-4). For example, an alchemical picture shows a group of armed men slaying a king[7] (see figure 6-5) Instead of the king it may be Sol, the sun, who is to be killed. For instance, in this text Sol says, "Unless ye slay me, your understanding will not be perfect, and in my sister the moon the degree of wisdom increases."[8] It may be the lion who undergoes *mortificatio*—the king of beasts and the theriomorphic aspect of the

---

[5] Jung, *Mysterium Coniunctionis, CW* 14, par. 548.

[6] Ibid., par. 168.

[7] Fig. 173 in Jung, *Psychology and Alchemy, CW* 12.

[8] *Mysterium Coniunctionis, CW* 14, par. 164.

FIGURE 6 – 3
Sol and Luna Kill the Dragon (Maier, *Atalanta Fugiens,* 1618.)

sun. In one version the lion has its paws cut off.[9] Again, an eagle may
have its wings clipped.

King, sun, and lion refer to the ruling principle of the conscious ego
and to the power instinct. At a certain point these must be mortified in
order for a new center to emerge. As Jung says, "Egocentricity is a
necessary attribute of consciousness and is also its specific sin."[10] On
the archetypal level the *mortificatio* of the king or the sun will refer to
the death and transformation of a collective dominant or ruling principle. This is alluded to in the following text, which, interestingly, equates
the king as old man with the dragon:

> I am an infirm and weak old man, surnamed the dragon; therefore am I shut
> up in a cave, that I may be ransomed by the kingly crown.... A fiery sword
> inflicts great torments upon me; death makes weak my flesh and bones....
> My soul and my spirit depart; a terrible poison, I am likened to the black
> raven, for that is the wages of sin; in dust and earth I lie, that out of Three
> may come One. O soul and spirit, leave me not, that I may see again the light
> of day, and the hero of peace whom the whole world shall behold may arise
> from me.[11]

---

[9]See Fig. 4 in Jung, *Psychology and Alchemy, CW* 12.

[10]*Mysterium Coniunctionis, CW* 14, par. 364.

[11]Ibid., par. 733.

FIGURE 6 – 4
Death Pours a Drink for the King (Holbein, *The Dance of Death*, 1538.)

The infirm and weak old man represents a conscious dominant or
spiritual principle that has lost its effectiveness. It has regressed to the
level of the primordial psyche (dragon) and must therefore submit to
transformation. The cave in which it is shut up is the alchemical vessel.
The torture is the fiery ordeal that brings about transformation in order
that "out of the Three may come One"; that is, that body, soul, and
spirit may be unified within an integrated personality.

The "hero of peace whom the whole world shall behold" is the
Philosophers' Stone, the reconciler of opposites, but this way of putting
it implies that what is undergoing *mortificatio* and rejuvenation is
nothing less than the collective God-image.

We get an interesting picture of *mortificatio* and *putrefactio* in the
so-called *Vision of George Ripley:*

> When busy at my book I was upon a certain night,
> This vision here expressed appeared unto my dimmed sight,

FIGURE 6 – 5
Death of the King (Stolcius, *Viridarium Chymicum,* 1624. Reprinted in Read,
Prelude to Chemistry.)

A Toad full red I saw did drink the juice of grapes so fast,
Till over charged with the broth, his bowels all to braast;
And after that from poisoned bulk he cast his venom fell,
For grief and pain whereof his members all began to swell,
With drops of poisoned sweat approaching thus his secret den,
His cave with blasts of fumous air he all be-whyted then;
And from the which in space a golden humor did ensue,
Whose falling drops from high did stain the soil with ruddy hue:
And when this corpse the force of vital breath began to lack,
This dying Toad became forthwith like coal for color black:
Thus drowned in his proper veins of poisoned flood,
For term of eighty days and four he rotting stood:
By trial then this venom to expel I did desire,
For which I did commit his carcass to a gentle fire:
Which done, a wonder to the sight, but more to be rehearsed,
The Toad with colors rare through every side was pierced,
And white appeared when all the sundry hues were past,
Which after being tincted Red, for evermore did last.
Then of the venom handled thus a medicine I did make;
Which venom kills and saves such as venom chance to take.

Glory be to him the granter of such secret ways,
Dominion, and honor, both with worship and with praise. Amen.[12]

This vision is a summary of the entire *opus*. The toad as *prima materia* is destroyed by its own greed or unbridled concupiscence. It is the theme of drowning in one's own surfeit. As it dies it turns black, putrefies, and is filled with poison. The alchemist then enters the picture and subjects the poison-laden carcass to the fire of the alchemical process. This brings about a progressive color change from black to many colors to white to red. At the same time the poison is changed to a paradoxical medicine that can kill or save, the elixir. The toad is a symbolic variant of the "poisonous dragon."[13] It also represents the "philosophic earth" that cannot be sublimated.[14] Earth signifies *coagulatio*, alluding to the fact that *mortificatio* must follow *coagulatio*. That which has become earth or flesh is subject to death and corruption. As the Apostle Paul says, "For if ye live after the flesh, ye shall die; but if ye through the Spirit do mortify the deeds of the body, ye shall live" (Rom. 8:13 AV).

Just as *coagulatio* is followed sooner or later by *mortificatio,* so likewise does consummation of the lesser *coniunctio* lead to *mortificatio.* Examples are Tristan and Isolde, Romeo and Juliet, and the sequence depicted in the *Rosarium* pictures.[15] This fact helps to account for the reluctance sensitive people have to committing themselves to the individuation process. They sense in advance the suffering they are letting themselves in for.

The poisonous toad was thought to have a jewel in its head, as does the dragon. Ruland says: "Draconites is a precious stone...to be found in the brain of serpents, but unless it is removed while they are alive, it will never become a precious stone, by the inbred malice of the animal who, conscious of death approaching, destroys the virtue of the stone. Therefore the head is removed from dragons while asleep, and thus the gem is secured.... The color of the Draconite is white, it drives away all poisonous animals and cures envenomed bites."[16]

The precious stone is the Philosophers' Stone extracted from the ugly *prima materia,* which is poison in its original form but panacea after undergoing the *mortificatio.* Shakespeare expresses this same idea:

---

[12]Ashmole, ed., *Theatrum Chemicum Britannicum,* p. 374.

[13]*Mysterium Coniunctionis, CW* 14, par. 30.

[14]Ibid., par. 2.

[15]Figs., 1–10 in Jung, *The Practice of Psychotherapy, CW* 16.

[16]Ruland, *Lexicon,* p. 128.

> Sweet are the uses of adversity,
> Which like the toad, ugly and venomous,
> Wears yet a precious jewel in his head;
> And this our life exempt from public haunt,
> Finds tongues in trees, books in the running brooks,
> Sermons in stones, and good in everything.[17]

The uses of adversity also come up in that great *mortificatio* manual, *The Imitation of Christ* by Thomas à Kempis. There we read the following:

> It is good that we sometimes have griefs and adversities, for they drive a man to behold himself and to see that he is here but as in exile, and to learn thereby that he ought not put his trust in any worldly thing. It also is good that we sometimes suffer contradiction; and that we be thought of by others as evil and wretched and sinful, though we do well and intend well; such things help us to humility, and mightily defend us from vainglory and pride. We take God better to be our judge and witness when we are outwardly despised in the world and the world does not judge well of us. Therefore, a man ought to establish himself so fully in God that, whatever adversity befall him he will not need to seek any outward comfort.[18]

> A clean, pure and constant heart is not broken or easily overcome by spiritual labors, for he does all things to the honor of God, because he is clearly mortified to himself. Therefore, he desires to be free from following his own will. What hinders you more than your own affections not fully mortified to the will of the spirit? Truly, nothing more.[19]

So far we have noted several possible subjects of *mortificatio,* namely, dragon, toad, king, sun, and lion. Another such subject is the figure of purity and innocence. One text reads:

> Take it fresh, pure, living white and clear,
> Then bind firmly both hands and feet
> With the very strongest cords,
> That it suffocate and die,
> In the closed house of Putrefaction.[20]

This corresponds to the classic victim for sacrifice which must be pure and unblemished like the Pascal lamb (Exod. 12:5). An alchemical drawing pictures Herod's massacre of the innocents as the "dissolution of the metallic seeds," which are then poured into the alchemical vessel[21] (see figure 6-6). The psychological idea behind these images is that the

---

[17]*As You Like It,* Act 2, sc. 1, lines 12–17.

[18]Kempis, *The Imitation of Christ* 1:12.

[19]Ibid., 1:3.

[20]Figulus, *A Golden and Blessed Casket of Nature's Marvels,* p. 319.

[21]Bessy, *A Pictorial History of Magic and the Supernatural,* p. 112.

Dissolution des germes métalliques représentés par les innocents qu'Hérode fait égorger.

FIGURE 6 – 6

Massacre of the Innocents (Alchemical drawing. Reprinted in Bessy, *A Pictorial History of Magic and the Supernatural.*)

childhood state of purity and innocence must be sacrificed. A woman who could not face this issue once dreamed that *a lamb was to be sacrificed and she couldn't bear to watch.*[22] Another patient, a young man who was moving toward maturity, dreamed that *a pure white turkey was being killed. In the process the dreamer is stained with blood.* In these cases the *nigredo* is not the initial stage. A preliminary *albedo* must be first destroyed. When something white has been killed it putrefies and turns black. It enters the "gate of blackness," Ruland

---

[22]Edinger, *Ego and Archtype,* p. 234.

says: "Putrefaction or corruption takes place when a body becomes black. Then it stinks like dung and true solution follows. The elements are separated and destroyed. Many colors are afterwards developed, until the victory is obtained and everything is reunited."[23]

Feces, excrement, and bad odors refer to the *putrefactio*. The common dreams of neglected or overflowing toilets which plague puritan-minded people belong to this symbolism. *Odor sepulcrorum* (the stench of the graves) is another synonym for the *putrefactio*. Since people today seldom smell a rotting corpse, this image does not appear often in dreams. One modern equivalent I have encountered is a dream of severe air pollution. Worms accompany putrefaction, and dreams of worms convey this image with powerful impact (see figure 6-7). In the *I Ching,* Hexagram 18 is entitled "Work on What has been Spoiled," and the text tells us that "the Chinese character *ku* represents a bowl in whose

FIGURE 6 – 7

Death Blowing the Worm Trumpet (J. Meydenbach, *Doten Dantz,* c. 1492. Mainz. Reprinted in Hind, *An Introduction to a History of Woodcut.*)

---

[23]*Lexicon,* p. 266.

contents worms are breeding. This means decay."[24] Typical of the paradoxical imagery of the unconscious, the despicable worm can turn into the supreme value. Thus the Messiah is equated with a worm in the messianic Psalm 22, verse 6: "But I am a worm and no man; a reproach of men, and despised of the people" (AV).

An alchemical text says, "Know, O Sons of the Doctrine, that it behooves you to allow the composition to putrefy for forty days."[25] This passage connects the *putrefactio* with the theme of the wilderness through the symbolism of the number 40. The Israelites wandered in the wilderness for forty years; Elijah fasted in the wilderness for forty days; and Jesus was tempted in the wilderness for forty days. Also, the Egyptian embalming procedure was said to take forty days (Gen. 50:3), and, analogously, forty days elapsed between Christ's resurrection and ascension. Concerning the alchemical *opus,* Jung says, "the blackening usually took forty days.... In this state the sun is surrounded by the *anima media natura* and is therefore black. It is a state of incubation or pregnancy."[26] The *anima media natura* corresponds to Sophia caught in the embrace of Physis and is equated with Divine Wisdom, the feminine counterpart of God (see figure 6–8). Even if it is caused by the wisdom of God, the blackening or eclipse of the sun remains a fearful experience. In fact, fear is proverbially linked to wisdom in the saying, "The fear of the Lord is the beginning of wisdom" (Prov. 1:7). Fear as an agent of *mortificatio* is described in this passage from Emerson's essay "Compensation":

Fear

> All infractions of love and equity in our social relations are speedily punished. They are punished by fear. Whilst I stand in simple relations to my fellow-man, I have no displeasure in meeting him....But as soon as there is any departure from simplicity and attempt at halfness, or good for me that is not good for him, my neighbor feels the wrong; he shrinks from me as far as I have shrunk from him; his eyes no longer seek mine; there is war between us; there is hate in him and fear in me.
>
> All the old abuses in society, universal and particular, all unjust accumulations of property and power, are avenged in the same manner. Fear is an instructor of great sagacity and the herald of all revolutions. One thing he teaches, that there is rottenness where he appears. He is a carrion crow, and though you see not well what he hovers for, there is death somewhere.[27]

A classic biblical description of the wilderness *nigredo* is that of Jeremiah. St. John of the Cross uses this passage in his description of

---

[24]Wilhelm, trans., *The I Ching or Book of Changes,* p 75.

[25]Waite, trans., *Turba Philosophorum,* p. 87, dictum 26.

[26]Jung, *Mysterium Coniunctionis, CW* 14, par. 729.

[27]Emerson, "Compensation," in *Selected Writings of Ralph Waldo Emerson,* p. 180.

the dark night of the soul.[28] Jeremiah here laments both his own sufferings and those of Zion (Lam. 3:1–20, NAB):

> I am a man who knows affliction from the rod of his anger,
> One whom he has led and forced to walk
> in darkness, not in light;
> Against me alone he brings back his hand
> again and again all the day.
> He has worn away my flesh and my skin,

FIGURE 6 – 8

Coniunctio in the Black Vas. The *Nigredo* (Paris, Bibliothèque de l'Arsenal, MS. 975, fol. 14. Reprinted in Derola, *The Secret Art of Alchemy*.)

---

[28]St. John of the Cross, *The Dark Night of the Soul,* pp. 109ff.

he has broken my bones;
He has beset me round about
with poverty and weariness;
He has left me to dwell in the dark
like those long dead.
He has hemmed me in with no escape
and weighed me down with chains;
Even when I cry out for help,
he stops my prayer;
He has blocked my way with fitted stones,
and turned my paths aside.
A lurking bear he has been to me,
a lion in ambush!
He deranged my ways, set me astray,
left me desolate.
He bent his bow, and set me up
as the target for his arrow.
He pierces my sides
with shafts from his quiver.
I have become a laughing stock for all nations,
their taunt all the day long;
He has sated me with bitter food,
made me drink my fill of wormwood.
He has broken my teeth with gravel,
pressed my face in the dust;
My soul is deprived of peace,
I have forgotten what happiness is;
I tell myself my future is lost,
all that I hoped for from the Lord.

Probably the biblical reference most frequently connected with *putrefactio* by the alchemists is this passage from the Gospel of John: "Truly, truly, I say to you, unless a grain of wheat falls into the earth and dies, it remains alone; but if it dies, it bears much fruit. He who loves his life loses it, and he who hates his life in this world will keep it for eternal life" (12:24–25 RSV).

For example, a text says, "As the grain of wheat sown in the earth putrefies before it springs up into a new growth or vegetation, so our Magnesia...being sown in the Philosophic Earth, dies and corrupts, that it may conceive itself anew."[29]

Another text refers to the sowing of gold:

The whole Fundament of the Philosophers' Stone consists in bringing to a new birth the primary matter of metals—i.e., Mercurial Water, the perfect *Corpus Solis*—that it be born again by water and of the spirit, just as Christ says: "Except a man be born again by water and the Spirit, he cannot see the

---

[29]Quoted in Atwood, *Hermetic Philosophy and Alchemy*, p. 115n.

Kingdom of God." So also here in this art, I tell thee, my son: Except *Corpus Solis* be sowed, all else is vain, and there will be no fruit. Even as Christ says: "Except the seed fall into the earth and die, it shall bear not fruit."[30]

The sowing of gold (*corpus solis*) is an interesting image. Gold signifies light, value, consciousness. To sow it means to sacrifice it, to offer it up to *mortificatio* in the hope that it will multiply. Just as seed grain is kept apart and not eaten, so seed consciousness will not be used to live on. Instead, it is offered up to the unconscious by a kind of voluntary death of one's psychic comfort, rightness, and rationality. One allows oneself to be less in order to be more—less nearly perfect, but more nearly whole.

The image of death and burial has always been associated with the planting of seeds and their germination. Pictures from ancient Egypt show stalks of grain sprouting from the dead body of Osiris (see figure 6-9). The Apostle Paul uses this image in his famous passage concerning the resurrection of the dead: "It is sown in corruption; it is raised in

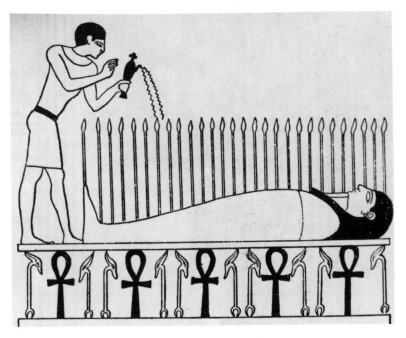

FIGURE 6 – 9
Grain Growing from the Corpse of Osiris (From a bas-relief at Philae. Reprinted in Budge, *Osiris: The Egyptian Religion of Resurrection.*)

---

[30]Figulus, *A Golden and Blessed Casket of Nature's Marvels,* p. 299.

incorruption. It is sown in dishonor; it is raised in glory; it is sown in weakness; it is raised in power. It is sown a natural body; it is raised a spiritual body" (1 Cor. 15:42–44, AV).

I was once told of a striking dream on this subject, which, incidentally, was dreamed on Halloween.

> *The dreamer was attending a party for a dead friend and perhaps other departed spirits. The dead friend recounts a dream that he had before his death. Its major image was a great circle of grain standing 80 inches high. It grew out of a pit in the earth which contained dead bodies that were also buried treasure. The dreamer was trying to convey to his friend the importance of the dream* (cf. figure 6-10).

It is to be noted that dead bodies equal buried treasure.

In a Gnostic text the perfect man, or *Anthropos*, is called a corpse because he is "buried in the body like a mummy in a tomb."[31] Jung points out that there is a parallel idea in Paracelsus, who says, "Life,

FIGURE 6 –10
Grain Growing from the Grave, Symbolizing Resurrection (*The Hermetic Museum*, trans. by A. E. Waite.)

---

[31]Jung, *Aion, CW* 9II, par. 334.

verily, is naught but a kind of embalmed mummy, which preserves the mortal body from the mortal worms."[32] It turns out that this *"mumia"* is symbolically identical with the original man or *Anthropos.* This Gnostic corpse or Paracelsian mummy is thus the Self as the product of *mortificatio*—the incorruptible body that grows out of the death of the corruptible seed. It corresponds to the alchemical idea that death is the conception of the Philosophers' Stone.[33]

Germination and decay, light changing to darkness, death and rebirth—all these belong to the symbolism of the moon, which dies and is reborn each month. One text states the following:

> The lion, the lower sun, grows corrupt through the flesh. Thus is the lion corrupted in his nature through his flesh, which follows the times of the moon, and is eclipsed. For the moon is the *shadow of the sun,* and with corruptible bodies she is consumed, and through her corruption is the lion eclipsed with the help of the moisture of Mercurius…the moisture of the moon, when she receives his light, slays the sun, and at the birth of the child of the Philosophers she dies likewise, and at death the two parents yield up their souls to the son, and die and pass away, *And the parents are the food of the son.*[34]

The statement that the lion or lower sun grows corrupt through the flesh can be understood to mean that the ego, by incarnating, by daring to exist as an autonomous center of being, takes on substantial reality but also becomes subject to corruption and death (see figure 6-11). The ego is eventually eclipsed—falls into the blackness of *mortificatio*—but from its death the "child of the philosophers"—the Philosophers' Stone—is born. Both sun and moon die and transfer their power to their offspring—the son of the philosophers.

Jung says that this passage may have inspired the picture of the death of the royal pair in the *Rosarium.*[35] In that picture[36] the king and queen, following intercourse, have merged into one body with two heads and are lying dead in a tomb. The picture is captioned "conception or putrefaction." The statement that "the parents are the food of the son" is particularly interesting. Psychologically this suggests that the conscious endurance of darkness and the conflict of the opposites nourishes the Self (cf. Figure 3-16 in chapter 3).

---

[32]Ibid.

[33]*The Practice of Psychotherapy, CW* 16, par. 473.

[34]Jung, *Mysterium Coniunctionis, CW* 14, par. 21.

[35]Ibid.

[36]*The Practice of Psychotherapy, CW* 16, fig. 6.

FIGURE 6 – 11

Death and the Landsknecht (Dürer. Reprinted in *The Complete Woodcuts of Albrecht Dürer.*)

A common term for the *nigredo* is *"corvus,"* crow or raven,[37] perhaps because it is black and is a carrion eater (see figure 6-12). The crow appears in Greek mythology in the birth of Asklepios. His mother was Coronis, the crow maiden, who, while pregnant with Asklepios by Apollo, had intercourse with Ischys. This infidelity was reported to Apollo by the crow, who was turned from white to black for bringing the bad news. Coronis was killed for her crime, but the infant Asklepios was snatched from her womb while she was on the funeral pyre. As Kerényi has demonstrated, the birth of healing power from the *nigredo* belongs to the archetype of the wounded healer. In Kerényi's words, the

---

[37]Jung, *Mysterium Coniunctionis, CW* 14, par. 727.

FIGURE 6 – 12

The *Nigredo* (Mylius, *Philosophia reformata,* 1622. Reprinted in Derola, *The Secret Art of Alchemy.*)

myth refers psychologically to the capacity "to be at home in the darkness of suffering and there to find germs of light and recovery with which, as though by enchantment, to bring forth Asklepios, the sunlike healer."[38]

Related to *"corvus"* is the term *"caput corvi,"* head of the raven. This in turn is synonymous with *"caput mortuum,"* dead head. It is not immediately evident why the *nigredo* should be associated with head symbolism. One reason seems to be the connection between the term "head" and top or beginning. Blackness was considered to be the starting point of the work.[39] A text says, "When you see your matter going black, rejoice: for that is the beginning of the work."[40] Another text speaks of the work as made up of three ravens: "The black which is the head of the art, the white which is the middle, and the red which brings all things to an end."[41]

[38]Kerényi, *Asklepios: Archetypal Image of the Physician's Existence,* p. 100.

[39]Jung, *Mysterium Coniunctionis, CW* 14, par. 729.

[40]Ibid., n. 182.

[41]Ibid.

The head is the principle thing. A capital offense is the gravest one, involving the loss of one's head. Thus, the connection of the *nigredo* with head imagery indicates the great importance alchemy attached to this experience. According to one derivation, the word "alchemy" derives from *khem* or *chemia* meaning black and referring to Egypt, the land of the black soil.[42] Decapitation or separation of the head from the body also belongs to the *mortificatio*. Jung writes: "Beheading is significant symbolically as the separation of the 'understanding' from the 'great suffering and grief' which nature inflicts on the soul. It is an emancipation of the '*cogitatio*' which is situated in the head, a freeing of the soul from the 'trammels of nature.' Its purpose is to bring about, as in Dorn, a *unio mentalis* in the overcoming of the body"[43] (see figure 6-13).

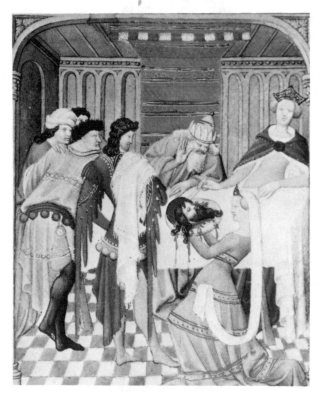

FIGURE 6 – 13
Salome with the Head of John the Baptist (*Les Belles Heures du Duc de Berry.* New York, The Metropolitan Museum of Art.)

---

[42]See Read, *Prelude to Chemistry,* p. 4n.; see also Jung, *Mysterium Coniunctionis, CW* 14, par. 14.

[43]Jung, *Mysterium Coniunctionis, CW* 14, par. 14.

From another standpoint, beheading extracts the *rotundum,* the round, complete man, from the empirical man. The head or skull becomes the round vessel of transformation. In one text it was the head of the black Osiris or Ethiopian that, when boiled, turned into gold.[44]

The term *"caput mortuum"* was used to refer to the residue left after the distillation or sublimation of a substance. A text describes this *caput mortuum:* "What remains below in the retort is our salt, that is, our earth, and it is of a black color, a dragon that eats its own tail. For the dragon is the matter that remains behind after the distillation of water from it, and this water is called the dragon's tail, and the dragon is its blackness, and the dragon is saturated with his water and coagulated, and so he eats his tail."[45]

The dead, worthless residue is the stuff of the *nigredo* phase. The fact that it is called a *caput* or head indicates a paradoxical reversal of opposites. The worthless becomes the most precious, and the last becomes first. This is a lesson that we each must learn again and again. It is the *psyche* that we find in the worthless, despised place. By the conventional standards of our environment the psyche is nothing, nothing at all. A personal example: I feel empty and out of sorts; I sit for hours in my chair seeking my lost libido. What a painful humiliation to be subjected to such catatonic impotence. Even active imagination refuses to function. Finally I get one meager image—a small, black, earthenware pot. Does it contain something, or is it empty like me? I turn it over. One drop of golden fluid comes, which solidifies on contact with the air. That was all I needed! That single drop of solid gold released a stream of associations, and with them, libido. It had come from the black pot, the black head of Osiris, which personified my dark and empty state, a state I despised while I was in it.

The death head also leads into the idea of a dialogue with a head or skull. Jung speaks of the oracular head,[46] which would symbolize the consulting of one's wholeness for information beyond the vision of the ego. The dramatic theme of soliloquy with a skull is a variant of this same archetypal image. The classic example is found in *Hamlet.* He contemplates Yorick's skull and concludes with these thoughts:

> To what base uses we may return, Horatio! Why may not imagination trace the noble dust of Alexander, till he find it stopping a bung-hole?... As thus: Alexander died, Alexander was buried, Alexander returneth into dust; the dust is earth; of earth we make loam, and why of that loam, whereto he was converted, might they not stop a beer-barrel?

---

[44]Ibid.

[45]Ibid., par. 244.

[46]Jung, *Psychology and Religion: West and East, CW* 11, par. 363ff; see also *Mysterium Coniunctionis, CW* 14, par. 626.

> Imperious Caesar, dead and turn'd to clay,
> Might stop a hole to keep the wind away;
> O! that that earth, which kept the world in awe,
> Should patch a wall to expel the winter's flaw.

(Act 5, sc. 1, lines 222–38)

Goethe's *Faust* also has a brief soliloquy to a skull near the beginning of the drama:

> Yon hollow skull, what has your grin to say,
> But that a mortal brain, with trouble tossed,
> Sought once, like mine, the sweetness of the day,
> And strove for truth, and in the gloom was lost.[47]

The skull as a *memento mori* is an emblem for the operation of *mortificatio*. It generates reflections on one's personal mortality and serves as a touchstone for true and false values. To reflect on death can lead one to view life under the aspect of eternity, and thus the black death head can turn to gold (see figure 6-14). In fact, the origin and growth of consciousness seem to be connected uniquely with the experience of death. Perhaps the first pair of opposites to penetrate the dawning awareness of primitive humans was the contrast between the living and the dead. Probably it is only a mortal creature that is capable of consciousness. Our mortality is our greatest and our ultimate weakness. And it is weakness, according to Jung, that gave Job the edge over Yahweh:

> What does man possess that God does not have? Because of his littleness, puniness, and defencelessness against the Almighty, he possesses, as we have already suggested, a somewhat keener consciousness based on self-reflection: he must, in order to survive, always be mindful of his impotence. God has no need of this circumspection, for nowhere does he come up against an insuperable obstacle that would force him to hesitate and hence make him reflect on himself.[48]

The earliest forms of religious expression—which indicate the first separation of the ego from the archetypal psyche—seem to be associated with burial rites. The outstanding example of death as the genesis of religion and consciousness is the elaborate mortuary symbolism of ancient Egypt. This is also clearly the origin of alchemy. The embalming of the dead king transformed him into Osiris, an eternal, incorruptible body. This is the prototype of the alchemical *opus,* which attempts to create the incorruptible Philosophers' Stone. The alchemical vessel

---

[47]Goethe, *Faust,* p. 3.

[48]Jung, *Psychology and Religion: West and East, CW* 11, par. 579.

FIGURE 6 – 14
The Death Head Points to the Cosmic Sphere (Holbein, *The Dance of Death,*
1538.)

has been equated with "the sealed tomb of Osiris, containing all the
limbs of the god."[49] The Egyptian mortuary symbolism is the first great
witness to the reality of the psyche. It is as though the psyche cannot
come into existence as a separate entity until the death of the literal, the
concrete, and the physical. The collective unconscious is equivalent to
the land of the dead or the afterlife, and a descent into the collective
unconscious is called a *nekyia* because an encounter with the autonomous psyche is felt as a death of this world.

Plato explicitly connects wisdom with death. For him, philosophy,
the love of wisdom, is quite literally a *mortificatio.* In the *Phaedo* he
writes:

---

[49]Jung, *Alchemical Studies, CW* 13, par. 97.

"Purification, as we saw some time ago in our discussion, consists in separating the soul as much as possible from the body, and accustoming it to withdraw from all contact with the body and concentrate itself by itself, and to have its dwelling, as far as it can, both now and in the future, alone by itself, freed from the shackles of the body. Does not that follow?"

"Yes, it does," said Simmias.

"Is not what we call death a freeing and separation of soul from body?"

"Certainly," he said.

"And the desire to free the soul is found chiefly, or rather only, in the true philosopher. In fact the philosopher's occupation consists precisely in the freeing and separation of soul from body. Isn't that so?"

"Apparently."

"Well then, as I said at the beginning, if a man has trained himself throughout his life to live in a state as close as possible to death, would it not be ridiculous for him to be distressed when death comes to him?"

"It would, of course."

"Then it is a fact, Simmias, that true philosophers make dying their profession, and that to them of all men death is least alarming. Look at it in this way. If they are thoroughly dissatisfied with the body, and long to have their souls independent of it, when this happens would it not be entirely unreasonable to be frightened and distressed? Would they not naturally be glad to set out for the place where there is a prospect of attaining the object of their lifelong desire—which is wisdom—and of escaping from an unwelcome association? Surely there are many who have chosen of their own free will to follow dead lovers and wives and sons to the next world, in the hope of seeing and meeting there the persons whom they loved. If this is so, will a true lover of wisdom who has firmly grasped this same conviction—that he will never attain to wisdom worthy of the name elsewhere than in the next world—will he be grieved at dying? Will he not be glad to make that journey? We must suppose so, my dear boy, that is, if he is a real philosopher, because then he will be of the belief that he will never find wisdom in all its purity in any other place."[50]

What stands out in this passage is the startling statement that "true philosophers make dying their profession." The same can be said of an important aspect of analysis. As we pursue the withdrawal of projections, we make dying our profession.

These ideas of Plato lead directly into Jung's discussion of the *unio mentalis* in *Mysterium Coniunctionis.* There he describes the *coniunctio* as taking place in three stages. In the first stage of this operation soul and spirit are united with each other. The united product is then separated from the body. This separation is experienced as a death. Jung writes:

The *unio mentalis,* the interior oneness which today we call individuation, he (Dorn) conceived as a psychic equilibration of opposites "in the overcoming of the body," a state of equanimity transcending the body's affectivity and

---

[50]Plato, *Phaedo,* 67c–68b, in *The Collected Dialogues.*

instinctuality. The spirit which is to unite with the soul, he called a "spiracle of eternal life," a sort of "window into eternity" (Leibnitz)....

But, in order to bring about their subsequent reunion, the mind (*mens*) must be separated from the body—which is equivalent to voluntary death—for only separated things can unite. By this separation (*distractio*) Dorn obviously meant a discrimination and dissolution of the "composite," the composite state being one in which the affectivity of the body has a disturbing influence on the rationality of the mind. The aim of this separation was to free the mind of the influence of "the bodily appetites and the heart's affections," and to establish a spiritual position which is supraordinate to the turbulent sphere of the body. This leads at first to a dissociation of the personality and a violation of the merely natural man.

This preliminary step, in itself a clear blend of Stoic philosophy and Christian psychology, is indispensable for the differentiation of consciousness. Modern psychotherapy makes use of the same procedure when it objectifies the affects and instincts and confronts the consciousness with them.[51]

Thus the *unio mentalis* corresponds precisely to the philosophers who make dying their profession.

In this preliminary step the "natural man" must be mortified and reminded that, in the words of Thomas Gray,

> The boast of heraldry, the pomp of power,
> And all that beauty, all that wealth e'er gave
> Await alike the inevitable hour:
> The paths of glory lead but to the grave."[52]

Or, in the words of the Apostle Paul, "You must kill everything in you that belongs only to earthly life: fornication, impurity, guilty passion, evil desires, and especially greed, which is the same thing as worshipping a false god" (Col. 3:5, JB). Of course this statement is to be taken symbolically, not literally. Desires are to be killed in their obsessive, projected forms.

Encounter with the unconscious is almost by definition a wounding defeat. In *Mysterium Coniunctionis* we find one of the most important sentences that Jung ever wrote: *"The experience of the self is always a defeat for the ego."*[53] And in another work he writes, "The integration of contents that were always unconscious and projected involves a serious lesion of the ego. Alchemy expresses this through the symbols of death, mutilation, or poisoning, or through the curious idea of dropsy."[54]

This "lesion of the ego" is what is symbolized by the figure of the sun-hero who is lame or has an amputated extremity. It is the meaning of

---

[51]Jung, *Mysterium Coniunctionis, CW* 14, par. 670ff.

[52]"Elegy Written in a Country Churchyard."

[53]Jung, *Mysterium Coniunctionis, CW* 14, par. 788.

[54]*The Practice of Psychotherapy, CW* 16, par. 472.

Jason as a *monosandolos* who had lost a sandal while carrying an unknown woman (Hera) across a river. It is also the meaning of Oedipus whose name means "swollen foot." I once dreamed that *while Jung was giving a brilliant lecture I noticed that his right foot was lame.*

Mortificatio is experienced as defeat and failure. Needless to say, one rarely chooses such an experience. It is usually imposed by life, either from within or from without. To some extent it can be experienced vicariously through that great cultural instrument of *mortificatio,* the tragic drama. In some cases the drama can provide even more than a vicarious experience. If the time is right, it can have an inductive effect and initiate an authentic transformation process in the individual. What I have written in another work is relevant here:

> Gilbert Murray has given us a valuable description of the origin and basic features of the classic tragedy [quoted in Harrison, *Themis,* 341ff]. It is his view that Greek tragedy started as the ritual re-enactment of the death and rebirth of the year-spirit (equated with Dionysus), and that this ritual re-enactment had four chief features. First there is an *agone* or contest in which the protagonist, the representative of the year-spirit, is in contest with darkness or evil. Secondly, there is a *pathos* or passion in which the hero undergoes suffering and defeat. Third is a *threnos* or lamentation for the defeated hero. And fourthly, there is a *theophany,* a rebirth of life on another level with a reversal of emotion from sorrow to joy. This sequence is basically the same as the ritual drama of Osiris and of Christ, each of which has the characteristic features of the death and rebirth of the year-spirit. In later Greek tragedy the final phase, the theophany, almost disappears, perhaps remaining only as a hint. In psychological terms we can say that the sequence of steps which constitute the tragic process involves the overcoming of the ego, the defeat of the conscious will, in order for the Self, the final epiphany, to manifest.[55]

The *pathos* and *threnos* stages of suffering and defeat correspond to the alchemical *mortificatio,* and the *theophany* corresponds to the reborn, incorruptible body that sprouts out of the corpse of Osiris. Shakespeare's *King Lear* is a particularly good example of tragedy as *mortificatio.* In a text previously quoted, the old man says he is "surnamed the dragon." Similarly, wrathful King Lear, early in the play, identifies himself with the dragon with his words to Kent, "Come not between the dragon and his wrath" (Act 1, sc. 1, line 124). The play then unfolds as a progressive stripping of authority, power, and control from the king. The will of the kingly ego undergoes total *mortificatio* to the point of madness. Out of this *nigredo* state is born the theophany of Lear's transformation. Through his madness he gets a glimpse of the transpersonal psyche that he is now willing to serve. After final defeat

---

[55] Edinger, "The Tragic Hero: An Image of Individuation."

by Edmund's forces, as Lear and Cordelia are being led to prison, the theophany comes in this stunning passage. Here the black death's head turns to gold.

> Come, let's away to prison:
> We two alone will sing like birds i' the cage:
> When thou dost ask me blessing, I'll kneel down
> And ask of thee forgiveness: so we'll live,
> And pray, and sing, and tell old tales, and laugh
> At gilded butterflies, and hear poor rogues
> Talk of court news; and we'll talk with them too,
> Who loses and who wins, who's in, who's out;
> And take upon's the mystery of things,
> As if we were God's spies: and we'll wear out,
> In a wall'd prison, packs and sects of great ones
> That ebb and flow by the moon.

> (Act 5, sc. 3, lines 8–18)

With this statement Lear has passed beyond the opposites. Self replaces ego. Blackness turns to gold. The modern poet Theodore Roethke describes a parallel experience of the Self's being born out of the *nigredo* in his poem "In a Dark Time":

> In a dark time, the eye begins to see,
> I meet my shadow in the deepening shade;
> I hear my echo in the echoing wood—
> A lord of nature weeping to a tree.
> I live between the heron and the wren,
> Beasts of the hill and serpents of the den.
>
> What's madness but nobility of soul
> At odds with circumstance? The day's on fire!
> I know the purity of pure despair.
> My shadow pinned against a sweating wall.
> That place among the rocks—is it a cave,
> Or winding path? The edge is what I have.
>
> A steady stream of correspondences!
> A night flowing with birds, a ragged moon,
> And in broad day the midnight come again!
> A man goes far to find out what he is—
> Death of the self in a long, tearless night,
> All natural shapes blazing unnatural light.
>
> Dark, dark my light, and darker my desire.
> My soul, like some heat-maddened summer fly,
> Keeps buzzing at the sill. Which I is I?
> A fallen man, I climb out of my fear.

> The mind enters itself, and God the mind,
> And one is One, free in the tearing wind.[56]

This remarkable poem has the ring of complete psychological authenticity. It is a modern expression of the same experience as lay behind *King Lear;* that is, it derives from the same archetype. The first stanza speaks of darkness bringing a new kind of vision. The ego's lordship over nature is overthrown. Weeping to a tree is analogous to the heath scene in *King Lear*. The unconscious as nature and as animal has erupted into consciousness. The second stanza is concerned with madness, as was Lear in the storm. What is madness? It is soul in conflict with circumstance. It is inner and outer reality confused. Illusions are being dissolved. One's dark side is pinned and must be acknowledged. The opposites come into view, and the ego must traverse the narrow edge between them. The third stanza speaks of a "stream of correspondences." When the depths of the unconscious open, "circumstance" cracks open, synchronicities occur, and transpersonal meanings shine through—"natural shapes blazing unnatural light." In the fourth stanza the author becomes disidentified from his desire and from his "soul"— that is, the unconscious. Like Lear, he had been bound to a wheel of fire, in a state of identity with the transpersonal energies of the Self. Now he is released and can realize the Self as separate from the ego. As Roethke says in another poem ("The Shape of Fire"), "the redeemer comes a dark way."

Another poetic expression of the *mortificatio* experience is found in these lines from "East Coker" by T. S. Eliot:

> I said to my soul, be still, and wait without hope
> For hope would be hope for the wrong thing; wait without love
> For love would be love for the wrong thing; there is yet faith
> But the faith and the love and the hope are all in the waiting.
> Wait without thought, for you are not ready for thought:
> So the darkness shall be the light, and the stillness the dancing.
>
> . . . .
>
> In order to arrive at what you do not know
>   You must go by a way which is the way of ignorance.
> In order to possess what you do not possess
>   You must go by the way of dispossession.
> In order to arrive at what you are not
>   You must go through the way in which you are not.
> And what you do not know is the only thing you know
> And what you own is what you do not own
> And where you are is where you are not.

---

[56]*The Collected Poems of Theodore Roethke,* p. 231.

Out of the experience of darkness and emptiness can come the encounter with the inner companion.

Jung speaks of such an experience:

> The state of imperfect transformation, merely hoped for and waited for, does not seem to be one of torment only, but of positive, if hidden, happiness. It is the state of someone who, in his wanderings among the mazes of his psychic transformation, comes upon a secret happiness which reconciles him to his apparent loneliness. In communing with himself he finds not deadly boredom and melancholy but an inner partner; more than that, a relationship that seems like the happiness of a secret love, or like a hidden springtime, when the green seed sprouts from the barren earth, holding out the promise of future harvests. It is the alchemical *benedicta viriditas,* the blessed greenness, signifying on the one hand the "leprosy of the metals" (verdigris), but on the other the secret immanence of the divine spirit of life in all things.[57]

Mortificatio leads us directly into the imagery of Christ's Passion—his mocking, flagellation, torture, and death (see figure 6-15). The alchemists sometimes explicitly connected the treatment of the material in the vessel with the treatment Christ received. For instance, one text says, "It is not unfitly compared with Christ when the putrefied body of the Sun lies dead, inactive, like ashes in the bottom of the phial.... So also did it happen to Christ himself, when at the Mount of Olives, and on the cross, he was roasted by the fire of the divine wrath (Matt. 26, 27), and complained that he was utterly deserted by his heavenly Father..."[58]

Another text reads:

> Again, as our chemical compound ... is subjected to the action of fire, and is decomposed, dissolved, and well digested, and as this process, before its consummation, exhibits various chromatic changes, so this Divine Man, and Human God, Jesus Christ, had, by the will of his heavenly Father, to pass through the furnace of affliction, that is, through many troubles, insults, and sufferings, in the course of which His outward aspect was grievously changed....
>
> Then again, the Sages have called our compound, while undergoing the process of decomposition, the Raven's Head, on account of its blackness. In the same way, Christ (Isaiah, 53) had no form nor comeliness—was despised and rejected of men—a man of sorrows and acquainted with grief—so despised, that men hid, as it were, their faces from Him....[59]

This passage connects the tortured *prima materia* not only with Christ but also with the suffering servant of Isaiah who personifies Zion and the Messiah yet to come.

This well-known saying of Jesus also belongs to *mortificatio* symbolism: "If anyone wants to be a follower of mine, let him renounce himself

---

[57]Jung, *Mysterium Coniunctionis, CW* 14, par. 623.

[58]Ibid., par. 485.

[59]Waite, trans., *The Hermetic Museum* 1:101ff.

FIGURE 6 – 15

The Scourging of Christ (Mair of Landshut, 15th century. London, British Museum. Reprinted in Hind, *An Introduction to a History of Woodcut.*)

and take up his cross and follow me. For anyone who wants to save his life will lose it; but anyone who loses his life for my sake will find it" (Matt. 16:24, 25 JB).

The same idea is expressed more starkly in the following noncanonical saying from a recently discovered Gnostic text: "Verily I say unto you, none will be saved unless they believe in my cross. But those who have believed in my cross, theirs is the kingdom of God. Therefore become seekers for death, like the dead who seek for life.... When you examine death it will teach you election. Verily I say unto you, none of those who fear death will be saved; for the kingdom of death belongs to those who put themselves to death."[60]

Psychologically we can understand this to refer to the law of opposites—the fact that the conscious experience of one side constellates its opposite in the unconscious. In Goethe's words, *stirb und werde*, die and become. To the extent that the ego consciously embraces death it constellates life in depth. This fact is related to the psychology of sacrifice. The outstanding alchemical example of the sacrificial theme is found in the visions of Zosimos, where we read: "I am Ion, the priest of the inner sanctuaries, and I submit myself to an unendurable torment. For there came one in haste at early morning, who overpowered me, and pierced me through with the sword, and dismembered me in accordance with the rule of harmony. And he drew off the skin of my head with the sword, which he wielded with strength, and mingled the bones with the pieces of flesh, and caused them to be burned upon the fire of the art, till I perceived by the transformation of the body that I had become spirit."[61]

Ion, the priest of the inner sanctuaries, is a personification of both the *prima materia* and the Philosophers' Stone. He is both the sacrificer and the sacrificed. In this respect he corresponds to the figure of Christ as pictured in Hebrews: "But now Christ has come, as the high priest of all the blessings which were to come. He has passed through the greater, the more perfect tent, which is better than the one made by men's hands because it is not of this created order, and he has entered the sanctuary once and for all, taking with him not the blood of goats and bull calves, but his own blood, having won an eternal redemption for us" (Heb. 9:11, 12 JB).

Ion, the priest who submits himself to an unendurable torment, is reminiscent of a remarkable passage in an unpublished letter by Jung:

> The problem of crucifixion is the beginning of individuation; there is the secret meaning of the Christian symbolism, a path of blood and suffering—like any other step forward on the road of the evolution of human consciousness. Can man stand a further increase of consciousness?...I confess that I submitted to the divine power of this apparently unsurmountable problem and I consciously and intentionally made my life miserable, because I wanted God to be alive and free from the suffering man has put on him by loving his own reason more than God's secret intentions.[62]

The idea of deliberately making oneself miserable is difficult doctrine. We must remember, however, that Jung is speaking to a particular

---

[60]*The Nag Hammadi Library,* pp. 31f.

[61]Jung, *Alchemical Studies, CW* 13, par. 86.

[62]Adler, "Aspects of Jung's Personality and Work," p. 12.

person in this letter. There is much evidence that Jung adjusted his mode of speaking to the reality of the person he was talking to. For instance, in talking to his American Indian friend, Mountain Lake, he told him that he, Jung, belonged to a cattle-breeding tribe that lived in the mountains. So I suspect that this letter is tailored to the psychology of the person to whom it is written. Nevertheless, its mode of expression gives us a fresh angle of vision. To pay attention to the unconscious does mean to deliberately make oneself miserable in order that the autonomous psyche will be able to function more freely. It has nothing to do with masochism but is rather a conscious participation in the process of actualizing the Deity. In the words of Meister Eckhart, "Suffering alone is sufficient preparation for God's dwelling in man's heart....God is always with a man in suffering; as he himself declared by the mouth of the prophet, 'Whosoever is sorrowful, I will myself be with him'" (probably Jer. 31:25).[63]

I am reminded of a woman who, in the course of her life, had more than her fair share of suffering and frustration. She struggled in analysis for many years to accept her fate and to master her bitterness. Her efforts were eventually crowned with a dream that contained this image:

> *I see a tree which had been struck by lightning. However, it seemed that it had not been destroyed completely, but that something of the electric power had gone through the tree and into its surroundings where it caused unusual fertility.*

This dream reminded her of a previous dream in which a goat had been sacrificed. In a picture that she drew of that dream, the blood of the sacrificed goat is fertilizing the surrounding vegetation (see figure 6-16). In fact, this woman does have a favorable effect on her surroundings. She is a gifted teacher, and her long *mortificatio* has heightened and matured her gifts. The dream of the lightning-struck tree has similarities to a dream that Jung had in 1914.

> *Frightful cold had again descended from out of the cosmos. This dream, however, had an unexpected end. There stood a leaf-bearing tree, but without fruit (my tree of life, I thought), whose leaves had been transformed by the effects of the frost into sweet grapes full of healing juices. I plucked the grapes and gave them to a large, waiting crowd.*[64]

As previously mentioned, the alchemical *mortificatio* has very close parallels to the imagery of Christ's Passion. In fact they are both expres-

63 *Meister Eckhart* 1:263.

64 Jung, *Memories, Dreams, Reflections,* p. 176.

FIGURE 6 – 16
Patient's Drawing

sions of the same archetype. However, the alchemical attitude to the Christ-image and the attitude of religious faith are very different. Jung takes great care to make the distinction in the following quotation:

> If the adept experiences his own self, the "true man," in his work, then... he encounters the analogy of the true man—Christ—in new and direct form, and he recognizes in the transformation in which he himself is involved a similarity to the Passion. It is not an "imitation of Christ" but its exact opposite: an assimilation of the Christ-image to his own self, which is the "true man." It is no longer an effort, an intentional striving after imitation, but rather an involuntary experience of the reality represented by the sacred legend.... The Passion happens to the adept, not in its classic form... but in the form expressed by the alchemical myth. It is the arcane substance that suffers those physical and moral tortures. ... It is not the adept who suffers all this, rather *it* suffers in him, *it* is tortured, *it* passes through death and rises again. All this happens, not to the alchemist himself but to the "true man," who he feels is near him and in him and at the same time in the retort.[65]

To conclude, as a previously quoted text implied, the motif of the *mortificatio* of the king has an application to the collective psyche. Our collective God-image is undergoing *mortificatio* as is indicated by the phrase "God is dead." The collective psyche is thus going through a

---

[65]Jung, *Mysterium Coniunctionis,* CW 14, par. 492.

nigredo. Jung alludes to this in his interpretation of Augustine's terms, "morning knowledge" and "evening knowledge." Morning knowledge is knowledge of the creator, evening knowledge is the knowledge of created things. Morning knowledge knows about God, evening knowledge knows about humanity. Morning knowledge is religion, evening knowledge is science. The transition from morning knowledge to evening knowledge corresponds to the fact that "every spiritual truth gradually turns into something material, becoming no more than a tool in the hand of man."[66] As more and more falls under the rational control of the ego, humanity's morning knowledge is increasingly darkened. As Jung says, "Modern man is already so darkened that nothing beyond the light of his own intellect illuminates the world. *'Occasus Christi, passio Christi.'* That surely is why such strange things are happening to our much lauded civilization, more like a *Gotterdammerung* than any normal twilight."[67]

"But just as evening gives birth to morning, so from the darkness arises a new light, the *stella matutina,* which is at once the evening and the morning star—Lucifer, the light-bringer."[68] In terms of the symbolism of the seven days of creation and the seven days of the week, it was thought that each day takes human beings farther away from their morning knowledge until "the growing darkness reaches its greatest intensity on the day of Venus (Friday), and changes into Lucifer on Saturn's day. Saturday heralds the light which appears in full strength on Sun-day.... The Sabbath is therefore the day on which man returns to God and receives anew the light of the *cognitio matutina* (morning knowledge). And this day has no evening."[69]

---

[66] *Alchemical Studies, CW* 13, par. 302.

[67] Ibid.

[68] Ibid., par. 299.

[69] Ibid., par. 301.

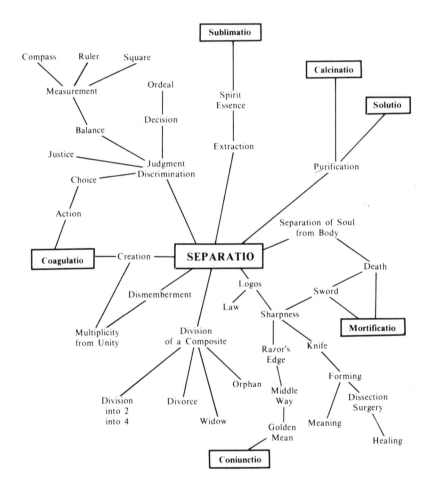

7 Separatio

THE *PRIMA MATERIA* WAS THOUGHT OF AS A COMPOSITE, a confused mixture of undifferentiated and contrary components requiring a process of separation. Images for this process are supplied by various chemical and physical procedures performed in the alchemical laboratory. Metal was extracted from its crude ore by heating, pulverizing, or various chemical means. Many substances when heated will separate into a volatile part which vaporizes and an earthy residue which remains behind. Amalgams, for instance, when heated release their mercury as vapor and leave the nonvolatile metal at the bottom of the vessel. The process of distillation will separate a more volatile liquid from a less volatile one, and evaporation separates a liquid solvent from the solid that had been dissolved in it. Filtration, sedimentation, and perhaps even crude centrifuging were available to the alchemist.

In all these examples, a composite mixture undergoes a discrimination of its component parts. Order is brought out of confusion in a process analogous to that in which cosmos is born out of chaos in creation myths. It is not surprising, therefore, that many cosmogonic myths describe creation as *separatio* (see figure 7-1). For instance, Ovid describes creation as follows:

> Before the sea was, and the lands, and the sky that hangs over all, the face of Nature showed alike in her whole round, which state have men called chaos: a rough, unordered mass of things, nothing at all save lifeless bulk and warring seeds of ill-matched elements heaped in one. No sun as yet shone forth upon the world, nor did the waxing moon renew her slender horns; not yet did the earth hang poised by her own weight in the circumambient air, nor had the ocean stretched her arms along the far reaches of the lands. And, though there was both land and sea and air, no one could tread that land, or swim that sea; and the air was dark. No form of things remained the same; all objects were at odds, for within one body cold things strove with hot, and moist with dry, soft things with hard, things having weight with weightless things.
>
> God—or kindlier Nature—composed this strife; for he rent asunder land from sky, and sea from land, and separated the ethereal heavens from the

FIGURE 7 –1
God Creating the World (Manuscript illustration, 13th century. Vienna,
Austrian National Library. Reprinted in Clark, *Civilization*.)

dense atmosphere. When thus he had released these elements and freed them
from the blind heap of things, he set them each in its own place and bound
them fast in harmony.[1]

Marie-Louise von Franz tells us that creation myths often begin with
a cosmic egg and that

after the egg has been created it is divided and generally into two parts....
Frequently one finds the same motif of a separation of a preconscious unit in
connection with the separation of the first parents. In many cosmogonic
myths the first parents, Father Heaven and Mother Earth, for instance, first
exist in a continuous embrace. They form, as it were, a hermaphroditic being

---

[1]Ovid, *Metamorphoses*, I, bk. 1, lines 5–25.

in constant cohabitation. In this state nothing can come into existence, because Father Heaven lies so closely on Mother Earth that there is no space for anything to grow between them.... The first act of creation is therefore the separation of this divine couple, pushing them sufficiently apart so that a space is created for the rest of creation. This can be compared to the cutting apart of the egg.[2] (See figure 7-2.)

An example of the separation of the World Parents is the following Egyptian creation myth:

Shu was the personification of the atmosphere and his name, meaning "to raise," derived from his most important act in mythology, the separation of his children, Geb, the earth, and Nut, the sky, which resulted in the creation of the world as men knew it. On the orders of Ra or, according to some, spurred by incestuous jealousy, Shu thrust himself between Geb and Nut, thus breaking their close embrace. Alternatively Shu was said to have been ordered by Ra to support Nut when, as a cow, she had become dizzy after raising Ra to the heights of heaven.

Shu was usually represented as a bearded man standing or kneeling over Geb with arms upraised to support Nut. On his head he wore an ostrich feather, the hieroglyph of his name, or four tall plumes, symbolising the four

FIGURE 7 – 2
Cutting the Philosophical Egg (Maier, *Atalanta Fugiens,* 1618.)

---

[2]von Franz, *Patterns of Creativity Mirrored in Creation Myths,* p. 150.

pillars of heaven which supported Nut. Sometimes he was represented as a lion, or as a column of air.

Shu's name is also said to mean "to be empty" and he was treated in some texts as emptiness deified. In others he was accorded rather more importance: as god of air, Shu was seen in the later texts as personifying the divine intelligence. He therefore became the immediate agent of Atum's creation, and hence an embodiment of Atum's supreme power. Shu was thus the god who set creation in motion, forming the world by separating earth and sky.[3] (See figure 7-3).

Alchemical texts speak of a separation of earth and sky taking place in the retort. For instance, Ripley says the following:

> Separation thus must thou oft times make,
> Thy matter dividing into parts two;
> So that the Simple from the gross thou take
> Till earth remain beneath in color blue,
> That earth is fix for to abide all woe:

FIGURE 7 - 3

The Separation of Heaven and Earth: Nut Lifted Above Geb by Shu (Drawing after an illustration in A. Jeremias, *Das Alte Testament im Lichte des Alten Orients,* Leipzig, 1904. Turin, Egyptian Museum. Reprinted in Neumann, *The Origins and History of Consciousness.*)

---

[3]Ions, *Egyptian Mythology,* p. 46.

> The other part is Spiritual and fleeing,
> But thou must turn them all into one thing.[4]

Again, in the *Emerald Tablet* we read, "Separate the earth from the fire, the subtle from the dense, gently with great ingenuity."[5] Psychologically, the result of *separatio* by division into two is awareness of the opposites. This is a crucial feature of emerging consciousness.

In the evolution of Western consciousness, the opposites (*enantia*) were discovered by the pre-Socratic philosophers. The Pythagoreans established a table of ten pairs of opposites:[6]

1. limit (*peras*) ——————: unlimited (*apeiron*)
2. odd (*peritton*) : even (*artion*)
3. one (*hen*) : many (*plēthos*)
4. right (*dexion*) : left (*aristeron*)
5. male (*arren*) : female (*thēlu*)
6. resting (*ēremoun*) : moving (*kinoumenon*)
7. straight (*euthu*) : curved, crooked (*kampulon*)
8. light (*phōs*) : darkness (*skotos*)
9. good (*agathon*) : bad (*kakon*)
10. square (*tetragōnon*) : oblong (*heteromēkes*)

The psychological significance of the discovery of the opposites can hardly be overestimated. Like numbers, the newly discovered opposites carried an aura of numinosity for the ancients. The world had been rent asunder, and between the separated opposites space had been created, room for the conscious human ego to live and to grow.

The elemental *separatio* that ushers in conscious existence is the separation of subject from object, the I from the not-I. This is the first pair of opposites. Shu can separate Geb from Nut only after achieving a prior separation of himself from them. Shu thus signifies the primordial ego, the splitter of opposites, who creates space for the existence of consciousness. To the extent that the opposites remain unconscious and unseparated, one lives in a state of *participation mystique*, which means that one identifies with one side of a pair of opposites and projects its contrary as an enemy. Space for consciousness to exist appears *between* the opposites, which means that one becomes conscious as one is able to contain and endure the opposites within.

A major aspect of psychotherapy is the process of *separatio*, of which the most important component is the separation of subject and object. The immature ego is notorious for its state of *participation mystique*

---

[4]Ashmole, ed., *Theatrum Chemicum Britannicum*, p. 140.

[5]Cf. *The Lives of the Alchemystical Philosophers*, p. 383.

[6]Aristotle, *Metaphysics*, 986a 22, in *The Basic Works of Aristotle*.

with both the inner and the outer worlds. Such an ego must go through a prolonged process of differentiation between subject and object. As this proceeds, disidentification with other pairs of opposites also occurs.

The alchemist says, "Separate the earth from the fire, the subtle from the dense." Psychologically this can be applied to the separation of the concrete, literal aspects of an experience from its attached libido and inner symbolic meaning—that is, a separation of the subjective and objective components. A common problem in psychotherapy is conflict and ambivalence concerning a practical decision. Should I take this job? Should I make this move? Should I marry or divorce? The basis of such conflicts is often a lack of distinction between the concrete and the symbolic meanings of the proposed action. It may be, for instance, that a person obsessed with the idea of divorce but unable to act is being required to bring about a psychic separation from his or her spouse, a symbolic divorce, rather than a literal one. At any rate, the concrete and the symbolic are two different levels of reality that need to be distinguished and considered separately. When this is done, the objective decision is often easily reached.

Creation by *separatio* is also described as division into four. Paracelsus says: "In the creation of the world, the first separation began with the four elements, when the first matter of the world was one chaos. From that chaos God built the Greater World, separated into four distinct elements, Fire, Air, Water, Earth."[7] Again, in the *Golden Treatise of Hermes* we read: "Understand ye then, O sons of wisdom, that the knowledge of the four elements of the ancient philosophers was not corporally or imprudently sought after, which are through patience to be discovered according to their causes and their occult operation.... Know, then, that the division that was made upon the Water, by the ancient philosophers, separates it into four substances."[8]

These passages hark back to Plato's account in the *Timaeus*, in which he speaks of chaos in the process of creation

> being full of powers which were neither similar nor equally balanced, was never in any part in a state of equipoise, but swaying unevenly hither and thither, was shaken by them, and by its motion again shook them, and the elements when moved were separated and carried continually, some one way, some another. As, when grain is shaken and winnowed by fans and other instruments used in the threshing of corn, the close and heavy particles are borne away and settle in one direction, and the loose and light particles in another. In this manner, the four kinds or elements were then shaken by the receiving vessel.[9]

[7] Waite, trans., *Hermetic and Alchemical Writings*, p. 160.

[8] *The Golden Treatise of Hermes* in Atwood, *Hermetic Philosophy and Alchemy*, p. 106.

[9] Plato, *Timaeus*, in *The Collected Dialogues*, p. 1179.

A more complex account of creation by *separatio* is found in Philo, as summarized by Goodenough:

> God projects the Logos which is the principle of unity and which at the same time is given the peculiar name the "Cutter." The Logos-Cutter forms first the intelligible world (world of archetypal forms) and then the material world after the manner and model of the intelligible world. Crude matter, which is again a datum of creation, was first bisected by the Logos-Cutter into light and heavy, then these two were each bisected to produce four, which became the four elements. Each of these was again divided, as earth into mainland and islands, water into fresh and salt. The process of division kept on until it had produced animate and inanimate objects, wild and cultivated fruits, wild and tame animals, male and female, and the rest. In every case the division was not only a separation but a reunion, for the Logos was the Glue as well as the Cutter; that is, it was the principle of cohesion which makes the universe a unit in spite of its manifold divisions.[10]

This passage is remarkable for its loyalty to the opposites in its description of the cosmogonic principle. What is here called Logos is actually Logos-Eros, since it is not only a cutting edge but also a glue. This way of thinking is absolutely alchemical and corresponds to some of the paradoxical descriptions of Mercurius.[11]

The motif of division into the four elements corresponds psychologically to the application of all four functions to a given experience. Sensation tells us what the facts are. Thinking determines in what general concepts the facts can be placed. Feeling tells us whether or not we like the facts. Intuition suggests where the facts may have come from, what they may lead to, and what connections they may have with other facts. It presents possibilities, not certainties.

It is important that the four functions be separated. For example, one's feeling reaction to a fact should not hinder one's ability to see its existence; or, a possibility should not be confused with a certainty. Although the four elements cannot be equated precisely with the four functions, there is an approximate parallel. There is a similar approximation with the four suits of the Tarot: Swords, Cups, Coins, and Staves (see figure 7-4). Each of these fourfold patterns is a particular embodiment of the Quaternity archetype, which structures undifferentiated matter. Specifically, the four elements signify the four different degrees of material aggregation, ranging from disembodied energy (fire) to full solidity (earth). Presumably, there are analogous degrees of aggregation of the psychic substance that remain to be elucidated.

Every newly encountered area of the unconscious requires a cosmogonic act of *separatio.* Each new increment of *prima materia* calls forth

---

[10]Goodenough, *An Introduction to Philo Judaeus,* pp. 107f.

[11]Jung, *Alchemical Studies, CW* 13, par. 267.

FIGURE 7 – 4
The Aces of the Four Tarot Suits: Swords, Staves, Coins, and Cups
(Marseilles Tarot.)

a sharp-edged action by Philo's "Logos-Cutter." The creation of consciousness requires that new contents be carved out of the unconscious. The dream of a middle-aged man of multiple talents and ambitions who was torn between different professions and different life-goals illustrates this issue:

> *Pieces of a map were to be cut out and assembled. A sharp blade was needed. In the dream I could not get the blade sharp enough.*

The dreamer needed a better contact with the Logos-Cutter than he had as yet achieved.

Swords, knives, and sharp cutting edges of all kinds belong to the symbolism of *separatio*. It is surely significant that one of the first tools of aboriginal human beings was a cutting edge. Logos is the great agent of *separatio*, that brings consciousness and power over nature—both within and without—by its capacity to divide, name, and categorize. One of its major symbols is the cutting edge that can dissect and differentiate on the one hand and can kill on the other. By separating the opposites, the Logos brings clarity; but, by making the opposites visible, it also brings conflict. An example of this paradoxical symbolism is the classic *separatio* text in the Gospels: "I have not come to bring peace, but a sword. For I have come to set a man against his father, and a daughter against her mother, and a daughter-in-law against her mother-in-law; and a man's foes will be those of his own household" (Matt. 10:34–36, RSV). (See figure 7-5.)

An even sterner version of the same idea is found in the Gnostic *Gospel of Thomas*: "Jesus said, 'Men think, perhaps, that it is peace which I have come to cast upon the world. They do not know that it is dissension which I have come to cast upon the earth: fire, sword, and war. For there will be five in a house: three will be against two, and two against three, the father against the son, and the son against the father. And they will stand solitary.'"[12]

Christ, the Self as Logos-Cutter, comes to dissect or dismember the *participation mystique* of the family psyche ("a man's foes will be those of his own household"). The Gnostic version states explicitly that the goal is to make the individual ("they will stand solitary").

Separatio may be expressed by images of death or killing. Death dreams and death wishes directed against a particular person often indicate the need for separation from a relationship of unconscious identification that has become suffocating. A *separatio* process may be heralded by increasing conflict and antagonism in a previously amicable

a second knowing that now unifies

---

[12]*The Nag Hammadi Library*, p. 120.

FIGURE 7 – 5
Christ of the Apocalypse (Dürer. Reprinted in *The Complete Woodcuts of
Albrecht Dürer.*)

relationship. If the participants lack an understanding of what they are experiencing the process may become dangerous or even violent. This will be especially likely if a relationship of unconscious identification is standing in the way of the activated urge to individuation. A man in such a situation had this dream:

> *It is night. There is the feeling that dawn is approaching. Two shepherds dressed in sheepskin, holding staffs and identical in looks are on a mountain path. There is an intense look in both their eyes that says they know they must go their separate ways. One has the look of the desire for vengeance and the other has a feeling of sadness. They embrace and kiss each other on the cheek with a kiss of peace and the one who had the feeling of sadness begins his climb up the mountain. The other shepherd pauses and looks at him as though to say, "I could have killed you!" and then turns and goes down the mountain and dawn has arrived.*

This dream pictures the purely archetypal aspect of the *separatio* process that was activated between the dreamer and his friend. Devoid of personal features, it is as though the dream were speaking to the ego about the loss of its friend in the same fashion as John Milton wrote his poem *Lycidas* to mourn the drowning of Edward King, or as Shelley wrote his *Adonais* at the death of John Keats. The archetypal pattern behind the personal event is revealed, which sets it in a larger context, brings comfort to the bereaved, and illuminates the tragedy with meaning. Such dreams are apt to come when the situation is particularly dangerous. It seems that, as with all instincts, archetypal wisdom is called forth in times of greatest need.

Eris, the Goddess of Discord and sister of Ares, presides over *separatio*. It was she who came uninvited to a marriage on Olympus and flung into the midst of the gathering an apple inscribed "to the fairest." Thus she brought about the judgement of Paris. Comparisons are odious and comparison is what the golden apple provoked. To determine what is "more" and what is "most" requires and leads to judgements. Such actions disturb the *participation mystique* of the status quo and generate conflict, but they may lead to greater consciousness. Thus Heraclitus says, "War (between the opposites) is the father of all and the king of all, and some he shows as gods, others as men; some he makes slaves, others free."[13] (See figure 7-6.)

---

[13]Kirk and Raven, *The PreSocratic Philosophers,* p. 195.

FIGURE 7 – 6

Joust Between Sol and Luna (*Aurora Consurgens,* 14th century. Zurich, Zentralbibliothek, Cod. rhenovacensis 172, fol. 10. Reprinted in Derola, *The Secret Art of Alchemy.*)

Eris' golden apple brought comparison, judgement, choice, and war. The burden fell on Paris, the human victim of divine buck passing, to make a judgement among Hera, Athena, and Aphrodite. The innocent shepherd was faced with an ordeal of manhood requiring him to choose his central life-value among power, knowledge, and beauty. His choice was an act of *separatio* and led him on to the next stage of development. In an alchemical picture (see figure 7-7), the judgement of Paris is accompanied by the awakening of a sleeping king. This suggests that such an act of judgement can bring into consciousness a connection with the Self.

Separatio may be wrongly applied, in which case it will be destructive. It is improper to divide an organic whole mechanically in the name of an arbitrary notion of equality. Paris tried to evade his responsibility by suggesting that the apple be divided into three equal parts, but this was not allowed. There is a similar idea in the story of the judgement of Solomon. Two women came before Solomon, each claiming to be the mother of the same child.

> Bring me a sword said the king; and a sword was brought into the king's presence. "Cut the living child in two," the king said, "and give half to one, half to the other." At this the woman who was the mother of the living child addressed the king, for she burned with pity for her son. "If it please you, my lord," she said, "let them give her the child; only do not let them think of

FIGURE 7 – 7
The Awakening of the Sleeping King as a Judgment of Paris (Thomas Aquinas
[pseud.], "De Alchemia," 16th century. Leiden, Bibliothek der Rijksuniversiteit,
Cod. Vossianus 29, fol. 78. Reprinted in Jung, *Psychology and Alchemy.*)

killing it!" But the other said, "He shall belong to neither of us. Cut him up."
Then the king gave his decision. "Give the child to the first woman," he said,
"and do not kill him. She is his mother." All Israel came to hear of the
judgement the king had pronounced, and held the king in awe, recognising
that he possessed divine wisdom for dispensing justice. (1 Kings 3:24–28, JB)

A living whole may not be carved up into equal portions in order to
satisfy opposing standpoints. This is a danger for one who knows the
theory of the union of opposites but not its living reality. A striking
image of *separatio* gone wrong is found in canto 28 of Dante's *Inferno,*

This is what we have done with the earth

in which the sowers of discord are subject to eternal mutilation by sharp blades (see figure 7–8):

> No cask without an end stave or a head
> E'er gaped so wide as one shade I beheld,
> Cloven from chin to where the wind is voided.
> Between his legs his entrails hung in coils;
> The vitals were exposed to view, and too
> That sorry paunch which changes food to filth.
> While I stood all absorbed in watching him
> He looked at me and stretched his breast apart,
> Saying: "Behold, how I now split myself!
> Behold, how mutilated is Mahomet!
> In front of me the weeping Ali goes,
> His face cleft through from forelock to the chin;
> And all the others that you see about
> Fomenters were of discord and of schism:

FIGURE 7 – 8
Schismatics (Doré, *Illustrations for Dante's Divine Comedy.*)

And that is why they are so gashed asunder.
"A demon stands behind here, unrelenting,
Who tricks us cruelly; for every one
Must taste again the keenness of his blade
When he has trod the path of anguish round;
And all the wounds are healed and well again
Ere one of us may pass once more before him."[14]

This passage reminds me of certain people who have nothing but the sharp blade of rational intellect with which to understand their tender and sensitive soul-life. Their self-examination is a perpetual torture of self-dissection.

Measurement, numbering, weighing, and quantitative consciousness in general belong to the operation of *separatio*. So, likewise, do applied arithmetic, the geometrical imagery of lines, planes, and solids, and the surveyor's and navigator's procedures of setting boundaries, measuring distances, and establishing locations within a system of coordinates. Thus, compass, ruler, square, scales, sextant, and plumb line all pertain to *separatio*, as do clocks and other modes of temporal reckoning. The very categories of space and time, the foundation of conscious existence, are the products of *separatio* (see figure 7-9).

The ancients held in high esteem their newly discovered insights regarding numbers, measurement, and relations between quantities. Proportion and the mean between extremes evoked particular fascination. According to Plato's account, the Demiurge created the world by means of proportion.[15] The early geometers attached special significance to an ideal proportion achieved by the so-called *golden section*. This is done by bisecting a line of given magnitude in such a way that the lesser part is to the greater part as the greater part is to the whole. Thus, if a line of length c is bisected into a shorter part a and a longer part b, the proportion will be $a \mid b = b \mid c$; b will be the so-called golden mean. This proportion was considered to be the most beautiful one.

The golden section is a very interesting *separatio* symbol. It expresses the idea that there is a particular way to separate the opposites that will create a third thing (the proportion or mean between them) of great value. The value is indicated by the term golden and by the presumed beauty of the proportion. The same image of the mean was used by Aristotle in an ethical context to define the nature of virtue. He writes: "Moral virtue is a mean. It is a mean between two vices, the one involving excess, the other deficiency. It is such because its character is to aim at what is intermediate in passions and in actions, . . . Hence also it is no

---

[14]Dante, *The Divine Comedy,* trans. Lawrence Grant White, p. 49.

[15]*Timaeus,* 31b–32c, in *The Collected Dialogues,* p. 1163.

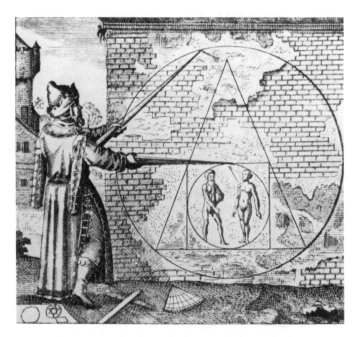

FIGURE 7 – 9
The Alchemist as Geometer (Maier, *Atalanta Fugiens,* 1618.)

easy task to be good. For in everything it is no easy task to find the middle, e.g., to find the middle of a circle is not for everyone but for him who knows."[16]

The image of the golden mean can be understood psychologically as a symbolic expression of the ego's relation to the Self. This accounts for the numinosity of the idea of the golden section to the ancients. This slender geometric parable contains the same mystery as the dogma of the Christian Trinity.

Not only is virtue associated with a mean or balance between the opposites, but also law (*jus*) and justice. The balance in the hand of the traditional personification of Justice indicates that justice is a balance between the opposites (see figure 7-10). Nature is just, but the coming of consciousness splits the opposites apart and is a crime, according to the myths. Anaximander says, "Things perish into those things out of which they have their birth, according to that which is ordained; for they give reparation to one another and pay the penalty of their injustice accord-

---

[16]Aristotle, *Nicomachean Ethics,* in *The Basic Works of Aristotle,* p. 963.

FIGURE 7 – 10
Justice (Marseilles Tarot.)

Present Moment

ing to the disposition of time."[17] Cornford interprets this to mean that "injustice was committed by the very fact of their birth into separate existence. The manifold world, in Anaximander's view, can arise only by robbery and misappropriation."[18] In other words, the separation of the opposites is the original crime, and justice can be served only by their reconciliation. This is achieved by death or perhaps, alternatively, by individuation.

original crime!!

---

[17]Cited in Cornford, *From Religion to Philosophy,* p. 8.
[18]Ibid., p. 10.

Just as the establishment of limit, measure, and line brings order out of chaos, so a loss of boundaries can reverse the process. Emerson describes such a situation in the following lines from his poem "Uriel." Uriel addressed the gods and

> Gave his sentiment divine
> Against the being of a line.
> "Line in nature is not found;
> Unit and universe are round;
> In vain produced, all rays return;
> Evil will bless, and ice will burn."
> As Uriel spoke with piercing eye,
> A shudder ran around the sky;
> The stern old war-gods shook their heads,
> The seraphs frowned from myrtle-beds;
> Seemed to the holy festival
> The rash word boded ill to all;
> The balance-beam of Fate was bent;
> The bounds of good and ill were rent;
> Strong Hades could not keep his own,
> But all slid to confusion.[19]

Robert Frost's poem "Mending Wall" takes up the same theme—that is, the conflict between the author's sentiment, "Something there is that doesn't love a wall," and his neighbor's idea that "Good fences make good neighbors."[20] Too much concern with *separatio* constellates its opposite, *coniunctio,* and Mercurius reverses himself from Logos-Cutter to Eros-Glue.

Another aspect of *separatio* is conveyed by the term *extractio.* Extraction is a particular case of separation. Ruland says, "Extraction is the separation of the essential part from its body."[21] A graphic description of *extractio* is presented in this recipe: "Go to the waters of the Nile and there you will find a stone that has a spirit (*pneuma*). Take this, divide it, thrust in your hand and draw out its heart; for its soul (*psyche*) is in its heart."[22]

The image of extraction from a stone is found also in Ripley:

> And of this separation I find a like figure
> Thus spoken by the prophet in the Psalmody.
> God brought out of a stone a flood of water pure,
> And out of the hardest stone oil abundantly:

---

[19]Emerson, "Uriel," in *Selected Writings of Ralph Waldo Emerson,* p. 764.

[20]Frost, "Mending Wall," in *Complete Poems of Robert Frost,* p. 47.

[21]Ruland, *A Lexicon of Alchemy,* p. 139.

[22]Cited by Jung, *Psychology and Alchemy, CW* 12, par. 405.

Right so of our precious stone if thou be witty,
Oil incombustible and water thou shalt draw.[23]

This text probably refers to Psalms 8:15 (RSV): "He cleft rocks in the
wilderness, and gave them drink abundantly as from the deep. He made
streams come out of the rock, and caused waters to flow down like
rivers" (see figure 7-11). The other reference may be to Job 29:5–7
(RSV): "When the Almighty was yet with me...when my steps were
washed with milk and the rock poured out for me streams of oil."

These texts that speak of the extraction of spirit, water, and oil from
a stone are expressing paradoxical, miraculous events and thus refer to
the Self. The miraculous agent is the Philosophers' Stone, which is
identified with Yahweh by the biblical associations. When the stony
facts of the world yield living meaning (as in events of synchronicity),
one glimpses the goal of the *opus*. In order for this to happen, spirit,
meaning, and libido must be extracted from matter—that is, from the
concrete objects of our yearning.

The separation of spirit and matter is an important feature of many
religions and philosophies. For instance, the thirteenth chapter of the

FIGURE 7 – 11
Moses Striking Water from the Rock (Biblia Pauperum Bavaria, 1414. Munich,
Bayerische Staatsbibliothek, Clm. 8201, fol. 86v. Reprinted in Evans, *Medieval
Drawings*.)

---

[23]Ashmole, ed., *Theatrum Chemicum Britannicum*, p. 139.

Bhagavad-Gita is entitled "The Book of Religion by Separation of Matter and Spirit" and concludes with these verses:

> That Ultimate, High Spirit, Uncreate,
> Unqualified, even when it entereth flesh
> Taketh no stain of acts, worketh in naught!
> Like to th' etherial air, pervading all,
> Which, for sheer subtlety, avoideth taint,
> The subtle Soul sits everywhere, unstained;
> Like to the light of the all-piercing sun
> (Which is not changed by aught it shines upon)
> The Soul's light shineth pure in every place;
> And they who, by such eye of wisdom, see
> How Matter, and what deals with it, divide;
> And how the Spirit and the flesh have strife,
> Those wise ones go the way which leads to Life![24]

In the texts previously cited, *separatio* has been described as the separation of the fixed earth from the fleeing spirit, the subtle from the dense, and the spirit from the stone that was imprisoning it. Another expression for it is the separation of the soul from the body. For example, Kelly speaks of "when the soul of gold has been separated from its body, or when the body, in other words, has been dissolved."[25] The separation of the soul from the body is synonymous with death.[26] For instance, Plato says, "We believe, do we not, that death is the separation of the soul from the body, and that the state of being dead is the state in which the body is separated from the soul and exists alone by itself and the soul is separated from the body and exists alone by itself."[27]

As indicated in the last chapter, *separatio* is closely connected to the symbolism of *mortificatio*, which means that *separatio* may be experienced as death. The extraction of the spirit from the stone or the soul from the body corresponds to the extraction of meaning or psychic value from a particular, concrete object or situation. The body—that is, the concrete manifestation of the psychic content—then dies. This corresponds to the withdrawal of a projection, which, if sizable, entails a mourning process. Thus, the death of a loved one is an aspect of individuation. The death of a parent, a sibling, a child, a lover, or a spouse is an individuation crisis that challenges elementary states of identification and *participation mystique*. The ego's unconscious connection

---

[24] *The Song Celestial or Bhagavad-Gita*, p. 121.

[25] Kelly, *The Alchemical Writings of Edward Kelly*, pp. 133f.

[26] Jung, *The Practice of Psychotherapy*, CW 16, fig. 7.

[27] Plato, *Phaedo*, 64c, in *Plato* 1:223ff.

with the Self is embedded in these primary identifications, and therefore the occasion of such a death is crucial. Either it will lead to an increased realization of the Self, or, if the potential for consciousness is aborted, then negative, regressive, and even fatal effects may follow. It is not unusual, after a major bereavement, for the surviving one to die soon after by suicide, accident, or fatal illness.

The images of widow, widower, or orphan belong to this symbolism.[28] They are separated ones who are on their way to the "indivisible." The ancient Greek philosophers were preoccupied with the idea of an indivisible magnitude (*atomon megethos*), which might be reached by an infinite series of divisions. The goal of *separatio* is to reach the indivisible—that is, the individual.[29] For Anaxagoras, the one indivisible entity is Nous, which also initiates the process of *separatio*. I quote in full his important Fragment 12 (Diels):

> All other things partake in a portion of everything, while Nous is infinite and self-ruled, and is mixed with nothing, but is alone, itself by itself. For if it were not by itself, but were mixed with anything else, it would partake in all things if it were mixed with any; for in everything there is a portion of everything, as has been said by me in what goes before, and the things mixed with it would hinder it, so that it would have power over nothing in the same way that it has now being alone by itself. For it is the thinnest of all things and the purest, and it has all knowledge about everything and the greatest strength; and Nous has power over all things, both greater and smaller, that have life. And Nous had power over the whole revolution, so that it began to revolve in the beginning. And it began to revolve first from a small beginning; but the revolution now extends over a larger space, and will extend over a larger still. And all the things that are mingled together and separated off and distinguished are all known by Nous. And Nous set in order all things that were to be, and all things that were and are not now and that are, and this revolution in which now revolve the stars and the sun and the moon, and the air and the aether that are separated off. And this revolution caused the separating off, and the rare is separated off from the dense, the warm from the cold, the light from the dark, and the dry from the moist. And there are many portions in many things. But no thing is altogether separated off nor distinguished from anything else except Nous. And all Nous is alike, both the greater and the smaller; while nothing else is like anything else, but each single thing is and was most manifestly those things of which it has most in it.[30]

The Nous of Anaxagoras can be understood psychologically as the Self in its dynamic aspect, which is both the source and goal of the *separatio* operation.

---

[28]Jung, *Mysterium Coniunctionis, CW* 14, pars. 13ff.

[29]The word "individual" is cognate with the word "widow." See Edinger, *Ego and Archetype,* p. 163.

[30]Burnet, *Early Greek Philosophy,* pp. 259f.

A very interesting *separatio* text is found in Hippolytus' account of the doctrine of Basilides, the Gnostic:

> All the events in our Lord's life occurred...he says, in order that Jesus might become the first-fruits of the distinction of the different orders (of created objects) that has been confused together. For when the world had been divided into an Ogdoad, which is the head of the entire world...and into a Hebdomad...the Demiurge of subjacent entities, and into this order of creatures (that prevails) amongst us, where exists Formlessness, it was requisite that the various orders of created objects that had been confounded together should be distinguished by a separating process performed by Jesus.... Jesus, therefore, became the first-fruits of the distinction of the various orders of created objects, and his Passion took place for not any other reason than the distinction that was thereby brought about in the various orders of created objects that had been confounded together.[31]

This text takes on special importance because Jung used a portion of it as a motto for his book *Aion*. It suggests the interesting psychological idea that Christ's Passion brings about a separation of personal and archetypal contents ("various orders of created objects"). This is reminiscent of another *separatio* image in the Gospel of Luke in which Jesus says, "I watched Satan fall like lightning from heaven" (10:18 JB). Jung says about this passage: "In this vision a metaphysical event has become temporal: it indicates the historic and—so far as we know—final separation of Yahweh from his dark son. Satan is banished from heaven and no longer has any opportunity to inveigle his father into dubious undertakings."[32]

The advent of Christian symbolism brought with it a decisive separation of the opposites, good and evil, in the Godhead. Christ offered himself as a sacrifice (first-fruits) to appease the wrathful side of Yahweh and thereby brought about the separation between Yahweh and Satan (see figure 7-12). At the same time, according to the Gnostic text, there occurred a "distinction in the various orders of created objects that had been confounded together." I take this to mean that Christ's Passion purged the human ego by separating personal from transpersonal contents, which had been confounded together in an inflated mixture.

Another powerful *separatio* document has also been expressed in the name of Basilides, namely, Jung's inspired writing entitled, "Seven Sermons to the Dead." The relevant portion is as follows:

> Our very nature is distinctiveness. If we are not true to this nature we do not distinguish ourselves enough. Therefore must we make distinctions of qualities. What is the harm, ye ask, in not distinguishing oneself? If we do not distinguish, we get beyond our own nature, away from creatura. We fall into

[31]Hippolytus, "The Refutation of All Heresies," in *The Ante-Nicene Fathers* 5:109.
[32]Jung, *Psychology and Religion, CW* 11, par. 650.

FIGURE 7 – 12
Crucifixion and Last Judgement (H. Van Eyck. New York, The
Metropolitan Museum of Art. Reprinted in *Masterpieces of Painting in
the Metropolitan Museum of Art.*)

indistinctiveness, which is the other quality of the pleroma. We fall into the pleroma itself and cease to be creatures. We are given over to dissolution in the nothingness. This is the death of the creature. Therefore we die in such measure as we do not distinguish. Hence the natural striving of the creature goeth towards distinctiveness, fighteth against primeval, perilous sameness. This is called the PRINCIPIUM INDIVIDUATIONIS. This principle is the essence of the creature. From this you can see why indistinctiveness and nondistinction are a great danger for the creature.

We must, therefore, distinguish the qualities of the pleroma. The qualities are PAIRS OF OPPOSITES, such as—

> The Effective and the Ineffective.
> Fullness and Emptiness.
> Living and Dead.
> Difference and Sameness.
> Light and Darkness.
> The Hot and the Cold.
> Force and Matter.
> Time and Space.
> Good and Evil.
> Beauty and Ugliness.
> The One and the Many, etc.

The pairs of opposites are qualities of the pleroma which are not, because each balanceth each. As we are the pleroma itself, we also have all these qualities in us. Because the very ground of our nature is distinctiveness, therefore we have these qualities in the name and sign of distinctiveness, which meaneth—

1. These qualities are distinct and separate in us one from the other, therefore they are not balanced and void, but are effective. Thus are we the victims of the pairs of opposites. The pleroma is rent in us.

2. The qualities belong to the pleroma, and only in the name and sign of distinctiveness can and must we possess or live them. We must distinguish ourselves from qualities. In the pleroma they are balanced and void; in us not. Being distinguished from them delivereth us.

When we strive after the good or the beautiful, we thereby forget our own nature, which is distinctiveness, and we are delivered over to the qualities of the pleroma, which are pairs of opposites. We labor to attain to the good and the beautiful, yet at the same time we also lay hold of the evil and the ugly, since in the pleroma these are one with the good and the beautiful. When, however, we remain true to our own nature, which is distinctiveness, we distinguish ourselves from the good and the beautiful, and, therefore, at the same time, from the evil and the ugly. And thus we fall not into the pleroma, namely, into nothingness and dissolution.[33]

A profound expression of the *separatio* archetype is encountered in the symbolism of the Last Judgment. The notion of a postmortem judgment is found in almost all cultures. Psychologically, this idea can be understood as a projection into the afterlife of an anticipated encounter with the Self that will determine whether or not one has reached

---

[33] Jung, *Memories, Dreams, Reflections* (New York: Vintage, 1963), Appendix 5, pp. 380ff. (This appendix is missing from the hard-cover edition.)

the condition of indivisibility. According to ancient Egyptian religion, the soul of the deceased was weighed on a balance against a feather signifying Maat, the Goddess of Truth. If it balanced, the deceased was escorted victoriously into the presence of Osiris. If not, the soul was fed to a waiting monster (see figure 7-13).

The Gospels present another version of *separatio* at the Last Judgement. "When the Son of man shall come in his glory, and all the holy angels with him, then shall he sit upon the throne of his glory: And before him shall be gathered all nations: and he shall separate them one from another, as a shepherd divideth his sheep from the goats: And he shall set the sheep on his right hand, but the goats on the left" (Matt. 25:31–33, AV).

The text informs us further that the sheep will inherit the kingdom, whereas the goats will be sent into everlasting fire. Again, this can be understood as an encounter with the Self transferred to the afterlife. It is as though the Last Judgment separates the completed ones from the incomplete. The incomplete ones are subjected to further *calcinatio* and perhaps other operations (see figure 7-14).

In spite of the apparent finality of the Egyptian and Christian versions of the Last Judgement, according to alchemy, *separatio* is not a final process. It is described as a beginning or intermediate operation that is a

FIGURE 7 – 13
The Soul of the Deceased is Weighed in the Balance (From the papyrus
of Ani, The British Museum. Reprinted in Budge, *The
Gods of the Egyptians.*)

FIGURE 7 -14

The Archangel Michael Weighing Souls (Van der Weyden, 15th century. Bourgogne, Hospice de Beaume. Reprinted in Brandon, The Judgement of the
Dead.)

prerequisite for the greater *coniunctio*. The *Aurora Consurgens* says,
"...a certain purification of things precedeth the work of perfect preparation, which by some is called administration or cleansing (*mundificatio*), by others rectification, and by some it is called washing (*ablutio*)
or separation."[34] Kelly quotes Avicenna: "Purify husband and wife
separately, in order that they may unite more intimately; for if you do
not purify them, they cannot love each other."[35] These texts state that
separatio must precede *coniunctio*, and they also speak of it as a cleansing operation. This corresponds psychologically to the fact that attitudes
contaminated by unconscious complexes give one the distinct impression
of being soiled or dirty. Kelly says:

> When the soul of gold has been separated from its body, or when the
> body, in other words, has been dissolved, the body of the Moon should
> be watered with its proper menstruum and reverberated.... For unless the
> moon or Earth is properly prepared and entirely emptied of its soul, it will
> not be fit to receive the Solar Seed; but the more thoroughly the earth is
> cleansed of its impurity and earthiness, the more vigorous it will be in the
> fixation of its ferment. This earth or moon of the Sages is the trunk upon
> which the solar branch of the Sages is engrafted.[36]

The product of the cleansing of the earth is the so-called "white
foliated earth."[37] This is then brought together with the purified "sun"
or "gold" principle by the recipe: "Sow your gold in white earth."[38] The
two protagonists—sun and moon, husband and wife, earth and spirit—
stand for all the pairs of opposites. They must be thoroughly cleansed
from contamination with each other, which means diligent and prolonged scrutiny of one's complexes. When the *separatio* is completed,
then the purified opposites can be reconciled in the *coniunctio*, which is
the goal of the *opus*.

---

[34]von Franz, *Aurora Consurgens*, pp. 94ff.

[35]Kelly, *The Alchemical Writings of Edward Kelly*, p. 35.

[36]Ibid., pp. 133f.

[37]Cited in Jung, *Mysterium Coniunctionis*, *CW* 14, par. 154 n. 181.

[38]Maier, *Atalanta Fugiens*, cited by Read in *Prelude to Chemestry*, facing p. 57. See
Figure 4-10, p. 106.

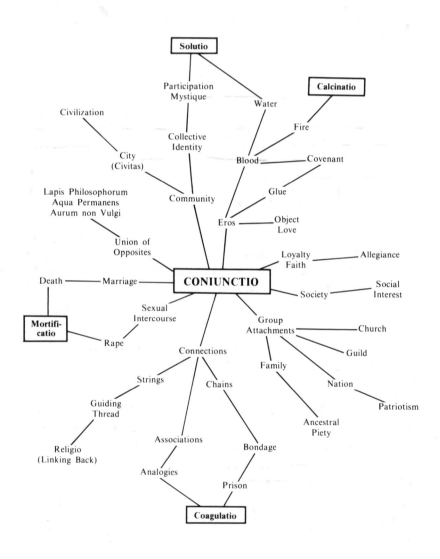

$\mathbf{8}$ Coniunctio

THE *CONIUNCTIO* IS THE CULMINATION OF THE *OPUS*. Historically, as well as psychologically, it has both an extraverted and an introverted aspect. The alchemists' fascination with the *coniunctio* on the extraverted side promoted a study of the miracle of chemical combination and led to modern chemistry and nuclear physics. On the introverted side, it generated interest in unconscious imagery and processes, leading to twentieth-century depth psychology.

The alchemists had the opportunity to witness in their laboratories many examples of both chemical and physical combination in which two substances come together to create a third substance with different properties. These experiences provided important images for alchemical fantasy. An impressive example of physical combination is the fusion of molten metals and, in particular, the formation of amalgams by the union of mercury with other metals. The common alchemical image of the sun and moon entering the mercurial fountain had its origin in the dissolving of gold and silver in mercury. In the realm of chemical combination an impressive example available to the alchemists is the union of mercury and sulphur to make red mercuric sulphide ($Hg + S \rightarrow HgS$). This chemical reaction may have been the original laboratory image that underlay the idea of the red stone of the philosophers.

In attempting to understand the rich and complex symbolism of the *coniunctio* it is advisable to distinguish two phases: a lesser *coniunctio* and a greater. The lesser *coniunctio* is a union or fusion of substances that are not yet thoroughly separated or discriminated. It is always followed by death or *mortificatio*. The greater *coniunctio*, on the other hand, is the goal of the *opus*, the supreme accomplishment. In actual reality these two aspects are combined with each other. The experience of the *coniunctio* is almost always a mixture of the lesser and the greater aspects. However, for descriptive purposes it is helpful to distinguish the two.

The Lesser *Coniunctio*

The union of opposites that have been imperfectly separated character-izes the nature of the lesser *coniunctio*. The product is a contaminated mixture that must be subjected to further procedures. The product of the lesser *coniunctio* is pictured as killed, maimed, or fragmented (an overlap with *solutio* and *mortificatio* symbolism). For example, refer-ring to the marriage of Mother Beya and her son Gabritius, a text reads: "But this marriage, which was begun with the expression of great joyfulness, ended in the bitterness of mourning. 'Within the flower itself there grows the gnawing canker: Where honey is, there gall, where swelling breast, the chancre.' For, 'when the son sleeps with the mother, she kills him with the stroke of a viper.'"[1]

Here we are in the familiar territory of the so-called Oedipus complex. However, for the alchemist, the mother was the *prima materia* and brought about healing and rejuvenation as well as death. This image of the *coniunctio* refers to one phase of the transformation process, death, to be followed, one hopes, by rebirth. Certainly the dangerous aspect of the *coniunctio* is pictured here. The immature son-ego is eclipsed and threatened with destruction when it naively embraces the maternal unconscious. However, other images indicate that such an eclipse can be inseminating and rejuvenating.

Another text, quoted earlier, speaks of the woman who slays her husband while he is in her embrace:

> Nevertheless the Philosophers have put to death the woman who slays her husband, for the body of that woman is full of weapons and poison. Let a grave be dug for that dragon, and let that woman be buried with him, he being chained fast to that woman; and the more he winds and coils himself about her, the more will he be cut to pieces by the female weapons which are fashioned in the body of the woman. And when he sees that he is mingled with the limbs of the woman, he will be certain of death, and will be changed wholly into blood. But when the Philosophers see him changed into blood, they leave him a few days in the sun, until his softness is consumed, and the blood dries, and they find that poison. What then appears, is the hidden wind.[2]

This text needs elucidation. As with dreams, the images are fluid and flow into one another. Who is the dragon that is to be chained fast to the woman? He is apparently the husband who is slain by the woman. The sequence of the text suggests that as the husband begins to lie with the woman he turns into a dragon; or, alternatively, as they lie together, the dragon aspect of the instinctual relationship (lust) is constellated.

---

[1] Quoted by Jung, *Mysterium Coniunctionis, CW* 14, par. 14.
[2] Ibid., par. 15.

The ensuing *coniunctio* is a dismemberment of the dragon (primitive desirousness) and is followed by its transformation into spirit (hidden wind). (See figure 8-1.)

The passage immediately preceding the above-quoted text proves that the woman whose embrace kills is associated with lust. It reads:

> In the same way that woman, fleeing from her own children, with whom she lives, although partly angry, yet does not brook being overcome, not that her husband should possess her beauty, who furiously loves her, and keeps awake contending with her, till he shall have carnal intercourse with her, and God make perfect the foetus, when he multiplies children to himself according to his pleasure. His beauty, therefore, is consumed by fire who does not approach his wife except by reason of lust.[3]

Lust as a lacerater brings to mind Shakespeare's great Sonnet 129:

> Th' expense of spirit in a waste of shame
> Is lust in action; and, till action, lust
> Is perjured, murd'rous, bloody, full of blame,
> Savage, extreme, rude, cruel, not to trust;

FIGURE 8 – 1
The Dragon Kills the Woman and She Kills It (Maier, *Atalanta Fugiens,* 1618.)

---

[3]Waite, trans., *Turba Philosophorum,* p. 178, dictum 59.

> Enjoyed no sooner but despised straight;
> Past reason hunted, and no sooner had,
> Past reason hated as a swallowed bait
> On purpose laid to make the taker mad;
> Mad in pursuit, and in possession so;
> Had, having, and in quest to have, extreme;
> A bliss in proof, and proved, a very woe,
> Before, a joy proposed; behind, a dream.
>> All this the world well knows, yet none knows well
>> To shun the heaven that leads men to this hell.

This is Shakespeare's negative *coniunctio* sonnet and should be contrasted with his positive Sonnet 116, quoted later in this chapter. Note the play of opposites so characteristic of *coniunctio* symbolism: enjoyed—despised, hunted—hated, reason—madness, bliss—woe, heaven—hell.

The woman who slays her husband with her embrace appears in the apocryphal Book of Tobit. Sarah, who is to be married to Tobias, has had seven previous husbands. Every wedding night, when the husband retired to bed with his bride, the demon Asmodeus killed him. Seven successive husbands had died that way. Raphael, his guardian angel, gives Tobias specific instructions on how to deal with the danger. On the way to his bride's house, Tobias encounters a huge fish that leaps out of the water at him. He is instructed to kill the fish and extract its heart, liver, and gall. On his wedding night he must burn the heart and liver as an incense offering to protect him from the evil demon. The gall is to be applied to the eyes of his blind father in order to restore his sight.

The symbolic idea behind this story is that the *coniunctio* leads to death—extinction of consciousness—until the energy of instinctual desirousness (fish) has been extracted from its original form and transformed into spirit (incense)—that is, conscious understanding. This interpretation is supported by a variant passage in the Vulgate. "Then the angel Raphael said to him, 'Listen and I will show you those whom the demon has power to overcome. They are those who at the time of their marriage put God out of their thoughts and so abandon themselves to their instincts that they have no more reason than horse or mule'" (Tobit 6:16f.)[4]

The gall of the fish, when applied to the eyes of Tobias' blind father, restores his sight. Gall is bitter, corresponding to the bitterness of frustrated desire. But the experience of bitterness, properly understood (applied to the eyes), brings wisdom. While discussing the symbolism of salt, Jung has made relevant comments about bitterness, as quoted earlier:

---

[4]The Jerusalem Bible, p. 613.

...the most outstanding properties of salt are bitterness and wisdom....The factor common to both, however incommensurable the two ideas may seem, is, psychologically, the function of feeling. Tears, sorrow and disappointment are bitter, but wisdom is the comforter in all psychic suffering. Indeed, bitterness and wisdom form a pair of alternatives: where there is bitterness wisdom is lacking, and where wisdom is there can be no bitterness. Salt, as the carrier of this fateful alternative, is coordinated with the nature of woman....The novilunium (darkness) of woman is a source of countless disappointments for man which easily turn to bitterness, though they could equally well be a source of wisdom if they were understood.[5]

The lesser *coniunctio* occurs whenever the ego identifies with contents emerging from the unconscious. This happens almost regularly in the course of the analytic process. The ego is exposed successively to identifications with the shadow, the anima/animus, and the Self. Such contaminated *coniunctios* must be followed by *mortificatio* and further *separatio.* A similar sequence occurs in the extraverted aspect of the process. The ego identifies with certain individuals, groups, institutions, and collectivities (individual and collective transferences). These identifications are contaminated mixtures, containing both the individual's potential for noble loyalties and object love and also unregenerate desires for power and pleasure. They must undergo further purification before the greater *coniunctio* is possible.

THE GREATER *CONIUNCTIO*

The goal of the *opus* is the creation of a miraculous entity variously called the "Philosophers' Stone," "Our Gold," "Penetrating Water," "Tincture," and so forth. It is produced by a final union of the purified opposites, and, because it combines the opposites, it mitigates and rectifies all one-sidedness. Thus the Philosophers' Stone is described as "a stone having power to give life to all mortal, to purify all corrupt, to soften all hard, and harden all soft bodies."[6] Again, the Stone (personified as the *Sapientia Dei*) says of itself: "I am the mediatrix of the elements, making one to agree with another; that which is warm I make cold, and the reverse; that which is dry I make moist, and the reverse; that which is hard I soften, and the reverse. I am the end and my beloved is the beginning. I am the whole work and all science is hidden in me."[7]

As the Stone is being prepared, the material is subjected to repeated reversals and turnings-into-the-opposite. The *Turba* says: "For

[5]Jung, *Mysterium Coniunctionis,* CW 14, pars. 330, 332.

[6]Figulus, *A Golden and Blessed Casket of Nature's Marvels,* p. 301.

[7]von Franz, *Aurora Consurgens,* p. 143.

the elements, being diligently cooked in the fire, rejoice, and are changed into different natures, because the liquefied...becomes not-liquefied, the humid becomes dry, the thick body becomes a spirit, and the fleeing spirit becomes strong and fit to do battle against the fire. Whence the Philosopher saith: Convert the elements and thou shalt find what thou seekest. But to convert the elements is to make the moist dry and the fugitive fixed."[8]

Another text says: "Now that the clearness may be manifest throughout without obscurity...the body must be repeatedly opened and made thin after its fixation and dissolved and putrefied....It is purified by separation, and is dissolved, digested, and coagulated, sublimed, incerated, and fixed by the reciprocated action of its own proper Identity, as agent and patient, *alternating to improve*" (Italics mine).[9]

The psychotherapeutic process is likewise an "alternating to improve." One is thrown back and forth between the opposites almost interminably. But very gradually a new standpoint emerges that allows the opposites to be experienced at the same time. This new standpoint is the *coniunctio*, and it is both releasing and burdensome. Jung says: "The one-after-another is a bearable prelude to the deeper knowledge of the side-by-side, for this is an incomparably more difficult problem. Again, the view that good and evil are spiritual forces outside us, and that man is caught in the conflict between them, is more bearable by far than the insight that the opposites are the ineradicable and indispensable precondition of all psychic life, so much so that life itself is guilt."[10]

The term "Philosophers' Stone" is itself a union of opposites, Philosophy, love of wisdom, is a spiritual endeavor, whereas a stone is crude, hard, material reality. The term thus suggests something like the concrete, practical efficacy of wisdom or consciousness. It is "a stone which is not a stone" about which Ruland says, "The Stone which is not a stone is a substance which is petrine as regards its efficacy and virtue but not as regards its substance."[11] The alchemical Philosophers' Stone is thus a forerunner of the modern discovery of the reality of the psyche. Jung says: "What unconscious nature was ultimately aiming at when she produced the image of the lapis can be seen most clearly in the notion that it originated in matter and in man...Christ's spirituality was too high and man's naturalness was too low. In the image of...the

---

[8] Waite, trans., *Turba Philosophorum,* p. 190, dictum 65.

[9] Scholium to "The Golden Treatise of Hermes," quoted in Atwood, *Hermetic Philosophy and Alchemy,* p. 115n.

[10] Jung, *Mysterium Coniunctionis, CW* 14, par. 206.

[11] Ruland, *A Lexicon of Alchemy,* p. 189.

lapis the 'flesh' glorified itself in its own way; it would not transform itself into spirit but on the contrary, 'fixed' the spirit in stone."[12]

A major symbolic image for the *coniunctio* is the marriage and / or sexual intercourse between Sol and Luna or some other personification of the opposites (see figure 8-2). This image in dreams refers to the *coniunctio,* either the lesser or the greater, depending on the context. An impressive example is a dream published by Esther Harding:

FIGURE 8 – 2

Coniunctio in the Alchemical Vessel (17th century. Paris, Bibliothèque de l'Arsenal, MS. 975, fol. 13. Reprinted in Derola, *The Secret Art of Alchemy.*)

---

[12]Jung, *Alchemical Studies, CW* 13, par. 127.

A woman dreamed that she went into an underground cavern that was divided into rooms containing stills and other mysterious-looking chemical apparatus. Two scientists were working over the final process of a prolonged series of experiments, which they hoped to bring to a successful conclusion with her help. The end product was to be in the form of golden crystals, which were to be separated from the mother liquid resulting from the many previous solutions and distillations. While the chemists worked over the vessel, the dreamer and her lover lay together in an adjoining room, their sexual embrace supplying the energy essential for the crystallization of the priceless golden substance. [13]

This dream has a close parallel in an alchemical text: "Do ye not see that the complexion of a man is formed out of a soul and a body; thus, also, must ye conjoin these, because the Philosophers, when they prepared the matters and conjoined spouses mutually in love with each other, behold there ascended from them a golden water!"[14] The image of sexual intercourse as producing the golden substance brings up the paradoxical aspect of the ego's relation to the Self. The usual formulation is that the Self unites and reconciles the opposites. However, this dream and the parallel text suggest, as is implicit in all of alchemy, that the operator—that is, the ego—brings about the union of opposites and thereby creates the Self, or at least brings it into manifestation. Thus is underscored the supreme importance of the conscious ego. It must unite the opposites, which is no easy task. To hold opposites simultaneously is to experience paralysis amounting to a veritable crucifixion. The symbolism of the cross includes the union of opposites, and many medieval pictures represent the crucifixion of Christ as a *coniunctio* of Sol and Luna (see figure 8-3). Augustine makes an amazingly explicit identity between the *coniunctio* and the crucifixion. "Like a bridegroom Christ went forth from his chamber, he went out with a presage of his nuptials into the field of the world.... He came to the marriage bed of the cross, and there, in mounting it, he consummated his marriage. And when he perceived the sighs of the creature, he lovingly gave himself up to the torment in the place of his bride...and he joined the woman to himself for ever."[15]

A classic and profound *coniunctio* image is the union of Zeus and Hera in book XIV of the *Iliad*. Leading Hera to his secret bower, Zeus says:

---

[13]Harding, *Psychic Energy: Its Source and Goal*, pp. 453–54.

[14]Waite, trans., *Turba Philosophorum*, p. 134, dictum 42.

[15]Quoted by Jung, *Mysterium Coniunctionis*, CW 14, par. 25, n. 176.

FIGURE 8 - 3

The Crucifixion as a *Coniunctio* Between Sol and Luna (Late 9th century. Paris, Bibliothèque Nationale, MS. lat. 257, fol. 12v. Reprinted in Swarzenski, *Monuments of Romanesque Art.*)

"Nor God, nor mortal shall our joys behold,
Shaded with clouds, and circumfus'd in gold,
Not ev'n the Sun, who darts thro' Heav'n his rays,
And whose broad eye th' extended earth surveys."
Gazing he spoke, and kindling at the view,
His eager arms around the Goddess threw.
Glad Earth perceives, and from her bosom pours
Unbidden herbs, and voluntary flowers;
Thick new-born violets a soft carpet spread,
And clust'ring lotos swell'd the rising bed,
And sudden hyacinths the turf bestrow,
And flamy crocus made the mountain glow.
There golden clouds conceal the heav'nly pair,
Steep'd in soft joys, and circumfused with air;

> Celestial dews, descending o'er the ground,
> Perfume the mount, and breathe ambrosia round.
> At length with Love and Sleep's soft power oppress'd,
> The panting Thund'rer nods, and sinks to rest.*

The image of a miraculous growth of flowers or vegetation comes up in dreams as evidence of proximity to the *coniunctio*. It is not invariably auspicious, since it can signify inflation for an immature ego.

Another traditional *coniunctio* image is the biblical Song of Songs. The rabbis interpreted it as referring to the marriage of Yahweh and Israel; the church fathers interpreted it as the marriage of Christ with the church; certain alchemists interpreted it as representing the alchemical *opus* (for example, *Aurora Consurgens*); and finally, the Jewish kabbalists interpreted it as the union of Yahweh with his exiled feminine essence, the *Shekinah*. The Song of Songs speaks of "love strong as death" (8:6), an allusion to the fact that the *coniunctio* is outside of time (see figure 8-4).

The major *coniunctio* image in the Christian Scriptures is the "Marriage of the Lamb" in Revelation:

> The marriage of the Lamb is come, and his wife hath made herself ready.
> (Rev. 19:7, AV)

> And I John saw the holy city, new Jerusalem, coming down from God out of heaven, prepared as a bride adorned for her husband. And I heard a great voice out of heaven saying, Behold, the tabernacle of God is with men, and he will dwell with them, and they shall be his people, and God himself shall be with them, and be their God. (Rev. 21:2,3, AV)

This is followed by a detailed description of the new Jerusalem as a beautiful, bejewelled city in the shape of a mandala. The new (that is, purified) Jerusalem is the bride of God (the Lamb). Heaven and earth, which were separated at the beginning of creation, are to be rejoined, healing the split in the psyche and reconnecting ego and Self ("the tabernacle of God is with men"). The city as an image of totality reminds us that the city is also the vessel for the collective transformation of humanity. The process of *civilization* takes place in the city (*civitas*). (See figure 8-5.)

The marriage of heaven and earth represented as Tifereth and Malchuth also appears in the Kabbala. Rabbi Simon ben Yochai, the reputed author of the Zohar is said to have described the sacred *coniunctio* on his deathbed in these words: "When...the mother is separated and conjoined with the King face to face in the excellence of the Sabbath, all things become one body. And then the Holy One—blessed be He!—sitteth on His throne, and all things are called the Complete Name, the Holy Name. Blessed be His Name for ever and unto the ages

---

*(XIV, 389-406 Pope tr.)

FIGURE 8 –4

The Circle of the Year as a *Coniunctio* of Sol and Luna (Medieval Drawing. Stuttgart, Wurttembergische Landesbibliothek, Cod. hist. fol. 415, fol. 17v. Reprinted in Evans, *Medieval Drawings*.)

of the ages.... When this Mother is conjoined with the King, all the worlds receive blessing, and the universe is found to be in joy."[16]

This is a profound vision of the *Unus Mundus* whose only equal in modern times is Jung's *coniunctio* vision. In *Memories, Dreams, Reflections* Jung describes his experience of the *coniunctio* during convalescence from a grave illness in 1944:

> Everything around me seemed enchanted. At this hour of the night the nurse brought me some food she had warmed—for only then was I able to take

---

[16]Mathers, trans., *The Kabbalah Unveiled*, p. 337.

FIGURE 8 – 5

The New Jerusalem as a *Coniunctio* of Sol and Luna (*The Cloisters Apocalypse,*
fol. 36. New York, the Metropolitan Museum of Art.)

any, and I ate with appetite. For a time it seemed to me that she was an old
Jewish woman, much older than she actually was, and that she was preparing ritual kosher dishes for me. When I looked at her, she seemed to have a
blue halo around her head. I myself was, so it seemed, in the Pardes
Rimmonim, the garden of pomegranates, and the wedding of Tifereth with
Malchuth was taking place. Or else I was Rabbi Simon ben Jochai, whose
wedding in the afterlife was being celebrated. It was the mystic marriage as it
appears in the Cabbalistic tradition. I cannot tell you how wonderful it was. I
could only think continually, "Now this is the garden of pomegranates! Now
this is the marriage of Malchuth with Tifereth!" I do not know exactly what
part I played in it. At bottom it was I myself: I was the marriage. And my
beatitude was that of a blissful wedding.

Gradually the garden of pomegranates faded away and changed. There
followed the Marriage of the Lamb, in a Jerusalem festively bedecked. I
cannot describe what it was like in detail. These were ineffable states of joy.
Angels were present, and light. I myself was the "Marriage of the Lamb."

That, too, vanished, and there came a new image, the last vision. I walked
up a wide valley to the end, where a gentle chain of hills began. The valley
ended in a classical amphitheater. It was magnificently situated in the green
landscape. And there, in this theater, the *hierosgamos* was being celebrated.
Men and women dancers came onstage, and upon a flower-decked couch

All-father Zeus and Hera consummated the mystic marriage, as it is described in the *Iliad.*

All these experiences were glorious. Night after night I floated in a state of purest bliss, "thronged round with images of all creation."[17]

That which goes by the name of love is fundamental to the phenomenology of the *coniunctio.* Love is both its cause and effect. The lesser *coniunctio* derives from love as concupiscence, whereas transpersonal love (analogous to Plato's Heavenly Aphrodite) both generates and is generated by the greater *coniunctio.* It has been said truly that object love is the extraverted aspect of individuation. Object love is *objective* love, a love purged of personal desirousness, not one side of a pair of opposites, but rather beyond the opposites. This transpersonal love is at the root of all group and social loyalties such as allegiance to family, party, nation, church, and humanity itself. The extraverted aspect of the *coniunctio* promotes social interest and the unity of the human race; the introverted aspect promotes connection with the Self and the unity of the individual psyche. That which holds things together is adhesive; thus, in alchemy, "glue," "gum," and "resin" are synonyms for the transforming substance. "This substance, as the life force *(vis animans),* is likened by another commentator to the 'glue of the world' *(glutinum mundi)* which is the medium between mind and body and the union of both."[18]

Beginning with Plato's *Symposium,* some of the world's most inspired texts bear witness to the transpersonal cosmogonic love. Lucretius expresses the pagan feeling in the beginning lines of *De Rerum Natura:*

> Mother of Rome, delight of Gods and men,
> Dear Venus that beneath the gliding stars
> Makest to teem the many-voyaged main
> And fruitful lands—for all of living things
> Through thee alone are evermore conceived,
> Through thee are risen to visit the great sun—
> Before thee, Goddess, and thy coming on,
> Flee stormy wind and massy cloud away,
> For thee the daedal Earth bears scented flowers,
> For thee the waters of the unvexed deep
> Smile, and the hollows of the sérene sky
> Glow with diffuséd radiance for thee!
> For soon as comes the springtime face of day,
> And procreant gales blow from the West unbarred,

---

[17]Jung, *Memories, Dreams, Reflections,* p. 294.

[18]Jung, *Psychology and Alchemy, CW* 12, par. 209.

First fowls of air, smit to the heart by thee,
Foretoken thy approach, O thou Divine,
And leap the wild herds round the happy fields
Or swim the bounding torrents. Thus amain,
Seized with the spell, all creatures follow thee
Whithersoever thou walkest forth to lead,
And thence through seas and mountains and swift streams,
Through leafy homes of birds and greening plains,
Kindling the lure of love in every breast,
Thou bringest the eternal generations forth,
Kind after kind. Since 'tis thou alone
Guidest the Cosmos.[19]

The classic description of transpersonal love for our era is that of the Apostle Paul:

If I speak in the tongues of men and of angels, but have not love, I am a noisy gong or a clanging cymbal. And if I have prophetic powers, and understand all mysteries and all knowledge, and if I have all faith, so as to remove mountains, but have not love, I am nothing. If I give away all I have, and if I deliver my body to be burned, but have not love, I gain nothing.

Love is patient and kind; love is not jealous or boastful; it is not arrogant or rude. Love does not insist on its own way; it is not irritable or resentful; it does not rejoice at wrong, but rejoices in the right. Love bears all things, believes all things, hopes all things, endures all things. (1 Cor. 13:1–7, RSV)

Dante continues the testimony in the description of his vision of eternal light, which concludes *The Divine Comedy* (see figures 8-6 and 8-7):

I saw that in its depths there are enclosed,
Bound up with love in one eternal book,
The scattered leaves of all the universe—
Substance, and accidents, and their relations,
As though together fused in such a way
That what I speak of is a single light.

. . . .

O Light Eternal, in Thyself contained!
Thou only know'st Thyself, and in Thyself
Both known and knowing, smilest on Thyself!
That very circle which appeared in Thee,
Conceived as but reflection of a light,
When I had gazed on it awhile, now seemed
To bear the image of a human face
Within itself, of its own coloring—
Wherefore my sight was wholly fixed on it.
Like a geometer, who will attempt
With all his power and mind to square the circle,

---

[19]Lucretius, *Of the Nature of Things*, pp. 3f.

FIGURE 8 – 6
The Heavenly Rose (Doré, *Illustrations for Dante's Divine Comedy.*)

Yet cannot find the principle he needs:
Just so was I, at that phenomenon.
I wished to see how image joined to ring,
And how the one found place within the other.
Too feeble for such flights were my own wings;
But by a lightning flash my mind was struck—
And thus came the fulfilment of my wish.
    My power now failed that phantasy sublime:
My will and my desire were both revolved,
As is a wheel in even motion driven,
By Love, which moves the sun and other stars.[20]

Three centuries later came Shakespeare's peerless description in
Sonnet 116:

---

[20]Dante, *The Divine Comedy,* trans. Lawrence Grant White, p. 188.

FIGURE 8 – 7
Star Trails Around the Pole (Photo Yerkes Observatory. Reprinted in Neely, *A Primer for Star-Gazers.*)

Let me not to the marriage of true minds
Admit impediments; love is not love
Which alters when it alteration finds,
Or bends with the remover to remove.
Oh, no, it is an ever-fixed mark,
That looks on tempests and is never shaken;
It is the star to every wand'ring bark,
Whose worth's unknown, although his height be taken.
Love's not Time's fool, though rosy lips and cheeks
Within his bending sickle's compass come;
Love alters not with his brief hours and weeks,
But bears it out even to the edge of Doom.
   If this be error, and upon me proved,
   I never writ, nor no man ever loved.

Jung describes his experience of transpersonal love in these words:

Eros is a *kosmogonos,* a creator and father-mother of all higher consciousness. I sometimes feel that Paul's words—"Though I speak with the tongues of men and of angels, and have not love"—might well be the first condition of all cognition and the quintessence of divinity itself. Whatever the learned interpretation may be of the sentence "God is Love," the words affirm the *complexio oppositorum* of the Godhead. In my medical experience as well as in my own life I have again and again been faced with the mystery of love, and have never been able to explain what it is.... For we are in the deepest sense the victims and the instruments of cosmogonic "love." I put the word in quotation marks to indicate that I do not use it in its connotations of desiring, preferring, favoring, wishing, and similar feelings, but as something superior to the individual, a unified and undivided whole. Being a part, man cannot grasp the whole. He is at its mercy. He may assent to it, or rebel against it; but he is always caught up by it and enclosed within it. He is dependent upon it and is sustained by it. Love is his light and his darkness, whose end he cannot see. "Love ceases not"—whether he speaks with the "tongues of angels," or with scientific exactitude traces the life of the cell down to its uttermost source. Man can try to name love, showering upon it all the names at his command, and still he will involve himself in endless self-deceptions. If he possesses a grain of wisdom, he will lay down his arms and name the unknown by the more unknown, *ignotum per ignotius*—that is, by the name of God. That is a confession of his subjection, his imperfection, and his dependence; but at the same time a testimony to his freedom to choose between truth and error.[21]

*   *   *   *

The Philosophers' Stone, once created, has the power to transform base matter into noble. This power is referred to in the texts by the operations of *proiectio* and *multiplicatio* (or *augmentatio*). Strictly speaking, these operations are performed not by the alchemist, but by the *lapis*. These so-called operations are thus really properties of the Philosophers' Stone, which, as a powder or liquid (elixir), projects itself upon base matter and thereby multiplies itself. A text says: "Alchimy is a Science, teaching how to transforme any kind of metall into another: and that by a proper medicine, as it appeareth by many Philosophers' Bookes. Alchimy therefore is a science teaching how to make and compound a certaine medicine, which is called *Elixer*, the which when it is cast upon metalls or imperfect bodies, doth fully perfect them in the verie projection."[22]

The Stone's power of *multiplicatio* is reminiscent of the widow's cruse of oil (1 Kings 17:14), the miracle of the loaves and fishes (Matt. 14:17–21), and the previously quoted miraculous multiplication of flowers during the *coniunctio* of Zeus and Hera.

The psychological implications of *multiplicatio* are very interesting. The image suggests that transformative effects emanate from the activated Self in process of conscious realization. Certainly it is true that all events, no matter how ordinary, take on import when they participate in

---

[21]Jung, *Memories, Dreams, Reflections,* p. 353f.

[22]Quoted by Read, *Prelude to Chemistry,* p. 24.

the process of individuation. Also, *multiplicatio* gives us a hint as to how psychotherapy may work. To some extent, the consciousness of an individual who is related to the Self seems to be contagious and tends to multiply itself in others. The *I Ching* speaks of such a phenomenon:

> Contemplation of the divine meaning underlying the workings of the universe gives to the man who is called upon to influence others the means of producing like effects. This requires that power in inner concentration which religious contemplation develops in great men strong in faith. It enables them to apprehend the mysterious and divine laws of life, and by means of profoundest inner concentration they give expression to these laws in their own persons. Thus a hidden spiritual power emanates from them, influencing and dominating others without their being aware of how it happens (See figure 8-8).[23]

However, for the patient to be influenced by the psychotherapeutic process, the ego must be open. This corresponds to the alchemical idea that the material must be open to receive the effects of the tincture. Paracelsus says, "For if the tincture is to tinge, it is necessary that the body or material which is to be tinged should be open, and in a state of flux: for unless this were so, the tincture could not operate."[24] In psychotherapy, openness (to the objective psyche) is required of both patient and therapist. Jung says: "The personalities of doctor and patient are often infinitely more important for the outcome of the treatment than what the doctor says and thinks.... For two personalities to meet is like mixing two different chemical substances: if there is any combination at all, both are transformed. In any effective psychological treatment the doctor is bound to influence the patient; but this influence can only take place if the patient has a reciprocal influence on the doctor. You can exert no influence if you are not susceptible to influence."[25]

Another feature of the Philosophers' Stone is its tendency to reciprocal action. This idea appeared in the dream of a man, who, the night before, had heard a lecture on alchemy. He dreamed that

> *a group of people had discovered the alchemists' secret. One aspect of that secret was that when alchemical studies are undertaken with the right attitude a reciprocity of interest is evoked; that is, when the adept takes an interest in alchemy, alchemy takes an interest in him.*

Likewise, an alchemical text says: "Understand ye Sons of Wisdom, the Stone declares: Protect and I will protect thee; give me my own,

[23]Wilhelm trans., *The I C   ok of Changes*, p. 83.

[24]Paracelsus, *Hermetic and   al Writings I*, 155.

[25]Jung, *The Practice of Psychotherapy*, *CW* 16, par. 163.

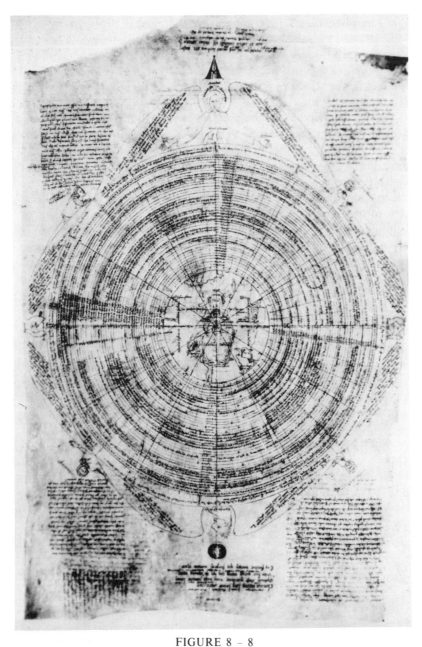

FIGURE 8 – 8

Autobiography as a Mandala. Events in the Life of Opicinus de Canistris Arranged Concentrically from his Conception on March 24, 1296, to Completion of Drawing on June 3, 1336. (Biblioteca Apostolica Vaticana, MS. Pal. lat. 1993, fol. 11r. Reprinted in Evans, *Medieval Drawings*.)

that I may help thee."[26] The same idea is expressed in Proverbs concerning wisdom: "Forsake her not, and she shall preserve thee; love her and she shall keep thee. Wisdom is the principle thing; therefore get wisdom: and with all thy getting get understanding. Exalt her, and she shall promote thee: she shall bring thee to honor, when thou dost embrace her" (Prov. 4:6–8, AV).

Further description of the marvelous powers of the Philosophers' Stone could continue almost indefinitely.[27] The reciprocal action of the Stone is a suitable stopping place because it is a reminder that paying attention to the imagery of the objective psyche (such as alchemy) generates auspicious reciprocal effects. The psychological rule is: the unconscious takes the same attitude toward the ego as the ego takes toward it. If one pays friendly attention to the unconscious it becomes helpful to the ego. Gradually the realization dawns that a mutual *opus* is being performed. The ego needs the guidance and direction of the unconscious to have a meaningful life; and the latent Philosophers' Stone, imprisoned in the *prima materia,* needs the devoted efforts of the conscious ego to come into actuality. Together they work on the Great Magistry to create more and more consciousness in the universe.

* * * *

In conclusion, I shall give the final word to the alchemists by quoting *in toto*, their most sacred text, *The Emerald Tablet of Hermes.* It was viewed "as a kind of supernatural revelation to the 'sons of Hermes' by the patron of their 'Divine Art.' "[28] According to legend, the original *Emerald Tablet* was found in the tomb of Hermes Trismegistus either by Alexander the Great or, in another version, by Sarah the wife of Abraham. It was at first known only in Latin, but in 1923 Holmyard discovered an Arabic version.[29] It is likely that an earlier text was in Greek and, according to Jung, was of Alexandrian origin.[30] The alchemists treated it with unique veneration, engraving its statements on their laboratory walls and quoting it constantly in their works. It is the cryptic epitome of the alchemical *opus*, a recipe for the second creation of the world, the *unus mundus.*[31]

---

[26]"The Golden Treatise of Hermes," in Atwood, *Hermetic Philosophy and Alchemy,* p. 128.

[27]For further material see Edinger, *Ego and Archetype,* ch. 10.

[28]Read, *Prelude to Chemistry,* pp. 51f.

[29]Holmyard, *Alchemy,* p. 96.

[30]Jung, *Mysterium Coniunctionis, CW* 14, par. 12.

[31]Ibid., pars. 759ff.

Tabula Smaragdina Hermetis

1. Verum, sine mendacio, certum et verissimum.
2. Quod est inferius, est sicut quod est superius, et quod est superius, est sicut quod est inferius, ad perpetranda miracula rei unius.
3. Et sicut omnes res fuerunt ab uno, meditatione unius: sic omnes res natae fuerunt ab hac una re, adaptatione.
4. Pater eius est Sol, mater eius Luna; portavit illud ventus in ventre suo; nutrix eius terra est.
5. Pater omnis telesmi totius mundi est hic.
6. Vis eius integra est, si versa fuerit in terram.
7. Separabis terram ab igne, subtile a spisso, suaviter, cum magno ingenio.
8. Ascendit a terra in coelum, interumque descendit in terram, et recipit vim superiorum et inferiorum. Sic habebis gloriam totius mundi. Ideo fugiat a te omnis obscuritas.
9. Hic est totius fortitudinis fortitudo fortis; quia vincet omnem subtilem, omnemque solidam penetrabit.
10. Sic mundus creatus est.
11. Hinc adaptationes erunt mirabiles, quarum modus est hic.
12. Itaque vocatus sum HERMES TRISMEGISTUS, habens tres partes Philosophiae totius mundi.
13. Completum est quod dixi de operatione Solis.

The Emerald Tablet of Hermes

1. Truly, without deception, certain and most true.
2. What is below is like that which is above, and what is above is like that which is below, to accomplish the miracles of the one thing.
3. And as all things proceeded from one, through mediation of the one, so all things came from this one thing through adaptation.
4. Its father is the sun; its mother the moon; the wind has carried it in its belly; its nurse is the earth.
5. This is the father of all, the completion of the whole world.
6. Its strength is complete if it be turned into (or toward) earth.
7. Separate the earth from the fire, the subtle from the dense, gently, with great ingenuity.
8. It ascends from the earth to the heaven, and descends again to the earth, and receives the power of the above and the below. Thus you will have the glory of the whole world. Therefore all darkness will flee from you.
9. Here is the strong power of the whole strength; for it overcomes every subtle thing and penetrates every solid.

10. Thus the world has been created.
11. From here will come the marvelous adaptations, whose manner this is.
12. So I am called HERMES TRISMEGISTUS, having the three parts of the philosophy of the whole world.
13. What I have said about the operation of the sun is finished.[32]

---

[32]The Latin text is taken from Jung, *E.T.H. Seminars: Alchemy,* pp. 55f. The English translation is taken from the same source with slight changes by comparison with other versions. In these notes Jung gives a brief psychological commentary on the *Emerald Tablet.*

❧ Bibliography ❧

Adler, Gerhard. "Aspects of Jung's Personality and Work." *Psychological Perspectives* (Spring 1975).

The Living Symbol. New York: Pantheon, 1961.

Studies in Analytical Psychology. New York: Norton, 1948.

Alexander, H. B. *The Mythology of All Races.* 13 vols. Boston: M. Jones, 1916.

Aristotle. *The Basic Works of Aristotle.* Edited by Richard McKeon. New York: Random House, 1941.

Ashmole, Elias, *Theatrum Chemicum Britannicum.* 1652. Reprint New York: Johnson Reprint Corp., 1967.

Atwood, M. A., *Hermetic Philosophy and Alchemy.* 1850. Reprint. New York: The Julian Press, 1960.

Augustine, Saint. *City of God.* Translated by Marcus Dods. The Modern Library. New York: Random House, 1950.

Confessions and Enchiridion. Library of Christian Classics. Philadelphia: Westminster Press, n.d.

Les Belles Heures du Duc de Berry. Metropolitan Museum of Art. New York: George Braziller, 1974.

Berthelot, M. P. E. *Collection des Anciens Alchemistes Grecs.* London: Holland Press, 1963.

Bertine, Eleanor. *Jung's Contribution to Our Time.* Edited by Elizabeth Rohrbach. New York: Putnam, 1967.

Bessy, Maurice. *A Pictorial History of Magic and the Supernatural.* London: Spring Books, 1964.

Bevan, Edwyn. *Stoics and Sceptics.* Oxford: Clarendon Press, 1913.

The Bhagavad-Gita. Translated by Edwin Arnold. Los Angeles: Self-Realization Fellowship, 1977.

Boehme, Jacob. *Aurora.* 1612. Translated by John Sparrow. Reprint. London: Watkins & Clarke, 1960.

"Forty Questions." In *Personal Christianity: The Doctrine of Jacob Boehme.* New York: Ungar, n.d.

The Signature of All Things. New York: Dutton, n.d.

Bonus of Ferrara. *The New Pearl of Great Price.* 1546. Translated by A. E. Waite. Reprint. London: Vincent Stuart, 1963.

Brandon, S. G. F. *The Judgment of the Dead.* New York: Scribners, 1967.

Breasted, James. *Development of Religion and Thought in Ancient Egypt.* New York: Harper Torch Books, 1959.

A History of Egypt. New York: Scribners, 1937.

Brehier, Emile. *The History of Philosophy: The Hellenic Age.* Chicago: University of Chicago Press, 1965.

Buber, Martin. *Ten Rungs: Hasidic Sayings.* New York: Schocken, 1970.

Budge, E. A. Wallis. *The Gods of the Egyptians.* Chicago: Open Court, 1904. Reprint. New York: Dover, 1969.

Osiris: The Egyptian Religion of Resurrection. 1911. Reprint. New Hyde Park, N.Y.: University Books, 1961.

Burland, C.A. *The Arts of the Alchemists.* New York: Macmillan, 1968.

Burnet, John. *Early Greek Philosophy.* Cleveland: World, Meridan Books, 1962.

Charles, R. H. *The Apocrypha and Pseudepigrapha of the Old Testament.* Oxford: Oxford University Press, 1969.

Chaucer, Geoffrey. *Canterbury Tales.* Rendered by J. U. Nicolson, Garden City, New York: Garden City Publishing Co., 1934.

Clark, Kenneth. *Civilization.* New York: Harper & Row, 1969.

The Cloisters Apocalypse. The Metropolitan Museum of Art. New York, 1971.

Collectanea Chemica. 16th century. Reprint. London: Vincent Stuart, 1963.

Cook, A. B. *Zeus: A Study in Ancient Religion.* Reprint. New York: Biblo and Tannen, 1965.

Cornford, F. M. *From Religion to Philosophy.* New York: Harper Torchbooks, 1957.

Plato's Cosmology. New York: Harcourt Brace, 1937.

Craven, Thomas, ed. *A Treasury of Art Masterpieces.* New York: Simon & Schuster, 1939.

Cumont, Franz. *Afterlife in Roman Paganism.* New Haven: Yale University Press, 1923.

The Mysteries of Mithra. New York: Dover, 1956.

Danielou, Jean. *Hindu Polytheism.* New York: Pantheon, 1964.

Dante, Alighieri. *The Divine Comedy.* Translated by John Ciardi. New York: New American Library, 1970.

The Divine Comedy. Translated by Lawrence Grant White. New York: Pantheon, 1948.

Derola, Stanislas Klossowski. *The Secret Art of Alchemy.* New York: Avon, 1973.

Dickinson, Emily. *The Complete Poems of Emily Dickinson.* Edited by Thomas H. Johnson. Boston: Little, Brown, 1960.

Dieterich, A. *A Mithraic Ritual.* A translation by G. R. S. Mead of *Eine Mithrasliturgie* (Leipzig, 1903). London: Theosophical Publishing Society, 1907.

Doré, Gustave. *The Dore Bible Illustrations.* New York: Dover, 1974.

The Doré Illustrations for Dante's Divine Comedy. New York: Dover, 1976.

Dürer, Albrecht. *The Complete Engravings, Etchings and Drypoints of Albrecht Dürer.* Edited by W. L. Strauss. New York: Dover, 1973.

The Complete Woodcuts of Albrecht Dürer. Edited by Willi Kurth. New York: Dover, 1963.

The Early Christian and Byzantine World. Landmarks of the World's Art. Text by Jean Lassus. London: Paul Hamlyn, 1967.

Edinger, Edward F. *Ego and Archtype.* New York: Putnam, 1972.

The Creation of Consciousness. Toronto: Inner City Books, 1984.

"The Tragic Hero: An Image of Individuation." *Parabola* 1, no. 1 (Winter 1976).

Eisler, Robert. *Orpheus the Fisher.* London: John M. Watkins, 1921.

Eliade, Mircea. *The Forge and the Crucible.* Translated by Stephen Corrin. New York: Harper, 1962

From Primitives to Zen. New York: Harper & Row, 1967.

Patterns in Comparative Religion. New York: World, 1963.

Shamanism: Archaic Techniques of Ecstasy. New York: Pantheon, 1964.

Eliot, T. S. *Four Quartets.* New York: Harcourt, Brace, 1943.

Emerson, Ralph Waldo. *The Journals and Miscellaneous Notebooks of Ralph Waldo Emerson.* Edited by W. H. Gilman et al. Cambridge, Mass.: Harvard University Press, Belknap Press, 1960.

Selected Writings of Ralph Waldo Emerson. The Modern Library, New York: Random House, 1940.

Evans, M. W. *Medieval Drawings.* London: Paul Hamlyn, 1969.

Evans-Wentz, W. Y., ed. *The Tibetan Book of the Dead.* London: Oxford University Press, 1951.

Figulus, Benedictus. *A Golden and Blessed Casket of Nature's Marvels.* 17th century. Translated by A. E. Waite. Reprint. London: Vincent Stuart, 1963.

Fitzgerald, Edward, trans. *The Rubaiyat of Omar Khayyam.* Garden City, N.Y.: Garden City Publishing Co., 1937.

Freeman, Kathleen. *Ancilla to the Pre–Socratic Philosophers.* Cambridge, Mass.: Harvard University Press, 1948.

Frost, Robert. *Complete Poems of Robert Frost.* New York: Henry Holt & Co., 1949.

Goethe. *Faust.* Translated by Philip Wayne. Baltimore: Penguin Books, 1969.

Goodenough, Erwin R. *An Introduction to Philo Judaeus.* Oxford: Basil Blackwell, 1962.

Grant, Robert M. *The Secret Sayings of Jesus.* London: Collins, 1960.

Grant, Michael and John Hazel. *Gods and Mortals in Classical Mythology.* Springfield, Mass.: Merriam, 1973.

Gray, Thomas. "Elegy Written in a Country Churchyard." In *The New Oxford Book of English Verse,* edited by Helen Gardner. New York and Oxford: Oxford University Press, 1972.

Harding, M. Esther. *Psychic Energy: Its Source and Goal.* New York: Pantheon, 1947.

Harrison, Jane. *Themis.* Cambridge: Cambridge University Press, 1927.

Hastings, James, ed. *Encyclopedia of Religion and Ethics.* New York: Scribner, 1922.

Hayes, Dorsha. *The Bell Branch Rings.* Dublin, N. H.: William L. Bauhan, 1972.

Hesiod. "Homeric Hymns to Demeter." In *The Homeric Hymns and Homerica.* Loeb Classical Library. Cambridge, Mass.: Harvard University Press, 1964.

Hind, Arthur M. *An Introduction to a History of Woodcut.* New York: Dover, 1963.

Hinsie, Leland E., and Robert J. Campbell. *Psychiatric Dictionary.* 3d ed. New York: Oxford University Press, 1960.

Hippolytus. "The Refutation of All Heresies." In *The Ante–Nicene Fathers,* Vol. 5. Grand Rapids, Mich.: Eerdmanns, 1975.

Holbein, Hans. *The Dance of Death.* 1538. Reprint. Boston: Cygnet, 1974.

Holmyard, E. M. *Alchemy.* Middlesex: Penguin, 1957.

Homer, *The Iliad,* Translated by Alexander Pope, in *The Complete Poetical Works of Pope.*

The Hours of Catherine of Cleves. The Guennol Collection and the Pierpont Morgan Library. New York: George Braziller, n.d.

Iamblichus. *On the Mysteries of the Egyptians.* Translated by Thomas Taylor. London: Stuart & Watkins, 1968.

Ions, Veronica. *Egyptian Mythology.* London: Paul Hamlyn, 1973.

Italian Painting: The Renaissance. Geneva, Paris, New York: Albert Skira, n.d.

Jaffé, Aniela. *The Myth of Meaning.* New York: Putnam, 1971.

James, M. R. *The Apocryphal New Testament.* Oxford: Oxford University Press, 1924.

The Jerusalem Bible. New York: Doubleday, 1966.

Jonas, Hans. *The Gnostic Religion.* Boston: Beacon Press, 1958.

Josephus, Flavius. *Antiquities of the Jews.* Grand Rapids, Mich.: Kregel, 1963.

Jung, C. G. *C. G. Jung Speaking.* Edited by William McGuire and R. F. C. Hull. Princeton, N.J.: Princeton University Press, 1977.

Collected Works. 20 vols. Princeton, N.J.: Princeton University Press.

E.T.H. Seminars: Alchemy. Notes on lectures given at the E.T.H. Zurich, Nov. 1940–July 1941. Zurich: Privately printed, 1960.

Letters. 2 vols. Edited by G. Adler and A. Jaffé. Princeton, N.J.: Princeton University Press, 1975.

Memories, Dreams, Reflections. Edited by A. Jaffé. New York: Pantheon, 1963, and New York: Vintage, 1963.

Psychology of the Unconscious. Translated by Beatrice Hinkle. New York: Moffat, Yard & Co., 1916.

The Visions Seminars. Zurich: Spring Publications, 1976.

Zarathustra Seminar. 10 vols. Notes on seminars given in Zurich, Spring 1934-39. Mimeographed.

Kazantzakis, Nikos. *The Saviors of God.* New York: Simon and Schuster, 1960.

Kelly, Edward. *The Alchemical Writings of Edward Kelly.* London: James Elliot, 1893.

Kempis, Thomas à. *The Imitation of Christ.* Edited by Harold C. Gardiner. Garden City, N.Y.: Doubleday, Image Books, 1955.

Kerényi, C. *Asklepios: Archetypal Image of the Physician's Existence.* New York: Pantheon, 1959.

Kirk, G. S., and J. E. Raven. *The PreSocratic Philosophers.* Cambridge: Cambridge University Press, 1957.

Kluger, Rivkah. "Flood Dreams." In *The Reality of the Psyche.* Edited by J. Wheelwright. New York: Putnam, 1968.

Kunz, G. F. *The Curious Lore of Precious Stones.* New York: Dover, 1971.

Lao Tse. *The Book of Tao.* Translated by Lin Yutang. The Modern Library. New York: Random House, 1942.

Larousse Encyclopedia of Mythology. New York: Prometheus Press, 1959.

The Lives of the Alchemystical Philosophers. London: John M. Watkins, 1955.

Longfellow, Henry Wadsworth. *The Poems of Henry Wadsworth Longfellow.* The Modern Library. New York: Random House, n.d.

Lucretius. *Of the Nature of Things.* Translated by W. E. Leonard. Everyman's Library. New York: Dutton, 1943.

Macrobius. *Commentary on the Dream of Scipio.* Edited by W. H. Stahl. New York: Columbia University Press, 1952.

Maier, Michael. *Atalanta Fugiens.* 1618. Pamphlet reprint. Berkeley, n.d.

Masterpieces of Painting in the Metropolitan Museum of Art. New York: New York Graphic Society.

Mathers, S. L. MacGregor, trans. *The Kabbalah Unveiled*. London: Routledge & Kegan Paul, 1962.

Mead, G. R. S. *Fragments of a Faith Forgotten*. London: Theosophical Publishing Society, 1906. Reprint. New Hyde Park, N.Y.: University Books.

Medieval Manuscript Painting. Edited by Sabrina Mitchell. New York: Viking 1965.

Meister Eckhart. Edited by Franz Pfeiffer. London: John M. Watkins, 1956.

Michelangelo. *The Sonnets of Michelangelo*. Translated by Elizabeth Jennings. Garden City, N.Y.: Doubleday, 1970.

Milton, John. "Paradise Lost." In *Milton: Complete Poetry and Selected Prose*. Edited by E. H. Visiak. The Nonesuch Library. Glasgow: The University Press, 1969.

Munch, Edvard. *Graphic Works of Edvard Munch*. Edited by Alfred Werner. New York: Dover, 1979.

The Nag Hammadi Library. Edited by James M. Robinson. San Francisco: Harper & Row, 1977.

Neely, Henry M. *A Primer for Star-Gazers*. New York: Harper & Brothers, 1946.

Neumann, Erich. *The Origins and History of Consciousness*. New York: Pantheon, 1954.

Nietzsche, Friedrich. "The Birth of Tragedy." In *Basic Writings of Nietzsche*. Translated by Walter Kaufman. The Modern Library. New York: Random House, 1967.

Oates, W. J., and Eugene O'Neill, eds. *The Complete Greek Drama*. New York: Random House, 1938.

Onians, R. B. *The Origins of European Thought*. New York: Arno Press, 1973.

Origen. *On First Principles*. Translated by G. W. Butterworth. New York: Harper & Row, Harper Torchbooks, 1966.

Otto, Walter. *Dionysus Myth and Cult*. Bloomington, Ind.: University of Indiana Press, 1965.

Ovid. *Metamorphoses*. Translated by F. J. Miller. Loeb Classical Library. Cambridge, Mass.: Harvard University Press, 1966.

Panofsky, Erwin. *The Life and Art of Albrecht Dürer*. Princeton, N.J.: Princeton University Press, 1971.

Paracelsus. *The Hermetic and Alchemical Writings of Paracelsus*. Edited and translated by A. E. Waite. New Hyde Park, N.Y.: University Books, 1967.

Philo. "On the Contemplative Life." In *The Essential Philo*. Edited by N. N. Glatzer. New York: Schocken, 1971.

Photo Atlas of the United States. Pasadena, Calif.: Ward Ritchie Press, 1975.

The Picture History of Painting. New York: Abrams, 1957.

Pindar. *The Odes of Pindar*. Translated by John Sandys. Loeb Classical Library. Cambridge, Mass.: Harvard University Press, 1941.

Plato. *The Collected Dialogues.* Edited by Edith Hamilton and Huntington Cairns. New York: Pantheon, 1961.

Plato. Translated by H. N. Fowler. Loeb Classical Library. Cambridge, Mass.: Harvard University Press, 1960.

Plutarch. *Moralia.* Translated by F. C. Babbitt. Loeb Classical Library. Cambridge, Mass.: Harvard University Press, 1962.

Rackham, Arthur. *Rackham's Color Illustrations for Wagner's "Ring."* New York: Dover, 1979.

Rahner, Hugo. *Greek Myths and Christian Mystery.* New York: Harper & Row, 1963.

Read, John. *Prelude to Chemistry: An Outline of Alchemy.* New York: Macmillan, 1937.

Rembrandt. *Rembrandt.* Text by Ludwig Munz. New York: Abrams, 1954.

Rembrandt's Life of Christ. New York: Abrams, Abradale Press, n.d.

Richter, G. M. A. *A Handbook of Greek Art.* London: Phaidon Press, 1965.

Rilke. *Sonnets to Orpheus.* Translated by C. F. MacIntyre. Berkeley: University of California Press, 1961.

Roethke, Theodore. *The Collected Poems of Theodore Roethke.* Garden City, N.Y.: Doubleday, Anchor Books, 1975.

Rohde, Erwin. *Psyche.* Translated by W. B. Hillis. New York: Harcourt, Brace, 1925.

Ruland, Martin. *A Lexicon of Alchemy.* Translated by A. E. Waite. London: John M. Watkins, 1964.

St. John of the Cross. *The Dark Night of the Soul.* Translated by E. Alison Peers. Garden City, N.Y.: Doubleday, Image Books, 1959.

Shakespeare, William. *The Complete Works of William Shakespeare.* London: Oxford University Press, 1965.

Scholem, Gershom. *Kabbalah.* New York: The New York Times Book Co., 1974.

Schopenhauer, Arthur. *The World as Will and Representation.* Translated by E. F. J. Payne. New York: Dover, 1967.

Swarzenski, Hanns. *Monuments of Romanesque Art.* Chicago: University of Chicago Press, 1974.

Titian. *Titian: The Colour Library of Art.* London: Paul Hamlyn, 1969.

Les Très Riches Heures du Duc de Berry. New York: George Braziller, 1969.

Trismosin, Solomon. *Splendor Solis: Alchemical Treatises of Solomon Trismosin.* London: Kegan Paul, Trench, Trubner and Co., n.d.

Vaughn, Henry. *The Complete Poetry of Henry Vaughn.* Edited by French Fogle. New York: Doubleday, 1964.

The Visconti Hours. New York: George Braziller, 1972.

von Franz, Marie–Louise. *Aurora Consurgens.* New York: Pantheon, 1966.

   The Passion of Perpetua. Irving, Tex.: Spring Publications, 1980.

   Patterns of Creativity Mirrored in Creation Myths. Zurich: Spring Publications, 1972.

Voragine, Jacobus de. *The Golden Legend.* Translated by G. Ryan and H. Ripperger. New York: Arno Press, 1969.

Wagner, Richard. *The Ring of the Nibelung.* Translated by Stewart Robb. New York: Dutton, 1960.

Waite, A. E., trans. *The Hermetic Museum.* London: John M. Watkins, 1953.

   The Holy Kabbalah. Reprint. New Hyde Park, N.Y.: University Books, n.d.

   trans. *Turba Philosophorum.* London: Wm. Rider & Sons, 1914.

Weitzmann, Kurt. *The Icon.* New York: George Braziller, 1978.

A Well of Living Waters. A Festschrift for Hilde Kirsch. Los Angeles: C. G. Jung Institute of Los Angeles, 1977.

Wickes, Frances. *The Inner World of Choice.* New York: Harper & Row, 1963.

Wilhelm, Richard, trans. *The I Ching or Book of Changes.* Translated from the German by Cary F. Baynes. Princeton, N.J.: Princeton University Press, 1971.

The World of Bruegel. New York: Time–Life Books, 1968.

Yerkes, Rayden Keith. *Sacrifice in Greek and Roman Religion and Early Judaism.* New York: Scribners, 1952.

Zimmer, Heinrich. *The Art of Indian Asia.* Completed and edited by Joseph Campbell. New York: Pantheon, 1960.

   Philosophies of India. New York: Pantheon, 1951.

Index

Abednego, 24
Actaeon, 59–60, fig. 3–8
Acts (of the Apostles), 131, 144–145
Acts of Thomas, 106
Adam, 31, 93, 109, fig. 4–14
Adler, Gerhard, 114&n, 130n, 177n
adversity, uses of, 155
Aeschylus, 42, 101
affect(s)
  and *coagulatio*, 100
  and a weak ego, 25
  immunity to, 44
  Holy Spirit or etherial fire as, 44
  and *mortificatio*, 150
  (affectivity) and *mortificatio*, 170–171
Agamemnon, 101
agathon, 187
Agni, 38–39
agone, 187
Aion, 204
air operation, 18; *see also sublimatio*
albedo, 147; *see also* white/whiteness
  defined, 40
  destruction of, in *mortificatio*, 156
  and *solutio*, 75
alchemical operations: *see* individual names
alchemical world-view, 3–4
alchemist, figs. 1–2, 7–9
alchemy
  dangers of, 7
  etymology of the word, 166
  and individuation, 2
  Jung's views on the significance of, 1–2
  mystery of, 7–8
  origin of, 168
  psychic component of, 19
  and psychotherapy, 5

secret nature of, 7
  understanding of, 14
alcoholism, 64
alcoolisation, 123
Alexander, H. B., 84n
Alexander the Great, 167, 230
Amalarius of Trier, 114
Ambrose, St., 71
analogy, use of, 100
analysis; *see also* psychoanalysis
  as a profession of dying, 170
Anaxagoras, 203
Anaximander, 10, 85, 198–199
Anaximenes, 10
Andrians, fig. 3–10
angels, fall of, fig. 4–3
anima
  and *coniunctio*, 215
  devils, 44
  as represented by Luna, 48
  mortificatio of, 150
  and possession, 45
anima candida, 120; *see also* white soul
anima media natura, 158
anima mundi, 144, 150
ANIMALS, figs. 2–2, 4–2
  birds (as *sublimatio* symbols), 120–122,
    129–130, 142
  crow, 164
  dove, 37, 122–123, fig. 5–3
  Dragon/dragon(s), 21, 22, 48, 137–139,
    143, 147, 150, 151–152, 154, 155,
    167, 172, 212–213, figs. 2–4, 3–9,
    6–3, 8–1
  eagle, 142, fig. 4–2
  fish, 214
  lamb/Lamb, 30, 38, 114, 155, 156, 220

lion, 18–19, 92, 95, 150–151, 155, 160, 163
mermaids/water nymphs, 54, 55, fig. 3–5
"peacock's tail," 147; see also cauda pavonis
pigeons, 122
raven, 165, 175
salamander, 100, fig. 2–6
serpent/viper, 212, figs. 4–12, 4–13, 5–10
sheep, 137, 207
toad, 152–155
turkey, 156
uroboros, 143
wolf, 18–19, 22, 97, fig. 2–1
worms, 157–158, 163, fig. 6–7
animus
    and coniunctio, 215
    devils, 44
    mortificatio of, 150
    and possession, 45
    as represented by Sol in solutio, 48n
antimony, 19
Antony, 123
Antony and Cleopatra, 123
Anthropos, 162–163
apeiron, 10, 12, 85, 187
Aphrodite, 37, 54, 194, fig. 3–4
Apocalypse, fig. 7–5
Apollo, 164
aqua mirifica, 75
aqua permanens, 72, 74, 75, 79
aqua sapentiae, 75; see also dew
Aquinas, Thomas (pseud.), fig. 7–7
arcanum/grand arcanum, 5
archetypal energies, 33
archetypal image(s), 98–99, 118
    of first matter, 10
    of parent figure, 98
archetypal psyche, 140, 168
    revelation of, in Mithraic individuation ritual, 128–129
archetype(s)
    and child development, 98–99
    indeterminacy of, 114
    parental, 98
    personalization of, 114
    Quaternity, 189
    of the wounded healer, 164
archons, planetary, 142
Ares, 193

Argonauts, the, 55
aristeron, 187
Aristotle, 10, 11, 187n, 197–198&n
Arnold of Villa Nova, 11
arren, 187
Artemis, 59, 60
artion, 187
asceticism, religious, 147
ash/ashes, 18, 40&n–42, 93, 104
Ashmole, Elias, 154n, 187n, 201n, fig. 3–9
Asklepios, 164
Asmodeus, 214
Athena, 194
athlon, 144; see also opus
Atman, 84
atomon megethos, 203
Atropos, 101
Atwood, M. A., 52n, 149n, 160n, 188n, 216n, 230n
Augustine, 17&n, 27&n, 28, 71, 137, 145, 180, 218
Aurora Consurgens, the, 209, 220, fig. 7–6
Avicenna, 79, 209
apathia, 125
augmentatio, 227
aurora, 147
Avichi, 28

Bacchae, The, 60
balneum regis, 19
baptism, 111
    in blood, 38, 72
    Christian, and solutio, 58–59
    and the fire-kneading woman, 24n
    imagery of in relation to Dionysian phallic symbolism, 63
    with lunar water and dragons, fig. 3–9
    and Noah's flood, 71
    as purification ritual, 72–74
Barchusen, J. K., fig. 1–2
Basilides, 204
Bathers, fig. 3–11
Bathsheba, 55, fig. 3–6
Baucis, 3
Beatrice, 139
being, three levels of, 19
Berthelot, M. P. E., 123&n
Bertine, Eleanor, 70n
Bessy, Maurice, 155n, fig. 6–6
Bevan, Edwyn, 35&n
Bhagavad-Gita, 202
Bible/Holy Scripture; see also New Testa-

ment, Old Testament, BIBLE
and symbolism of ashes, 40n
and food imagery, 111
and imagery of *putrefactio*, 158–160
BIBLE
OLD TESTAMENT
Daniel, 23
Exodus, 111, 155
Ezekiel, 127
Genesis, 35, 88, 158
Isaiah, 32, 40–41, 109
Jeremiah, 131, 177, 178
Job, 40n, 201
1 Kings, 194–195, 227
2 Kings, 131
Lamentations, 159
1 Maccabees, 131
Proverbs, 109, 158
Psalms, 32, 33, 68, 80, 109, 158, 201,
fig. 3–13
2 Samuel, 55
Song of Songs, 220
Zechariah, 32
NEW TESTAMENT
Acts of the Apostles, 131, 144–145
Colossians, 171
Corinthians, 40–41, 71, 162, 224
Ephesians, 66
Galatians, 87, 95
Luke, 204
Hebrews, 177
John, 80, 87, 104, 111, 160
Luke, 34, 204
Matthew, 28, 33, 90, 93, 111, 175, 176,
191, 207, 227
1 Peter, 71
2 Peter, 31
Revelation, 29–30, 38, 72, 220
Romans, 95, 154
2 Timothy, 41
APOCRYPHA
Daniel and Susanna, 55
Tobit, 214
biblical characters: *see* individual names
birds; *see also* crow, eagle, dove, pigeon,
raven, turkey
as *sublimatio* symbols, 120–122, 129–
130, 142
bismuth, 77
black/blackness/blackening, 20, 21, 26,
110, 147, 154, 156, 158, 163, 164, 175,
fig. 6–8; *see also nigredo* devil,

fig. 4–15
and symbolism of the head in *mortificatio*, 165–168, 173
as hallmark of *mortificatio*, 148–149
and *putrefactio*, 157, 158
as referring to the shadow, 149–150
and *solutio*, 51–52
black mass, 111
black *prima materia*, 118
blood, 38, 156, 178, 212
and baptism, 72
and *mortificatio*, 156
as *rubedo*, 147
body: *see also* flesh/flesh principle
perfection of, in *sublimatio*, 117–118
Boehme, Jacob, 35&n, 87–88&n, 91&n,
96&n
Bonus of Ferrara, 47n, 91n
Brahman, 84
Brahmanism, 44
bread, 109, 111; *see also* food, imagery of
Breasted, James, 131&n, 132n
Brehier, Emile, 10n
Bruce Codex, 36
Bruegel, Pieter the Elder, fig. 5–12
Buber, Martin, 137n
Budge, E. A. Wallis, 132–133, 134n, figs.
5–8, 6–9, 7–13
Buddhism, 44
Burnet, John, 85n, 203n

calcinatio, 17–46, 47, 72, 79, 83, 104, 117,
207, figs. 2–2, 2–3, 2–8
Book of Job as description of, 40n
chief feature of, 42–43
derivation from chemical procedure, 17
and desirousness, 22–23
fire of, 22–40, 42
and the king, 19–20, figs. 2–1, 2–14
product/end product of, 42–43
and punishment, 27–28
and purgatory, 26–27
and sexuality, 20–21
substance of, 42
Basil Valentine's recipe for, 18
calcination, chemical process of, 17, 43
Campbell, Robert J., 118&n
candle(s), 113, 114; *see also* wax
caput corvi, 165
caput mortuum, 165, 167
cauda pavonis, 147; *see also* peacock's tail
Celeus, 40

Cerberus, fig. 1–4
ceration, 76–77; see also liquifactio
chains and imprisonment, motif of, 93
Charles, R. H., 104n
Chaucer, 91&n
chemia, 166; see also khem
child
    development, 97–99
    image of, 11, 194
    of the philosophers, 163
    wolf children, 97
childhood innocence, 156
Christ; see also Jesus
    of the Apocalypse, fig. 7–5
    ascension of, 131, 144–145, 158
    baptism of, 73–74
    on baptism and rebirth, 161
    blood of, 66, 72
    as bread, 111
    and calcinatio, 33n
    cross of, 139
    crucifixion of, 64, 218, figs. 4–11, 7–12,
        8–3
    and evil, 93
    and fire, 27, 34
    as high priest, 177
    image, 179
    Incarnation of, 104–107
    and the Last Supper, fig. 4–15
    as Logos-Cutter, 191
    marriage with the Church, 220
    compared to Osiris, 172
    Passion of, 139, 175, 204
    as personal foundation, 27
    as Philosophers' Stone, 80
    resurrection of, 158
    scourging of, fig. 6–15
    Second Coming of, 31, 144–145
    spirituality of, 216
    and sulphur symbolism, 86
Christian/Christianity
    coniunctio imagery, 220
    and the dangers of unworthy practice of
        alchemy, 7
    and the Dionysian principle, 66
    and the use of honey, 91, 114
    martyrs, 137
    and mortificatio, 171
    mystics and mysticism, 137, fig. 5–9
    myth of the Incarnation, 104
    and the sacrament of Holy Communion,
        111

and solutio, 58–59
and sublimatio, 139, 144
symbolism, 204
Trinity, dogma of, 198
Chrysostom, Dio, 67
Circle of the Year, fig. 8–4
circulatio, 68, 142–144
Clotho, 101
coagulatio, 18, 47, 83–115, 117, 142, 143,
    154
    agents of, 86–87
    alchemical recipe for, 85
    churning as image of, 84–85
    and the Christian incarnation myth,
        105–107
    and clothing symbolism, 101–104
    and creation/creation myths, 83–85, 100
    defined, 83
    and desirousness, 87–90
    earth as synonym of, 83
    and ego development, 113–115
    and fate, 100–101
    and the flesh, 95–96, 107–109
    and food imagery, 109–111
    and honey, 90–91, 114
    and the parent-child relationship, 97–99
    and sin and evil, 91–93
    substance of, 85
    and wax symbolism, 114
cogitatio, 166
cogitatio matutina, 180
collectivization of the individual, 58–59
COLORS; see also gold, silver
    black/blackness, 20, 22, 26, 51–52, 110,
        118, 147, 148–150, 154, 156, 157,
        158, 163, 164, 165–168, 173, 175
    blackening, 147, 158
    nigredo, 26, 51, 147, 156, 158, 164,
        165–167, 172, 173, 180
    red/redness, 72, 147, 154, 165
    rubedo, 147
    white/whiteness, 26, 139, 147–148, 149,
        154, 156, 164, 165
    albedo, 40, 75, 147, 156
    white foliated earth, 104, 123, 209, fig.
        4–10
    white soul, 120
Colossians, Book of the Bible, 171
complex(es), 42, 85, 144, 209
    Oedipus complex, 212
compulsion, 86
concretion, 83n

concupiscence/*concupiscentia,* 27, 37, 42, 44, 95, 154, 223; *see also* desirousness, lust
coniunctio, 30, 111, 154, 200, 209, 211–232, figs. 6–8, 8–2, 8–3, 8–4, 8–5
  and death, 212–214
  defined, 211
  and fish imagery, 214
  greater, 215–232
  Jung's vision of, 221
  lesser, 212–215
    and the ego, 215
    product of, 212
  lesser and greater distinguished, 211
  and love, 223–227
  and lust, 212–214
  and *multiplicatio,* 227–228
  and the union of opposites, 217–220
  and the Philosophers' Stone, 215–216, 227, 228–230
  and psychotherapy, 228
  and marriage or sexual union, 217–221
  three stages of, 170–171
consciousness, 105, 140, 161, 187, 198, 216
  centers of, 20
  differentiation of, 171
  of one's own evil, 93
  evolution of, 8
  and the individual psyche, 9
  masculine, 95
  motive factor in, 86
  nature and, 8
  objective, 20
  origin and growth of, 168
  pure, 84
  ruling principle of, 19
  space for, 187
contained and the container, problem of, 56
Cook, A. B., 134n
copper, 3
Corinthians, Book of the Bible, 40–41, 71, 162, 224
Cornford, F. M., 100n, 199&n
corpus solis, 160, 161; *see also* gold
Coronis, 164
corvus, 164, 165; *see also* crow, raven
creation
  in alchemical recipes, 8–9
  and *coagulatio,* 83–84
  of humans, 93
  myths of, 47, 93, 100, 183–186, 197, 204

  according to Plato, 100
  and *separatio,* 188–189
  seven days of, 180
  symbolism of, 180
creativity, Dionysian, 64
crow, 164; *see also corvus,* raven
crucifixion, 113, figs. 4–11, 4–12; *see also* Christ, crucifixion of
Cumont, Franz, 27–28&n, 38n
cutting edges, 191, fig. 7–2; *see also* Logos-Cutter

Daniel, fig. 2–5
Daniel, Book of the Bible, 23
Daniel and Susanna, 55
Danielou, Jean, 39n, 84n
Dante, Alighieri, 139&n, 195–196, 197n, 224–225&n, fig. 5–11
David, 30, 55
death, 32, 95, 103–104, 129, 147–148, 154, 162–163, 168–171, 176–177, 199, 202, 212, 214, figs. 6–2, 6–4, 6–5, 6–7, 6–11, 6–14
  and *coniunctio,* 214
  of God, 179–180
  inner, 81
  Jung on corpses and, 162&n, 163&n, 168–169, 170–171&n
  Plato's view of, 170&n, 188&n
  and rebirth in baptism, 58
  and rebirth in Mithraism, 128
  and *separatio,* 191–193
death head, 167, 173, fig. 6–14
defeat and failure, 171–173
Deianeira, 38
Delacroix, E., fig. 4–7
Demeter, 40
demon(s): *see* devil(s)
Demophoon, 40
De Rerum Natura, 223
desire/desirousness, 22, 42, 44–45, 85–86, 90, 105, 212–213, 214; *see also* concupiscence, lust
  autoerotic, 19–20
  and *coagulatio,* 87
Deucalion/Deucalion's flood, 67–68
devekut, 136
Devil/devil(s), 44, 110, 147, 214, figs. 2–13, 4–15; *see also* Lucifer, Mephistopheles, spirit of, Satan
  and alchemy, 5
  animus and anima, 44

and psychotherapy, 5
and sulphur symbolism, 86
devouring parent, fig. 2–3
dexion, 187
dew, 74–75, 91, fig. 3 16; *see also aqua
     sapentiae*
diamond, 44, 107–108
Diana, fig. 3–8
Dickinson, Emily, 99&n
Dies Irae, 30
Dieterich, A., 34n, 128n
Dionysia, the, 63
Dionysian principle, the, 64–66
Dionysus, myth of, 60, 63–66, 93
dissociation, 126
divine water, 79
Djed pillar, 134
Don Juanism, 64–65
Doré, Gustave, figs. 2–7, 2–10, 3–12, 5–6,
     5–11, 7–8, 8–6
Dorn, Gerhard, 75, 90, 166, 170–171
double quaternity, 110
dove, 37, 122–123, fig. 5–3
Dragon/dragon(s), 21, 22, 48, 137–139,
     143, 147, 150, 151–152, 154, 155, 167,
     172, 212–213, figs. 2–4, 3–9, 6–3, 8–1
dreams; *see also* dreams, classification
     according to alchemical operation,
     DREAMS, DESCRIPTION BY
     CONTENT
   pertaining to alchemical operations, 20–
     21
   and circular motion, 144
   relating to floods, 68–71
   images of, 100
   pertaining to planets as metals, 3
   pertaining to the *prima materia,* 10–11
   symbols of *solutio* in, 58
dreams, classification according to alchemi-
     cal operation
   containing *calcinatio* imagery, 23
   —and fire, 24, 37
   containing *coagulatio* imagery, 90, 99,
     103, 113, 114
   —and clothing or fabric, 103, 104
   —and death, 103–104
   —and heavenly bodies, 90
   —with diamond imagery, 108
   —with food imagery, 109–111, 113
   containing *coniunctio* imagery, 228
   containing *mortificatio* imagery, 172, 178

—and Hades, 150
—and death/dead spirits, 162
containing *separatio* imagery, 193
—and cutting edges, 191
containing *solutio* imagery, 54–55, 57,
     61–63, 66, 69–70
—and creativity, 63–64
containing *sublimatio* imagery
—and birds, 121, 129–130
—with elevated places or ladders, 126,
     127, 130–131, 137
DREAMS, DESCRIPTION BY CON-
     TENT
the alchemists' secret is discovered, 228
birds are viewed from a tower through-
     out their life-cycle as time speeds
     up, 129–130
black slimy expanse surrounds dreamer
     whose struggles help to solidify it
     and free him, 85
black tar covers everyone in Hades dur-
     ing a sexual orgy, 150
candles are carried which signify life and
     death, 114
a carpet's completion represents the wov-
     en soul-work of a father's life, 103
chemists conduct experiments in an un-
     derground cavern while lovers lay
     in sexual embrace, 218
communion service turns into a rec-
     onciliation between two men after
     drinking the red wine of the ser-
     vice, 66
crashing down from atop a tall Man-
     hattan building, a boulder almost
     hits dreamer, 90
cremation with liquid gold as end prod-
     uct, 20
crucifixion intaglio is used in ritual meal
     during which dreamer reflects on
     the eating of metals, 113
daughter engages in indirect group sex
     after mother leaves the party, 63
dead friend tells a dream at a party at-
     tended by dreamer, 162
diamond is given to a pregnant woman
     dreamer in a subway, 108
after dinner is served at a monastery,
     a dessert of "cow-dung cookies"
     causes dreamer's distress, 111
dragon waits below a dangerous ladder

to capture climbers, but the dreamer (St. Perpetua) ascends to the top, 137–139

drowning, a dreamer exerts much effort and is saved by Jung in a Noah's ark, 70

in an elevator, dreamer frighteningly ascends skyward, 126

father deserts his children to follow a beautiful beckoning woman, 54–55

father is dressed in new clothes, 104

fire and smoke engulf dreamer in an underground cave, 23

flaming dinner table is reminiscent of Pentecost, 37

flight over the Alps, 129

floating in celestial Ether, a dreamer eats the shrunken world, 126

flood at night destroys all, followed by a new world life on the next day, 70

flood-stream of humanity passes by a fascinated dreamer, 70

food cooked and eaten by dreamer is taken by strange man in black, 110

four squares containing circles appear in connection with the dreamer's attitudes about femininity, 99

group lovemaking, 61

infancy and the *prima materia,* 11

king is killed with a sword; flames and a sword spring from his body, 20n

a ladder is removed, leaving dreamer stranded on a high platform, 126

a ladder is climbed by dreamer who is impelled skyward, 126

lame, Jung delivers a brilliant lecture, 172

a map must be cut by dreamer, 191

metal-clad visitors descend from the air, 3

moonlike body explodes, throwing a fragment into the dreamer's apartment, 90

mother is covered with hot slate, 20–21

pregnant dreamer in hospital is visited by girl with birds in her mouth, 121

roast is left too long in the oven, 103

shepherds embrace; one climbs a mountain, 193

tapestry is described and studied closely by dreamer, 103

tower is climbed by man daily, but dreamer is reluctant to do so, 127

tree covers earth, signifying love and individuation, 130

tree struck by lightening causes fertility in surroundings, 178

tree transforms frost into grapes, 178

turkey is killed, staining dreamer with blood, 156

water streams from mouth of dreamer's analyst, 80

waves flood a beach house while mother fears for the safety of his children, 69–70

waves splash onto the classroom audience who watches a beach exhibit containing fishing nets, 62

drowning, 47, 154, fig. 3–14; *see also* floods

drug addiction, 64

Dürer, Albrecht, figs. 2–12, 4–6, 4–8, 4–14, 6–11, 7–5

eagle, 142, fig. 4–2

earth
 feminine nature of, 95
 nursing the *Filius Philosophorum,* fig. 4–1
 operation, 18; *see also coagulatio*
 separation of sky from, 186, fig. 7–3
 as synonym for *coagulatio,* 83
 white (foliated), 104, 123, 209, fig. 4–10

Eckhart, Meister, 178&n

Edinger, Edward F., 19n, 40n, 66n, 140n, 156n, 172n, 203n, 230n

egg, philosophical, fig. 7–2

ego, 12, 19–20, 29, 56, 81, 85, 144, 150, 168, 171, 172, 174, 198, 202
 archetypal constituents of, 3
 -attitude, 48n
 and *calcinatio,* 44
 and *coagulatio,* 83, 85, 95, 111
 and *coniunctio,* 215
 and the ruling principle of the conscious, 151
 -consciousness, 24, 126
 creation of, 10
 destruction of, 65
 development, 88–90, 93, 97–98, 113–115
 and differentiation of subject and object, 187–188
 and the Dionysian principle, 65

and evil, 93
and food imagery, 109–110
incarnation of, 163
infantile, 49
inflated, 24, 53
as king, 52–53
neurotic, 49
primordial, 187
and psychotherapy, 228
and punishment, 93
purification of, 35
and Red Sea imagery, 72
and the Self, 114, 218
and *separatio,* 204
and *solutio,* 48–49, 59, 60, 68, 78
transpersonal value of, 105
and the unconscious, 230
egocentricity, 151
egohood
criminal aspects of, 93
redemptive function of, 107
egotism, 77
Egypt, ancient, 161, 166, 168–169
Egyptian
creation myth, 185–186
embalming, 158
myth of translation, 131–133
religion and *separatio,* 207
eight, significance of the number, 71
Eisler, Robert, 91n, 114n
elements, the four, 10, 30, 67–68, 83, 105,
188–189, 215–216
Eleusinian Mysteries, 7, 72
Eleusis, 40
Eliade, Mircea, 24&n, 58&n, 83n, 128n
Elijah, 131, 158, fig. 5–6
Eliot, T. S., 37–38&n, 174
Elisha, 131
elixir, 227
Elixir of Life, 9
elixir vitae, 79
Emerald Tablet of Hermes, the, 3, 8, 142,
144, 187, 230–232
Emerson, Ralph Waldo, 95&n, 126&n,
158&n, 200&n
Empedocles, 92–93&n
empiricism, psychological, 144
enantia, 187
end of the world, 29–31
Enobarbus, 123
Enoch, 128

Enoch, Book of, 104
Ephesians, Book of the Bible, 66
Ephreum, 24n
eremoun, 187
Eris, 193, 194
Eros, 226
principle, 54
as realm of the feminine principle, 21
symbolized as salt, 42
eternity
psychological meaning of, 140–142
symbolism of, 128–139
translation into, 134
Ethiopian/black Ethiopian, 21, 167
Eucharist, 111, 114, 118
Euripides, 60
euthu, 187
Evans-Wentz, W. Y., 87n
Eve, 93, 109, fig. 4–14
evening star, 180; *see also* Venus
evil, 91–93, 149, 172, 204
exhydrargyrosis, 123
exodus, the, 71–72, 158
Exodus, Book of the Bible, 111, 155
extractio, 200
extraction, 200–201
Eyck, Van, fig. 7–12
Ezekiel, 127
Ezekiel, Book of the Bible, 127

faith, religious, 144, 179
fantasies, alchemical, 211
fantasy images, 19
Fates/fate, 100–101, 103
Faust, 85, 168
fear, 158
feeling
function, 10, 189
realm of, 76
feminine
the archetypal, 59
principle, 48, 96–97
Figulus, Benedictus, 10n, 155n, 161n, 215n
filius macrocosmi, 144
filius philosophorum, 144, fig. 4–1
fire, 10, 17, 20–24&n, 26, 27, 29, 73, 99–
100, 118, 131, 152, 154, 174, 175, 188,
189, figs. 2–6, 2–9, 2–11
archetypal energies as, 33
astral and natural, 99–100
-bath, 40

as blood, 38
of *calcinatio,* 22–40, 42, figs. 2–4, 2–5
etherial and terrestrial, 44
associated with God, 33
and Hindu thought, 39
and the Holy Ghost, 35
mastery of, 24–25
operation, 18; *see also calcinatio*
punishment by/as punishment, 26–36,
    fig. 2–7
as purifier of the soul, 33
as quicklime, 17&n
sacrificial, 38
symbolism of, 18, 19
as tree of life, 35
two types of, 34
first matter, 10, 78; *see also prima materia*
fish, 59, 214
Fitzgerald, Edward, 76n
fixatio, 105; *see also coagulatio*
flesh/flesh principle, 95–96, 106–109, 114,
    163, 217
floods and flooding, 31, 67–72, 81, 83, 84,
    fig. 3–12; *see also* drowning, water
foliation, 123; *see also* earth, white (foliated)
food, imagery and symbolism of, 109–111,
    139, 163
Form/form(s), 96
    and baptism, 58
    eternal, 98, 125
    and matter, 10, 113–114
    Platonic, 118
    watery, 52
forty, significance of the number, 158
Freeman, Kathleen, 42n, 52n, 93n
Freud, Sigmund, 118
Frey, Liliane, 129
Frost, Robert, 31&n, 200&n
functions, the four, 10, 189

Galatians, Book of the Bible, 87, 95
gall, symbolism of, 214
gate of blackness, 156
Geb, 185–187, fig. 7–3
Genesis, Book of the Bible, 35, 88, 158
Gideon's dew, 75
Glauce, 38
glue, 189, 223
glutinum mundi, 223

Gnosticism/Gnostic thought, 1, 34, 36, 71,
    92, 162–163, 175–176, 191, 204
goat, 178
God
    actualization of, 178
    and alchemy, 5–6, fig. 1–2
    and *coagulatio,* 83
    concept of, according to Jung, 115
    and creation, fig. 7–1
    death of, 179–180
    feminine counterpart of, 158
    and fire, 33
    and flood myths, 67–72, 81
    and mortality, 168
    and the *opus,* 5–6
    and *sublimatio,* 127
god(s); *see also* GODS, INDIVIDUAL,
    goddesses, GODDESSES, INDIVIDUAL
    and the ego, 3
GODS, INDIVIDUAL
    Agni, 38–39
    Apollo, 164
    Ares, 193
    Dionysus, 60, 63–66, 93
    Eros, 21, 42, 54, 226
    Geb, 185–187, fig. 7–3
    Helios, 74
    Horus, 133, 134
    Jupiter, 3, 134, 135
    Mars, 1, 134, 135
    Mercury, 3, 134
    Mithra(s), 33, 114, 128
    Nut, 185–187, fig. 7–3
    Osiris, 60, 74, 133, 134, 161, 167, 168–169,
        172, 207, figs. 5–8, 6–9
    Poseidon, 67–68
    Ra/Re, 132, 133
    Saturn, 3, 86, 91–92, 96, 134, 135, 139
    Set, 133
    Shiva, fig. 2–11
    Shu, 185, fig. 7–3
    Sol, 48&n, 51, 96, 150, 151, 217, 218,
        figs. 6–3, 7–6, 8–4, 8–5; *see also* Helios
    Zeus, 93, 218, 227
goddess(es); *see also* god(s), GODS, IN-
    DIVIDUAL, GODDESSES, INDI-
    VIDUAL
    of birth, 101
    of Discord, 193
    of Truth, 207

GODDESSES, INDIVIDUAL

Aphrodite, 37, 54, 194, fig. 3–4
Artemis, 59, 60
Athena, 194
Atropos, 101
Clotho, 101
Demeter, 40
Diana, fig. 3–8
Eris, 193, 194
Fates, 100–101, 103
Hebe, 101
Hera, 27, 67, 101, 172, 194, 218, 227
Hestia, 67
Lachesis, 101
Luna, 48&n, 51, 75, 96, 217, 218, figs. 6–3, 7–6, 8–4, 8–5
Maat, 207
Persephone, 40
Venus, 3, 53–54, 134, 135, 180
Godhead, the, 204
God-image, 152, 179
Goethe, 60, 63n, 85n, 168&n, 177
gold, 3, 8, 18, 19, 48, 76, 104, 118, 160–161, 167–168, 173, 202, 209, 211, 215, fig. 4–10
golden mean, 197–198
golden section, 197, 198
golden water, 218
Golden Treatise of Hermes, the, 52, 188
Goodenough, Erwin R., 189&n
Gospel of Thomas, the, 34, 191
grace, 75
grand arcanum, 5
Grant, Robert M., 34n
Gray, Thomas, 171
Great Magistery, the, 230
Great Mother, 49
grinding, symbolism of, 123
guilt, 93

Hamlet, 91, 167
hammering, meaning and symbolism of, 123
Hades, 30, 74, 150; see also hell
Harding, Esther, 19–20&n, 217–218&n
Harding, St. Stephen, fig. 2–5
Hasidism, 136
Hastings, James, 28n, 31n, 32n, 68n
hate, 92–93
Hayes, Dorsha, 25, 26n

head, symbolism of, 165–167, 173, fig. 6–13; see also death head
Heavenly Rose, the, fig. 8–6
Hebe, 101
hell, 19, 28–29, 79, 86; see also Hades
Hebrews, Book of the Bible, 177
Helios, 74
hen, 187
Hera, 27, 67, 101, 172, 194, 218, 227
Heracles, 38, 55, 131
Heraclitus, 10, 31, 42n, 52, 193
Hermes Trismegistus, 230, 232
Hermetic Museum, the, 33n, fig. 1–1, 6–10
hero, imagery of, 152, 172
Herod, 155
Hesiod, 40n
Hestia, 67
heteromékes, 187
hierosgamos, the, 222
Hinduism / Hindu
    and coagulatio, 83
    and fire, 39
    myth of the flood, 84
Hinsie, Leland E., 118&n
Hippolytus, 204&n
Holbein, Hans, figs. 6–4, 6–14
Holmes, Oliver Wendell, 101
Holy Spirit / Holy Ghost, 35, 36, 37, 142, 160
    as affect, 44
    as etherial fire, 44, 79
honey, 86–87, 90–91, 114, 212
Honorius of Autun, 72
Horus, 133, 134
Howell, Alice, 130n
Hylas, 55, fig. 3–5

Iamblichus, 39, 40n
I Ching, the, 77, 127&n, 157, 228
id, 118
idealism, 125
Iliad, the, Homer's, 33, 218
illness, mental, 126
Il Penseroso, Milton's, 127
imagery / images; see also specific subjects
    of animals: see ANIMALS
    astrological, 142
    fantasy, 19
    of a child, 11
    of clothing, 101, 104
    of drowning, 52–53, 57

of *mortificatio*, 148
of planets as metals, 3-4
of *putrefactio*, 157
of sublimation, 120, 145
of swords, 35
Imitation of Christ, the, 155
immortality, 128
incarnation, 87, 96, 101, 106, 107-108, 112, 115, 130-131, 142, 163
Incarnation of the Divine Logos, 104
incense, 214
incest
    and *solutio*, 48
    uroboric, 49
increatum, the, 12
Indians, North American
    creation myths of, 83-84
individuation, 2, 15, 85, 104, 110, 111, 115, 140, 154, 170, 199, 202, 223, 227-228
    and alchemy, 2
    as world-creating process, 9
Inferno, Dante's, 195-197
inflation, 64
    solipsistic, 9
inner partner/inner companion, 175
innocence, 11, 75, 155-156, fig. 6-6
instinct(s), 118, 171
    power of, 151
instinct bath, 60
intuition (function), 10, 189
Ion, 177
Ions, Veronica, 186n
Iphigenia, 101
iron, 3, 132-133, 137
Isaiah, 12, 29, 40, 111, 175
Isaiah, Book of the Bible, 32, 40-41, 109
Ischys, 164
Isis, 60, 74, 133
Israelites, 158
Isolde, 50
Ixion, 27

Jacob of Batnae, 139
Jacoby, E., fig. 2-9
Jaffe, Aniela, 86&n
James, M. R., 30n, 32n, 106n
Jason, 38, 172
Jeremiah, 158-159
Jeremiah, Book of the Bible, 131, 177-178
Jeremiah, A., fig. 7-3
Jesus, 6, 11, 158, 175-176; *see also* Christ

as separater of created objects, 204
Jesus patibilis, 105
Job, 40n, 168
Job, Book of the Bible, 40n, 201
John the Baptist, 24n, fig. 6-13
John of the Cross, St., 158-159&n
John the Evangelist, 41-42, 80, fig. 2-12
John, Gospel of, 80, 87, 104, 111, 160
Jonas, Hans, 106n
Josephus, 31&n
Judas, 95, fig. 4-15
Jung, C. G., 3n, 8, 9&n, 12n, 15&n, 18n, 21n, 24n, 33n, 45n, 47n, 49n, 51n, 54n, 72n, 85n, 101, 151n, 189n, 200n, 203n, 209n, 212n, 217n, 218n, 230&n, 232n
    on the alchemists' understanding of matter, 1
    on alchemy, 1-2&n, 15
    on the indeterminacy of archetypes, 114&n
    on ash and glass, 40n
    on bitterness, 214-215
    on blackening, 158&n
    on blackness, 164n, 165&n
    on the distinction between the Christian and the alchemical attitude, 144&n
    on Christ's crucifixion and suffering, 177
    on Christ's Passion, 204&n
    on *circulatio*, 143&n
    on *coagulatio*, 86&n
    on compulsion, 86&n
    on *coniunctio*, 216
    coniunctio vision of, 221-223&n
    on the experience of darkness, 175&n
    on death and corpses, 162&n, 163&n, 168-169&n, 170-171&n
    on desirousness, 44
    on dissolution by identification with creative powers, 64&n
    on the slaying of the dragon, 150
    on dream interpretation, 80&n
    dream of, concerning the tree of life, 178&n
    on drowning imagery, 52&n
    on the death of the ego-personality, 129&n
    on emotions, 100&n
    on the Eucharist, 111&n
    on evil, 93&n
    on the distinction between faith and the alchemical attitude, 179&n

on the feminine principle, 97
on fire symbolism, 100&n
on Freud, 118&n
on Gnosticism, 71&n
on God, 115
on guilt, 95n
on the symbolism of the head, 166&n,
   167n
on the oracular head, 167
on honey symbolism, 91&n
on images and emotions, 100&n
on individuation, 115&n, 128&n
on the inner companion, 175&n
on Job and Yahweh, 168&n
on transpersonal love, 226 227&n
on the Mithraic ritual of individuation,
   128&n
on moon and dew symbolism, 74 75&n
on "morning" and "evening" knowledge,
   180&n
on mortality, 168
on *mortificatio,* 150&n, 154&n, 166
on the opposites, 206&n, 216&n
on the *opus,* 147&n, 158
on personality, 65, 228&n
on possession, 86&n
on psychotherapy, 78&n, 228
on punishment and torment, 30n
on the symbolism of the raven and blackness, 164n, 165&n
on the *Rosarium,* 163
on sacrifice, 177&n
on salt symbolism, 42&n
on the Self, 115
on self and ego, 171
on *separatio,* 204n-205
on *solutio,* 56&n, 58&n, 78&n, 80&n,
   81&n
sublimatio vision of, 140 142&n
on sublimation and *sublimatio,* 118,
   140 142&n
on suffering, 42&n, 177, 215&n
on sulphur symbolism, 86&n
on the tree of life, 178
on the *unio mentalis,* 170 171
Jupiter, 3, 134, 135
jus, 198
justice/Justice, 198 199, fig. 7 10

Kabbala, 220
kabbalists, 136, 220, 222
kakon, 187

kampulon, 187
Kazantzakis, Nikos, 31n
Keats, John, 193
Kelly, Edward, 10n, 47n, 56n, 79&n, 123n,
   202&n, 209&n
Kempis, Thomas à, 29n, 155&n
Kerenyi, C., 164 165&n
khem, 166; *see also chemia*
king/King, 47, 52, 132, 155, 163, 172, 194,
   fig. 7 7
   and *calcinatio,* 19 20, figs. 2 1, 2 14
   and drowning imagery, 52 54, fig. 3 3
   and *mortificatio,* 150 151, 168, 179, figs.
      6 4, 6 5
   and *solutio,* 51 54, 75, figs. 3 2, 3 3,
      3 16
   transfixion of, fig. 4 13
King, Edward, 193
King Lear, 172 174
1 Kings, Book of the Bible, 194 195, 227
2 Kings, Book of the Bible, 131
kinoumenon, 187
Kirk, G. S., 193n
Kluger, Rivkah, 68, 70n
knowledge
   "morning" and "evening," 180
   philosophical, 75
Kuhul, 85; *see also* lead
Kunz, G. F., 107n

Lachesis, 101
ladder, symbolism of, 133 134, 136 139,
   145, figs. 5 8, 5 9, 5 11
lamb/Lamb, 30, 38, 114, 156, 220
   Marriage of the, 220
   Paschal, 155
Lamentations, Book of the Bible, 159
Lao Tse, 77
lapis Lydius, 30n
lapis philosophorum, 30n, 216, 217; *see
   also* Philosophers' Stone
Last Judgment
   and fire imagery, 29 31
   and *separatio* symbolism, 206 209, figs.
      7 12, 7 13, 7 14
Last Supper, fig. 4 15
lead, 3, 76, 86, 93 95
Lear, King, 172 173
leukosis, 147
Liberty, fig. 4 7
libido, 18, 76, 90, 167, 188, 201
   infantile forms of, 150

lion
  and *calcinatio*, 18–19
  and *coagulatio*, 92, 95
  and *mortificatio*, 150–151, 155, 160, 163
liquefactio, 76–77
Logos, 12, 34, 189, 191
  Divine, 104
Logos-Cutter, 189, 191, 200
logos spermatikos, 35
Longfellow, Henry Wadsworth, 145
love, 27, 38, 75, 77, 112–113, 220, 223–227
  divine, 17n
  as agent of *solutio*, 55
  transpersonal, 223–227
Lucian, 28
Lucifer, 180; *see also* Devil/devil(s), Satan
Lucretius, 223, 224&n
Luke, Book of the Bible, 34, 204
Luna, 48&n, 51, 75, 96, 217, 218, figs. 6–3,
  7–6, 8–4, 8–5; *see also* moon
lust, 60, 212–214; *see also* concupiscence,
  desire/desirousness
  as agent of *solutio*, 55
Lycidas, 193

Maat, 207
1 Maccabees, Book of the Bible, 131
MacIntyre, C. F., 123n
Macrobius, 88n, 134&n
madness, 172, 174
Maenads, the, 60, 65
Magistery, 7
  Great Magistery, 230
magnesia, 86, 160
Maier, Michael, 209n, figs. 2–1, 2–6, 2–8,
  2–14, 3–15, 4–1, 4–4, 6–3, 7–2, 7–9,
  8–1
Mair of Landshut, fig. 6–15
Malchuth, 220
mandala, fig. 8–8
Mandara, 84
Maneros, 60
Manicheans/Manicheanism, 44, 105
Manu, 84
Marolles, M. de, fig. 1–3
Mars, 3, 134, 135
Marseilles Tarot, figs. 7–4, 7–10
masculine principle, the, 19, 48
mater, 96; *see also* matter
materiality, principle of, 104–105
Mathers, S. L. MacGregor, 221n
matter, 11, 96, 105, 125

and alchemy, 1
attenuation of, 123
and evil, 92
first, 10; *see also* prima materia
and form, 10
living, 114
separation of, from spirit, 201–202
suffering of, 147
transformation of, 10
Matthew, Book of the Bible, 28, 33, 90, 93,
  111, 175, 176, 191, 207, 227
Matthew, the Evangelist, 28
Mead, G. R. S., 36n
Medea, 38
Melchior, 21n
Melito of Sardis, 73
melting, 76–77, 78; *see also* liquefactio
Mephistopheles, Spirit of, 85
Mercurius, 85–86, 95, 150, 163, 189, 200,
  fig. 5–5
Mercury, 3, 134
mercury, 48, 85, 122, 211
mermaids/water nymphs, 54, 55, fig. 3–5
Meschach, 24
Messiah, the, 158, 175
metals, 3, 10, 19, 183; *see also* individual
  names
  and *coniunctio*, 211
  dissolution of, 155
  "leprosy of the," 175
  nobility of, 77
  purification of, 31
  chemical processing of, in *solutio*, 48, 78
  transmutation of, 78
Metaneira, 40
Meydenbach, J., fig. 6–7
Michael, the Archangel, fig. 7–14
Michelangelo, 37&n
Michelspacher, Steffan, *frontispiece*
Milton, John, 88&n, 127, 193
Mithraic ritual of initiation, 128
Mithraism, taurobolium rite of, 38, 72
Mithra(s), 33, 114, 128
Mohammad, 128
monosandolos, 172
moon, 3, 60, 74–75, 95–96, 123, 134, 150,
  163, 209, 211, fig. 4–6; *see also* Luna
  as *aqua mirifica*, 75
Moreau, G., fig. 4–5
morning star, 180; *see also* Venus
mortificatio, 19, 35, 52, 91, 95, 111, 147–
  180, 202, 211, 212, 215

agent of, 158
and blackness/*nigredo,* 148–149, 158–160, 167, 173
Christian imagery of, 155, 160–161, 171, 175–179
and the collective psyche, 179–180
and death/burial, 161–163, 167–171
as defeat and failure, 172
defined, 147–148
distinguished from *putrefactio,* 148
and dragon imagery, 150–152, 154
and gold imagery, 160–161, 173
and symbolism of the head/skull, 165–168, 173
and the inner companion, 175
and symbolism of the king, 150–151, 163, 168, 179, figs. 6–4, 6–5
and the number forty, 158
and the law of opposites, 177
and purity/innocence, 155
putrefactio imagery in, 157–158
and raven imagery, 164–165
Ripley's vision of, 152–154
and the psychology of sacrifice, 177–179
and the Self, 173–174
and the shadow, 149
Shakespearean imagery of, 154
skeleton, fig. 6–1
Moses, 127, fig. 7–11
Moses and Khidr, Moslem legend of, 58n
Mother, Great, 49
mourning, 202
multiplicatio, 227, 228
mummy/*mumia,* 163
Munch, Edward, fig. 5–4
mundificatio, 209
Murray, Gilbert, 172
Mylius, J. D., figs. 3–2, 6–12
Mysterium Coniunctionis, 2, 86, 170–171
mysteries, alchemical, 7–8
myths: *see also* GODS, GODDESSES, individual subjects
of Actaeon, 59
concerning animals: *see* ANIMALS
of Asklepios, 164–164
Christian, of Divine Incarnation, 104, 106
creation, 83
of Dionysus, 60
Egyptian, of life after death, 132–134
concerning floods, 67–72, 84

Gnostic, of incarnation, 106
Greek, 67, 164
of the hero, 150
concerning water, 52–55

nature, 11, 48, 65, 166, 173, 183, 191, 198
and art, 8
and the *opus,* 8
and quicksilver, 123
Nebuchadnezzar, 23–24
nekyia, 169
Nemean Odes, Pindar's, 101n
Neoplatonism, 88
Nemesis, fig. 4–8
Nessus, 38
Neumann, Erich, 49&n, 98&n
New Testament, 87; *see also* BIBLE
Nietzsche, Friedrich, 64, 65, 66n
nigredo, 26, 51, 147, 156, 158, 164, 165–167, 172, 173, 180, figs. 6–8, 6–12; *see also* black/blackness, blackening
Noah's flood, 67, 71
Norton, Thomas, 5
Nous: *see* Logos
numinosum, the, 81, 123
Nut, 185–187, fig. 7–3

Oates, W. J., 42n, 101n
Odes of Pindar, the, 101n
odor sepulcrorum, 157
Oedipus, 172
Oedipus complex, 212
Old Testament; *see also* BIBLE
and food imagery, 109
metallurgical metaphors in, 31–32
and *solutio,* 55, fig. 3–12
O'Neill, Eugene, 42n, 101n
Onians, R. B., 101n
Opicinus de Canistris, fig. 8–8
opposites
combination of, 79, 80, 214, 215, 216, 217, 223
law of, 149
pairs of, 57, 59, 187, 206
separation of, 186–187, 189, 195, 198–199, 204, 206, 209
transit through/realization of, 143
opus, 4–9, 20, 44, 47, 72, 75, 80, 144, 147, 150, 154, 158, 168, 201, 209, 211, 215, 220, 230, *frontispiece*
Ordinal of Alchemy, Thomas Norton's, 5

Origen, 28–29&n
Osiris, 60, 74, 133, 134, 161, 167, 168–169,
    172, 207, fig. 5–8
Otto, Walter, 60&n, 63&n
Ovid, 183–184&n

panta rhei, 71
Paracelsus, 32&n, 90&n–91, 125&n, 149n,
    162–163, 188, 228n
Paradiso, Dante's, 139
Paris, 193, 194, fig. 7–7
participation mystique, 187, 191, 193, 202
particulars, concrete, 79
Paschal lamb, 155
Passion of Christ, 175, 178–179, 204
pathos, 172
Paul, the Apostle, 8, 27, 29, 41, 58, 66, 71,
    87, 95, 104, 154, 161, 171, 224, 226;
    see also BIBLE: NEW TESTAMENT
"peacock's tail," 147; see also cauda pavonis
Pentecost, 36–37, fig. 2–10
Pentheus, 60
Pepi, 134
peras, 187
Peratics, the, 71
peritton, 187
Perpetua, St., 137–139
Persephone, 40
persona, 101
personality, 11, 144, 152, 228
    of the child, 97
    dissolution of, 19
    fragmentation of, 12
    integration of, through calcinatio, 30
    and the patient-therapist relation, 78–79
    solidification of, 85
personalization
    of archetypes, 99
    secondary, 98
1 Peter, Book of the Bible, 71
2 Peter, Book of the Bible, 31
Phaedo, 169–170
Phaedrus, 101
Phaethon, 68
phallus, 63, 128
Pharaoh's army, fig. 3–14
Philalethes, 51
Philemon and Baucis, 3
Philo, 2&n, 189, 191
Philosophers' Stone, 3, 6, 8, 9, 11, 14, 30n,
    43, 45, 68, 72, 80, 104, 120, 152, 154,

160, 163, 168, 177, 201, 215, 216, 227,
    228–230
philosophical egg, fig. 7–2
philosophical water, 79
philosophic earth, 154, 160
phos, 187
Physis, 158
pigeons, 122
Pindar, 101
planets, 142
    alchemical view of, 3
PLANETS
    Jupiter, 3, 134, 135
    Mars, 3, 134, 135
    Mercury, 3, 134
    Saturn, 3, 12, 86, 91–92, 96, 134, 135,
        139, figs. 4–4, 5–11
    Venus, 3, 134, 135, 180; see also evening
        star, morning star
    fountains of, 53–54
Plato, 100&n, 101, 125, 169, 170&n, 188&n–
    189, 197&n, 202&n, 223, 225
Platonic forms, 118
pleroma, 12, 206
plethos, 187
Plutarch, 60&n, 63
pneuma, 122; see also spirit
Poseidon, 67–68
possession, 44, 64, 86, 118
potentiality, pure, 10, 11
pre-Socratic philosophers, 9–10, 47, 187;
    see also Anaximenes, Anaxagoras,
    Anaximander, Empedocles, Heracli-
    tus, Pythagoreans, Thales
Priestley, J. B., 129, 131
prima materia, 9–15, 18, 21, 47, 68, 72, 78,
    79, 80, 85, 118, 150, 154, 175, 177, 183,
    189, 212, 230, figs. 1–3, 1–4, 2–1, 2–6;
    see also prime matter
prime matter, 86, 160; see also prima ma-
    teria
projection(s), 1, 10, 147, 170, 202, 206
Prometheus, 93, figs. 4–5, 5–5
proiectio, 227
Proverbs, Book of the Bible, 109, 158
Psalms
    No. 8, 201
    No. 22, 158
    No. 63, 80
    No. 66, 32
    No. 69, 68, fig. 3–13

No. 80, 109
No. 104, 33
psyche
  adult, 20
  archetypal, 14, 24, 40, 44, 85, 144
  autonomous, 169
  collective, 179
  dissociation of, 126
  individual, 9, 223
  instinctual, 150
  and *mortificatio,* 167
  objective, 3, 98, 100, 228, 230
  personal, 144
  primordial, 152
  reality of, 131, 169, 216
  and the Red Sea, 72
  secret of the, 8
  transpersonal, 172
  transpersonal center of, 79
  transpersonal level of, 6
  unconscious, 1
  understanding of, 1
psychoanalysis
  and *mortificatio,* 170
  and *solutio,* 60
  and sublimation, 118
Psychology of the Transference, The,
  Jung's, 75
psychosis, 9
psychotherapy, 1, 2, 10
  and alchemy, 1, 6
  and *calcinatio,* 42–43
  and *circulatio,* 144
  and *coagulatio,* 88, 97, 99
  and *coniunctio,* 216
  depth, 2
  etymology of the word, 2
  ·and *mortificatio,* 150, 171
  and *multiplicatio,* 228
  and the *prima materia,* 12, 48
  and *separatio,* 187–188
  and *solutio,* 47–48, 57, 78
  and *sublimatio,* 142
punishment, fig. 4–5
  by fire, 26–30
  Jung's views on, 64
purgatory, 26–27
purification, 170, 209, 215, fig. 3–16
purity, 155
putrefactio, 95, 147–148, 152, 157, 158,
  160; *see also* putrefaction/putrefication

putrefaction/putrification, 78, 149, 155; *see*
  also putrefactio
Pyrrha, 67
Pythagoreans, 187

Quaternity archetype, 189
quaternity, double, 110
queen
  and putrefaction, 163
  and *solutio,* 51, 75, figs. 3–2, 3–16
quicklime, 17&n, 23
quicksilver, 3, 85, 123

Ra/Re, 132, 133
Rackham, Arthur, fig. 3–1
Rahner, Hugo, 71n, 74n
Raphael, the angel, 214
Raven, J.E., 193n
raven/crow, 165, 175; *see also corvus*
Read, John, 3n, 19&n, 47n, 166n, 209n,
  227n, 230n
reason, 5, 125, 134
  Divine, 35
red/redness, 72, 147, 154, 165; *see also*
  rubedo
red stone, 211
Red Sea, imagery of, 71–72, fig. 3–14
reincarnation, 87, 130–131
Rembrandt, figs. 3–6, 4–9
Renoir, fig. 3–11
repentance, 40&n
Reusner, H., fig. 5–5
revelation, 127–128
Revelation, Book of the Bible, 29–30, 38,
  72, 220
Rhine Maidens, fig. 3–1
rhinisma (filings), 123
Rilke, 123n
Ring of the Nibelung, The, 49
Ripley, Sir George, 21n, 43, 186, 200
rites and rituals, 77; *see also* baptism
  concerning ascent and descent, 128
  of burial, 168–169
  concerning death, 172
  concerning the number eight, 71
  of Holy Communion, 111
  of individuation, 111
  Mithraic, of initiation, 128
  involving wax, 114
Roethke, Theodore, 173, 174&n
Rohde, Erwin, 33&n

Romans, Book of the Bible, 95, 154
Rosarium Philosophorum, the, 51, 75, 154, 163, fig. 3-16
Rosinus, 12
rotundum, 167
Rubaiyat of Omar Khayyam, the, 75
rubedo, 147; *see also* red/redness
Ruland, Martin, 76, 77n, 83n, 86&n, 154, 156-157, 200n, 216&n

sacrifice, 177, 204
  burnt, 38
  victim of, 155, 156
sacraments, the, 111; *see also* Eucharist
saints: *see* individual names
salamander, 100, fig. 2-6
Salome, fig. 6-13
salt, 42, 214f
salvation, 147
  and *solutio,* 71
Samson, 92
2 Samuel, Book of the Bible, 55
Sapientia Dei, the, 215
Sarah, 214, 230
Satan, 40n, 204; *see also* Devil/devil(s), Lucifer
Saturn, 3, 86, 91-92, 134, 135, 139, figs. 4-4, 5-11
Saturn's child, 12
Saturn's day, 180
schizophrenia, 99
schizmatics, 196-197, fig. 7-8
Scholem, Gershom, 136&n
Schopenhauer, Arthur, 9, 125&n
secondary personalization, principle of, 98
Secrets of Enoch, 128
seed consciousness, 161
seeds and planting, 160-162, 163, figs. 6-9, 6-10
Sefirah/Sefirot, 136
Self, the, 11, 24, 71, 72, 81, 105, 123, 163, 171, 172-173, 174, 191, 194, 198, 201, 215, 223, 227
  and *coagulatio,* 86
  as symbolized by crucifixion intaglio, 113
  and diamond symbolism, 108
  as unconscious prefiguration of the ego, 115
  in relation to the ego, 218
  -energy, 29

as fire-kneading woman, 24&n
and food imagery, 111
latent, 56
as product of *mortificatio,* 163
and the *opus,* 6
projection of, 57
and *separatio,* 201, 202, 207
and *solutio,* 58, 79, 80
transpersonal, 85
Senior, 40n
sensation (function), 10, 189
separatio, 20, 35, 122, 183-209, 215
serpent/viper, 212, figs. 4-12, 4-13, 5-10
Set, 133
Seven Sermons to the Dead, Jung's, 204-206
sexuality, 20, 60
shadow, the, 6, 12, 21, 72-73, 93, 149, 215
Shadrach, 24
Shakespeare, William, 114n, 123-125, 154-155&n, 167-168, 170, 172-173, 213-214, 225-226
shamans/shamanism, 24, 128
sheep, 137, 207
Shekinah, the, 220
Shelley, Percy Bysshe, 193
Shiva, fig. 2-11
Shu, 185-187, fig. 7-3
skotos, 187
Sibyl/Sibyline Oracles, 30, 32
silver, 3, 31-32, 48, 211
Simeon Stylites, fig. 5-10
Simmias, 170
Simon bar Yochai, 220, 222
sin/sinfulness, 29&n, 72, 86, 87, 151
skull, 167-168; *see also* head, death head
Sol, 48&n, 51, 96, 150, 151, 217, 218, figs. 6-3, 7-6, 8-4, 8-5; *see also* sun, Helios
Solomon, 194-195
solutio, 17, 18, 31, 47-81, 83, 99, 117, 212, fig. 3-15
  agents of, 55-56
  alchemical recipe for, 48
  seven major aspects of, 78
  and baptism, 58, 71-72
  blissful, 49-51
  chemical basis of, 48
  Christian imagery of, 66, 71-73, 80
  defined, 47, 55
  and dew symbolism, 74-75, fig. 3-16
  Dionysian, 60-66

and drowning, 52–53, 57, fig. 3–14
twofold effect of, 51
and ego development, 49, 53, 56–58
and flood myths or imagery, 67–72
as fragmentation and dismemberment, 59–60
within a group, 57, 60–61
imagery of, 51
and symbolism of the king, 52–53, figs. 3–2, 3–3, 3–16
lesser and greater aspects of, 79
and *liquifactio,* 76–77
and symbolism of the moon, 74
and *mortificatio,* 51–52
Old Testament imagery of, 55, 80
and psychoanalysis, 60, 78–79
and psychotherapy, 57
and Red Sea imagery, 71–72, fig. 3–14
and reduction of *prima materia,* 47–48, 79
and salvation, 71
as leading to the Self, 79, 81
as solution to problems, 75–76
symbolism/symbolic equivalents for, 58, 78
as descent into the unconscious, 48–49
and uroboric incest, 49
water as goal of, 79–80
and imagery of the womb, 48
son-ego, 212
Song of Songs, the, 220
Sophia, 158
soul(s), 29, 31, 51, 101–102, 117, 120, 122, 147, 152, 159, 174, 209
fall of, 92
incarnation and reincarnation of, 87–88
integration of, 147
Kabbalist doctrine of, 136
and *mortificatio,* 166, 170–171
and *separatio,* 202, figs. 7–13, 7–14
translation to eternity of, 134
white, 120
spheres, planetary, 134–136, 142, fig. 6–14
spirit(s)
coagulation of, 79, 100, 114
consolidation of, 79
and *mortificatio,* 152, 170–171
planetary deities as, 3
of the *prima materia,* fig. 2–6
and *separatio,* 201–202
of *sublimatio,* 139
sublimation of, 117, 123, 125

transpersonal, 86
as hidden wind, 213
year-, 172
spiritus phantasticus, 64
stars, 74, fig. 8–7
stella matutina, 180
Stephen Harding, St., fig. 2–5
stoics/stoicism, 30–31, 34, 125, 171
Stolcius, figs. 4–2, 6–5
stone, the: *see* Philosophers' Stone
subject and object, separation of, 187–188
sublimatio, 18, 47, 83, 100, 117–145, fig. 5–2
as attenuation of matter, 123
and bird imagery, 120–122, 142
Christian imagery of, 137–139, 142, 144–145, fig. 5–9
and *circulatio,* 142–144
dangers and misuse of, 126–127
defined, 117–118
and extraction procedure, 122–123
etymology of the word, 117
and grinding or hammering imagery, 123–125
images and symbolism of, 117–118, 120, 126–127, 142–143
as purification, 125
psychological significance of, 139–143
and sublimation, 118–120
distinguished from Freudian sublimation, 118
and towers, ladders, or high places, 126–139, 142–143
and translation to eternity, 131–142
sublimation, 38, 117–120
Freudian theory of, 118
substance, 51
of *calcinatio,* 42–44
and *coagulatio,* 114
mineral, 11–12
orignial: *see* first matter, *prima materia*
purification of, 26, 32, 44
transformation of, 47
transforming, 223
suffering, 147, 177–178
sulphur, 85–87, 211
sun, 3, 73–74, 134, 150–151, 155, 158, 163, 209, 211; *see also* Helios, Sol
Sun-day, 180
sun-hero, 171
Sun Mithras, 128
Susanna, 55, fig. 3–7

sweetness: *see* honey
swords and cutting edges, 189–191, 194, figs. 7–2, 7–4
symbols/symbolism; *see also* individual subjects
  alchemical, 1–2, 15
  of animals: *see* ANIMALS
  Book of Job as symbolic description of *calcinatio,* 40n
  of the number eight, 71
  of fire, 18
  of the head, 165
  on incest, 48
  of the lion, 19
  mortuary, 168–169
  of the planets as metals, 3–4
  of purgatory, 26–27
  of the Self, 11
  of *separatio,* 197
  of *solutio,* 58
  of *sublimatio,* 117
  of sulphur, 86–87
  of transformation, 15
  of translation to eternity, 128–139
  of white earth, 104–105
  of the wolf, 19
Synesius, Bishop, 64

Tantrism, 44
Tao, the, 77
Tarot, Marseilles, figs. 7–4, 7–10
Tarquin Priscus, 142
Tet pillar, 134
tetragonon, 187
Thales, 10, 47
thèlu, 187
theophany, 172
therapeuein, 2
Therapeuts, 2
thinking (function), 10, 189
threnos, 172
thysia, 38, 39
Tibetan Book of the Dead, the, 87
Tifereth, 220
Timaeus, 110, 188
2 Timothy, Book of the Bible, 41
tin, 3
tincture/Tincture, 72, 78, 79, 215, 228
Tintoretto, fig. 3–7
Titans, 60, 93
Titian, figs. 3–8, 3–10
toad, 152–155

Tobias, 214
Tobit, Apocryphal Book of the Bible, 214
tower, imagery of, 127, fig. 5–12
tragedy/tragic drama, 172–173
Traini, Francesco, fig. 6–2
transference, 57, 90, 215
transformation, 11
  of matter, 10
  symbols of, 15
tree of life, 35, 178
Trismosin, Solomon, 8n, figs. 2–4, 3–3, 5–3
Tristan and Isolde, 50, 154
Turba Philosophorum, the, 83, 85, 215–216
turkey, 156
Twelve Keys, the, of Basil Valentine, 18
tyrean dye, 72
Tyson, Carroll, fig. 3–11

unconscious (the), 103, 115, 158, 171, 174, 178, 189, 213, 230
  collective, 169
  descent into, 48
  maternal, 212
  psyche, 1
  psychology of, 1–2
  and Red Sea symbolism, 72
  as latent Self, 56
  as sin, 72
  undifferentiated, 10
  as water, 52
unio mentalis, 166, 170–171
universals, 79
universal solvent, 79
Unus Mundus, the, 221, 230
Upanishads, the, 84
Uriel, 200
uroboros, 143; *see also* dragon

Valentine, Basil, 18, 26
Van der Weyden, fig. 7–14
Van Eyck, Hubert, fig. 7–12
van Loben Sels, Robin, 104n
Varro, 63
Vaughn, Henry, 112, 113n, 134–136&n
Venus, 3, 134, 135, 180
  fountains of, 53–54
vijnanam, 84
Virgin Mary, the, 104, 131, figs. 4–6, 4–9, 5–5, 5–7
virtue(s), 197–198
  as prerequisites for the *opus,* 5

vis animans, 223
Vision of George Ripley, the, 152–154
von Franz, Marie-Louise, 139n, 184, 185n, 209n, 215n
Voragine, Jacobus de, 42n

Wagner, Richard, 49&n, 50, fig. 3–1
Waite, A. E., 5n, 6n, 11n, 12n, 17n, 18n, 26n, 33n, 35n, 43n, 52n, 62–63, 77n, 79n, 83n, 158n, 175n, 188n, 213n, 216n, 218n, figs. 1–1, 6–1, 6–10
water, 1, 47–48, 49–50, 68, 73–74, 75, 77, fig. 7–11; *see also* drowning, floods
   in alchemical recipes, 8–9
   as Dionysian fertility principle, 62
   divine, 79
   as generative or fertility substance, 63
   golden, 218
   lunar, fig. 3–9
   Mercurial, 160
   operation, 18; *see also solutio*
   Penetrating, 215
   as symbol of *solutio,* 79, fig. 3–13
   symbolism of, 47, 52–60
Waterhouse, John William, fig. 3–5
wax, 86, 114
White, Lawrence Grant, 197
white/whiteness/whitening, 26, 139, 147–148, 149, 154, 156, 164, 165; *see also albedo,* earth, white (foliated)

white soul, 120
Whitmont, Edward, 104n
Wickes, Frances, 20n
widow/widower/orphan, symbolism of, 203
Wilhelm, Richard, 77&n, 93, 127n, 158n, 228n
wisdom, 158, 169, 214, 215, 216
   archetypal, 193
   divine, 75, 150, 158
wolf, 18–19, 21, fig. 2–1
   as antimony, 19
   children, 97
womb as symbol of *solutio,* 47–48
World Parents/first parents, 184–186
worms, 157–158, 163, fig. 6–7
wrath, divine, 30, 32–33&n, 43

Yahweh, 31–32, 35, 40n, 168, 201, 204, 220
Yerkes, Rayden Keith, 38n
Yorick, 167

Zagreus, 64
Zechariah, Book of the Bible, 32
Zeus, 93, 218, 227
Zimmer, Heinrich, 84n
Zohar, the, 35, 220
Zosimos, 8, 177

ABOUT THE AUTHOR

Edward F. Edinger, a Jungian analyst, teaches at the C. G. Jung Institute of Los Angeles. He attended Indiana University and Yale Medical School, receiving the M.D, degree in 1946. He is a former supervising psychiatrist of Rockland State Hospital, a founding member of the C. G. Jung Foundation of New York, and the former chairman of the C. G. Jung Training Center in New York. Dr. Edinger is the author of *Ego and Archetype, Melville's Moby Dick: A Jungian Commentary,* and *The Creation of Consciousness: Jung's Myth for Modern Man.*

p5 – haste, Despair, Deception.

p 8   Misuse of secret.